Praise for *Lessons from the Poor*

"*Lessons from the Poor* shows that the mightiest soldiers in the war on poverty are poor people themselves. This fascinating book documents the remarkable creativity and entrepreneurship of the poor, ranging from the family grocer in Kenya that became a supermarket giant to the makers of traditional dyed cloth in the informal sector in Nigeria, who make as much money as corporate managers in the formal sector. The message of the book is profoundly hopeful—as governments remove obstacles to entrepreneurship, there is much potential for the poor to lift themselves out of poverty."

— **WILLIAM R. EASTERLY**, Professor of Economics and
Director, Development Research Institute, New York University

"Many people are naturally entrepreneurial, but the spirit of enterprise can be easily discouraged by government restrictions or a culture of conformity. Many poor countries have suffered from bad government and unnecessary regulations that discourage small-firm formation and growth. The important book *Lessons from the Poor* provides informative case studies of how good government has fostered entrepreneurship and economic development in some of the poorest countries of the world."

— **MARK C. CASSON**, Professor of Economics and Director,
Centre for Institutional Performance, University of Reading

The INDEPENDENT INSTITUTE

THE INDEPENDENT INSTITUTE is a non-profit, non-partisan, scholarly research and educational organization that sponsors comprehensive studies of the political economy of critical social and economic issues.

The politicization of decision-making in society has too often confined public debate to the narrow reconsideration of existing policies. Given the prevailing influence of partisan interests, little social innovation has occurred. In order to understand the nature of and possible solutions to major public issues, the Independent Institute adheres to the highest standards of independent inquiry, regardless of political or social biases and conventions. The resulting studies are widely distributed as books and other publications, and are publicly debated in numerous conference and media programs. Through this uncommon depth and clarity, the Independent Institute expands the frontiers of our knowledge, redefines the debate over public issues, and fosters new and effective directions for government reform.

THE INDEPENDENT INSTITUTE
100 Swan Way, Oakland, California 94621-1428, U.S.A.
Telephone: 510-632-1366 • Facsimile: 510-568-6040
Email: info@independent.org • Website: www.independent.org

Lessons from the Poor

Triumph of the Entrepreneurial Spirit

Edited by
Alvaro Vargas Llosa

The INDEPENDENT INSTITUTE

Oakland, California

The Independent Institute
100 Swan Way, Oakland, CA 94621-1428
Telephone: 510-632-1366 · Fax: 510-568-6040
Email: info@independent.org
Website: www.independent.org

Cover Design: Gail Saari
Cover Photo: © Steven Vidler / Eurasia Press / Corbis
Figure Illustrations: Leigh McLellan Design and Roland de Beque

Library of Congress Cataloging-in-Publication Data

Lessons from the poor : triumph of the entrepreneurial spirit / edited by Alvaro
Vargas Llosa.
    p. cm.
  Includes bibliographical references and index.
  ISBN 978-1-59813-020-1 (alk. paper)
  1. Entrepreneurship--Developing countries. I. Vargas Llosa, Alvaro.
  HB615.L46 2008
  338'.04091724--dc22

                            2008012175

Printed in the United States of America

12 11 10 09 08   1 2 3 4 5

Contents

Foreword

Entrepreneurship as a source of economic growth and as a weapon against poverty is underappreciated. The case studies of this book vividly illustrate this point. Adam Smith noted more than 230 years ago that people have a natural tendency to "truck and barter." They also have a natural tendency to act entrepreneurially—to discover opportunities and better ways of doing things.

Innovative thinking and alertness to opportunity is present in all societies. Indeed, it is often found in unusual places. Who would have thought a poorly educated young Peruvian, washing cars in downtown Lima, would go on to develop the country's largest textile business? Or who could have anticipated that a small retail shop selling blankets, mattresses, and clothing would develop into a giant supermarket chain that is improving the lives of millions of Kenyan consumers and workers? Or who could have known that women with little or no education in southwestern Nigeria would establish thousands of small indigo dyeing and design businesses, and thereby earn a living similar to that of managers and government employees in their native country? No central planner or development official would have chosen any of these people or business options as a tool to reduce poverty. Nonetheless, as this book highlights, all of these entrepreneurial activities have substantially upgraded the lives of millions of poor people.

In order to be successful in a market economy, entrepreneurs must produce goods that consumers value more highly than their cost. When this is the case, their actions will increase wealth. Others, including the poor, will be helped by the lower prices, improved products, and more attractive employment opportunities generated by the actions of the entrepreneurs.

The case studies presented here provide a fascinating story of entrepreneurs who succeeded under very difficult conditions. The roadblocks placed in their paths were many and varied. They included confiscation of property, pollution of the currency, bureaucratic corruption and inefficiency, excessive taxation, and unnecessary regulation. Remarkable entrepreneurs, like the ones presented here, are sometimes able to overcome these obstacles. Still, one cannot help but wonder how many other beneficial projects were derailed by the roadblocks.

Growth and prosperity are the result of entrepreneurship and gains from trade. When regulations limit trade and require people to get permission from the government in order to start a business and try out an innovative idea, they restrict economic progress. They also restrict basic human rights. People should not have to acquire permission from some government official in order to start a business. Neither should they have to get permission from the government before buying productive resources or selling their goods and services to consumers. Furthermore, regulations that force them to do so are nothing more than the raw materials for economic backwardness and political corruption.

There is a major difference among nations with regard to how they treat entrepreneurial activity. Some provide access to money of stable value, keep taxes low, protect property rights, enforce contracts in an evenhanded manner, and allow markets to direct and regulate the actions of entrepreneurs. When residents have substantial freedom to trade with others and keep what they earn, both entrepreneurs and the general populace will have a strong incentive to engage in productive activities. Further, as they help others in exchange for income, their actions will promote economic progress.

However, in many societies, the rules of the game incorporate barriers that restrict entrepreneurial activity and allow political officials to play favorites. This institutional structure undermines the operation of markets and encourages people to seek wealth through "legal plunder"—the use of the political process to take from some and give to others, particularly those in political power. When this incentive structure is present, even entrepreneurs will try to get ahead by seeking political favors. Rather than focusing on the production of better products at lower prices, many entrepreneurs will seek tax favors, subsidies, "sweetheart" government contracts, protected markets, regulations that harm potential rivals, and so on. Counterproductive actions will replace productive ones. Political corruption and arbitrary use of government power will be widespread. These societies will stagnate, and poverty will be a way of life for most of their citizens.

Institutions and policies that are consistent with economic freedom and allocation through markets are the key to growth and prosperity. In turn, economic growth will lead to lower rates of poverty, higher living standards, better education and health, and improvements in the quality of the environment. If you favor these things, you should be zealous in your support of economic freedom, particularly the freedom of entrepreneurs to start businesses, introduce new products, and engage in voluntary exchange with others. This book will enhance your understanding of these vitally important sources of economic progress.

James D. Gwartney
Gus A. Stavros Eminent Scholar
Professor of Economics
Florida State University

Introduction

Lessons from the Poor

ALVARO VARGAS LLOSA

Entrepreneurial ability and energy are present almost everywhere. But in those countries that still languish in backwardness, the labyrinthine intervention of the state and the absence of adequate institutions have kept that ability and energy from translating into full development. For that reason, it is important to study both the entrepreneurial potential of poor countries and the success of the countries that used to be poor but have ascended from poverty to prosperity in recent decades.

The example of the countries that have achieved prosperity fairly recently tells us that the removal and elimination of certain obstacles, and the establishment of an institutional framework that is friendly to the process of creating wealth, can harness entrepreneurial activity for the social good. In all places where free-market reforms were carried out with boldness, consistency, and depth, we have seen an explosion of wealth creation through private enterprise, small and large. These nations demonstrate precisely which types of reforms unleash a proliferation of enterprises and make it possible for millions of people to become successful entrepreneurs in societies whose economies were once unproductive.

The center I direct at the Independent Institute has conducted a series of case studies of entrepreneurial success in Latin America and Africa, as well as studies of countries that have recently gone from underdevelopment to development, thanks to free-market reform in Asia and southern Europe. In the first type of study (published in this volume), we researched specific companies; in the second (to come in subsequent publications), we looked at overall reform in certain countries and its impact on wealth creation. The underlying questions to which we sought answers were these: Is there an entrepreneurial reserve in poor countries? If so, what facilitates its development and what hinders it? What is the relationship between the development of private enterprise and the reduction of poverty, or, to phrase it in a positive manner, what triggers prosperity?

The case studies you will find in this and successive publications illustrate the central idea defended by the theoreticians of entrepreneurial activities, from Richard Cantillon to Israel Kirzner to Mancur Olson: that the decisive element in the voyage from poverty to prosperity in any society is the development of the entrepreneurial reserves that exist in its men and women, and that the institutions that grant more freedom to their citizens and more security to their citizens' possessions are those that best facilitate the accumulation of wealth.

All of the stories that make up this series were extensively researched on location by the various authors and their support teams. Together, they provide a tantalizing account of the potential and the achievements of poor people in Peru, Argentina, Nigeria, and Kenya, and of the way in which countries that were once deemed poor and hopeless, such as Spain, Vietnam, and Estonia, have seen their economic fortunes turn despite persistent problems (in the case of Vietnam, a dictatorial government that calls itself Communist, of course). In a couple of other cases, the authors address the link between the exploitation of natural resources and the environment in Mexico, a country that still treats its hydrocarbon resources as a government monopoly, and the perversion of democratic majoritism in Uruguay, which has validated increasing forms of government intervention over the years, reversing the fortunes of a nation that was once prosperous.

As you will see, entrepreneurship was a major factor in helping the Añaños family, which two decades ago was making its living on a small farm in the Peruvian Andes, an area that was being terrorized by a Maoist organization, become the biggest manufacturer of nonalcoholic beverages in Latin America. Entrepreneurship was also the determining element in the rise of Topy Top, Peru's biggest textile exporting company, from the humble beginnings of its founder, Aquilino Flores, who used to wash cars. No less impressive are the achievements of Nakumatt, a major retailer in Kenya whose origins go back to a small shop in the town of Nakuru in the 1980s—and whose success led it to involve itself in that nation's unhealthy political process more than it should have, a fate that contains important lessons about the limits of entrepreneurship in countries where successful enterprises are the exception because of the prevailing environment. Equally deserving of attention, if not more, is the clothing design industry that the heroic women of Abeokuta, in southwestern Nigeria, have established, with no outside help and against all odds.

These stories could easily replicate themselves throughout the developing world if major obstacles to enterprise were removed. That is the lesson we learn from the case studies that focus on free-market reform in Spain, Estonia, and Vietnam.

Estonia is a tiny country in the Baltic region, below the Gulf of Finland, with no more than 1.5 million inhabitants. It is also the nation that, along with Poland, has experienced the most radical reforms among the nations of the former Communist bloc in Europe. Thanks to these reforms, which occurred between 1991 and 2000, it has also seen the most economic growth in the region in the past several years. This achievement is all the more impressive when we consider that, unlike many countries in central Europe, Estonia was not only governed by the Communist Party but was also inserted into the asphyxiating economic structure of the Soviet Union.

The case of Spain is particularly interesting and instructive for those who think that certain nations are doomed forever by virtue of their culture. In the past two decades, Spain, whose culture was once inimical to notions such as self-reliance and individual initiative, has experienced an economic and social transformation. Beginning with institutional changes that were more or less liberal in nature, Spanish companies have learned to operate in the global economy. Family enterprises, cooperatives, and large companies have become increasingly competitive. Thanks to the dynamism of its enterprises, Spain today has a per capita income that represents almost 90 percent of the median revenue of the fifteen nations of the European Union (EU) before the EU expanded to twenty-five members. Thus, the Iberian Peninsula has practically caught up with its more prosperous and developed neighbors.

Each one of the studies presented in this series speaks to us of entrepreneurship as a transforming force in the developing world, and as by far the best bet against poverty. After half a century of failure, foreign aid can no longer be the preferred tool for lifting the masses of Africa and Latin America out of their economic prostration. After more than a century of welfare policies that have failed to deliver the goods, redistribution can no longer be seen as the best hope for those who aspire to the wealth of nations.

To judge by the cases described here, the best antidote to the scourge of economic misery is to recognize the entrepreneurial energy of the people and to replicate, and even improve on, the recent "miracles" in central Europe, Asia, and southern Europe.

In recent years, governments, international bodies, and nongovernmental organizations have started to recognize the importance of the business climate—that is, of the regulatory framework in which business is conducted—in fostering or hampering economic growth and the reduction of poverty. The World Bank's "Doing Business" report measures the ease of doing business in most countries using several parameters, including how many days it takes and how costly it is to start a firm, how many licenses are required to stay in operation, how cumbersome it is to register property, how onerous it is to hire and fire workers, and other aspects. The conclusion, as can be seen from Figure I.1, is that in poor countries the political and legal systems interfere with business more than in prosperous nations.

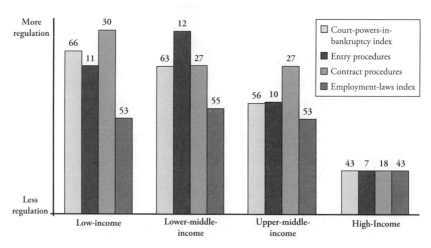

NOTE: The indicators for high-income countries are used as benchmarks. The average value of the indicator is shown above each column.

FIGURE I.1. Poor Countries Regulate Business the Most

SOURCE: *Doing Business* database.

The fact that Puerto Rico, an island in the Caribbean that is tied to the United States through a commonwealth, has a per capita income of $19,100 (in terms of purchasing power parity, or PPP) while the Dominican Republic, another Caribbean island, has a per capita gross domestic product (GDP) of no more than $8,000 (PPP) (CIA, World Factbook) seems to mirror the relative position of those two countries in the world ranking of business climates. Whereas Puerto Rico is reasonably well situated in 19th place, the Dominican Republic is 117th. Similarly, Botswana, which is ranked in the 48th position, has a per capita income (PPP) that is ten times greater than that of Nigeria, which is ranked 108th (in this case, the comparison is more poignant since Nigeria is actually a bigger nation than Botswana and is richer in natural resources) (World Bank, 2006).

The business climate, of course, is not responsible for the existence of entrepreneurship in a society. But it plays a big part in making it possible for entrepreneurship to flourish and to boost a nation's productivity or, conversely, in forcing much of that energy to go underground, into what is known as the informal economy, while those who choose to operate legally need to devote excessive time and resources to doing so. The fact that in Peru, despite significant reforms in recent years, starting a business continues to require at least ten procedures over a period of seventy-two working days and costs the equivalent of one-third of the nation's per capita income probably means that many Peruvians who could replicate the success of the two Peruvian companies studied in this volume are put off by the system. Similarly, the fact that in Nigeria it costs a person more than half of the nation's per capita income to open a business makes it hard to create industries as innovative as the one that the women of Abeokuta have successfully engaged in for years (World Bank, 2006).

Although it is true that regulatory barriers hinder entrepreneurship, it is also true that resourceful entrepreneurs have found and continue to find ways of creating wealth within the law by overcoming those obstacles. As the authors of the two Peruvian case studies indicate, the creators of Topy Top, the textile company, were able to use the opportunities afforded by the opening of trade in the 1990s to formalize their business. This case and others point to the fact that regulatory barriers do not necessarily prevent entrepreneurship, although they force entrepreneurs to devote more of their time and more resources than they would otherwise spend to the objective of operating within the law. And there are many different ways in which an economy can benefit from the informal economy long before the barriers are eliminated. Recognizing that the poor are entrepreneurial can thus be extremely advantageous for formal companies in the developing world. A recent article pointed out how Cemex, the largest cement producer in the world, built its wealth on its "ability to serve micro-markets—selling a bag at a time to poor folks" (Schaefer, 2006).

Other studies have shown that certain policies that were once seen as a panacea for wealth creation may not be enough to turn potential entrepreneurship into economic development. For example, the issuing of property titles—the formalization of squatter settlements—has not necessarily produced the democratization of credit that was expected. More than 1.2 million property titles were given away by the Peruvian authorities between 1998 and 2002. One recent study indicates, however, that "there is no evidence that titles increase the likelihood of receiving credit from private sector banks" (Field and Torero, 2006). In some cases, commercial banks seem to suspect that those who have obtained titles through well-publicized government titling programs are less trustworthy as loan recipients because they feel politically protected. Existing inadequacies in the institutional environment of the nation and the politicization of titling programs probably account in part for the fact that the formalization of property titles has not triggered a multiplication of entrepreneurial activity.

From the days of Richard Cantillon, an essayist of Irish origin who wrote in the first decades of the eighteenth century, until now, scholars have studied entrepreneurship and tried to determine what institutions facilitate or hinder its development.[1] If the rules of the game in a given society do not act to benefit some parties at the expense of others, and people can reasonably expect that their property will be respected and contracts will be fulfilled, entrepreneurship will bring about an accumulation of capital through innovation and a corresponding rise in productivity. Conversely, when the prevailing political and legal arrangements are such that people perceive the government as an intrusive force or an unreliable enforcer of the law that will neither respect their property nor guarantee protection against third-party violation, entrepreneurship will tend to express itself in marginal, unproductive ventures that might permit the poor to sustain themselves but will not amount to the kind of continuous wealth accumulation that fosters development. If the political and legal system creates incentives for entrepreneurship, the result will be an expansion of the small, medium-sized, and large companies investing in the future, and therefore an ever-increasing number of goods and services that will raise the standard of living of the population.

That prodigious expansion is precisely what has happened in the West in the last couple of centuries, after the rise of liberal democracy under the rule of law allowed commercial and contract societies to extend beyond the limited confines of the past and provide millions of people with the kinds of safeguards that had previously been the privilege of a minority. Although they had many flaws, the societies that emerged after the eighteenth century in Europe and, by extension, in the United States flourished under arrangements that were much more conducive to entrepreneurship than those of previous centuries and of other regions of the world. That is why the conquest of poverty is very recent. Over the last two centuries, the world's income has increased by an average of almost 1,000 percent, while the preceding ten centuries saw only a 50 percent increase (Norberg, 2007).

Prosperity, however, as the guilty consciences of the West remind us every day, is very unevenly spread out throughout the world. The fact that, today, millions of people manage to eke out a living in very creative ways under stifling bureaucracies, elitist systems, and despotic governments indicates that entrepreneurship is part of the human spirit and not the exclusive preserve of those countries that have generated astronomical wealth. But there are important differences between what happens to entrepreneurial activities in open societies and what happens to them in exploitative environments. One difference involves productivity; the other is perhaps best explained by William Baumol's characterization of private enterprise as "parasitic" in societies that are not governed by neutral and limited governments (Baumol, 1990). By this he means that in societies dominated by politics, entrepreneurial energies are diverted to dividing the existing wealth rather than increasing it. Entrepreneurial energy is present in many types of societies, but only in countries with limited government, adherence to the rule of law, and respect for individual rights does this energy foster economic growth. Although a certain degree of parasitism is also present in what we call the free societies of today, the dimensions of the problem are infinitely worse in other types of societies. This, and not Western capitalism, is what keeps the poor stuck in their current condition, despite half a century of foreign aid.

In Ibero-America and in Africa, with some exceptions, the prevailing climate has rewarded parasites because economic competition has been politicized and the government has tended to pick the winners and losers. Those who have been able to work most efficiently through the political and bureaucratic system have tended to secure privileges for themselves that made it difficult, costly, and even unsafe for potential competitors to access the economic markets.

When looking at many developing countries, I am often reminded of Stanislav Andreski's opinion that the countries of Latin America have traditionally constituted "a parasitic involution of capitalism," meaning "the tendency to seek profits and alter market conditions by political means in the widest sense of that word" (Andreski, 1969, 77). That tendency, sustained both by interventionist governments and by the culture that they have generated over time, explains, to a large extent, why in the last thirty years every Latin American country except Chile has seen its per capita income fall as a proportion of U.S. per capita income, whereas Thailand and Indonesia, two middle-of-the-table Asian nations, have seen theirs rise by 40 percent. It also explains why, despite the fact that only twelve years ago Brazil's economy was similar in size to that of China, the Asian giant, which is gradually shedding its parasitic economic system, now produces three and a half times more goods and services than Brazil (Vargas Llosa, 2006), and why Nigeria, a major oil producer, is ranked 145th in terms of income per capita.

But even under oppressive conditions, the enterprising spirit of individuals can be detected. Historical evolution suggests that people have, over time, developed an interest in property and private enterprise that we might call intuitive. This allows Richard Pipes to maintain that, even before the emergence of the modern state, in most countries property was possession, a claim based not on legal documents but on a prolonged holding that custom recognized as proof of ownership (Pipes, 1999, 117). In modern times, we have numerous examples of societies in which enterprise has tried and continues to try to defy the prevailing conditions. Many studies have been conducted in Africa and Latin America of the way in which, when forced to act under a large but incompetent state that did not provide the services it promised, the poor have organized spontaneous legal systems to bring security to their possessions and a certain predictability to their social activities (Vargas Llosa, 2005, 112–118). Those systems have not given rise to prosperous economies, but they have made the living conditions of the poor much less harsh than they would otherwise be.

Parasitism has, paradoxically, given private enterprise a very bad name in the developing world. Winston Churchill's words are perhaps more applicable to the developing world than they were to his own country when he expressed them: "Some people regard private enterprise as a predatory tiger to be shot. Others look on it as a cow they can milk. Not enough people see it as a healthy horse, pulling a sturdy wagon" (quoted in Magleby, 2005). Instead of associating entrepreneurship with innovation and progress, with job creation and the abundant supply of goods and services, many people, both educated and uneducated, associate it with corruption, privilege, and predation.

Corporativism, state mercantilism, privilege, the transfer of wealth, and a politicized law—what I like to call the five principles of oppression—have hindered entrepreneurship among the poor, preventing it from realizing its potential. The result, for millions of people, is an economy of survival rather than ever-increasing wealth. The potential is certainly there. It is expressed, for instance, in the fact that those Latin Americans who have emigrated to the United States generate enough capital in their adopted country to send home between $40 and $50 billion every year, according to the Inter-American Development Bank. But the mercantilist system under which economic success depends on political intervention has impeded the development of the undeveloped. Because of the preservation of such a system in Mexico after the half-baked reforms of the last few decades, China has overtaken that country as the United States' second-ranked trading partner.

One manifestation among many in the mercantilist system is the scant connection between research centers and producers—which explains why, with the exception of Mexico and Brazil, the Latin American economies are overwhelmingly dependent on natural resources and commodities (Brazil depends on them for a third of its exports, Peru for 70 percent.) The four largest firms in the region are government monopolies in oil exploitation and refining. A few years ago, economic nationalists decried the "unjust terms of trade" whereby Latin America and Africa sold cheap commodities and bought expensive industrial and capital goods. Today, those nations are basking in commodity dependence, which is making their governments—but not their people—rich. The countries that are prospering are those that did not stake their future on natural resources and are now buying them from Africa and Latin America.

Brazil has created some clusters of innovation in the form of tech parks; has made some breakthroughs in bioenergy, including ethanol fuel and biodiesel; and is now experimenting with biokerosene fuel for aviation. But these efforts are heavily dependent on government funds. In Jalisco, Mexico, some foreign investors are also developing technology. But a study by the Council on Competitiveness stated that the government forces the local pharmaceutical industry to sell cheaply to the state for its social security program, thereby making it very hard to invest in research and development. Only 0.4 percent of the country's GDP is invested in R&D (Council on Competitiveness, 2005).

Entrepreneurship is a fascinating phenomenon. Austrian economist Ludwig von Mises pointed out that economics is interested in studying how individuals choose the means necessary to achieve specific ends. Because the means are scarce, entrepreneurs try to achieve their goals for a profit at the least possible cost. The entrepreneur tries to assign limited resources to create a supply that will seek to satisfy the unlimited needs and preferences of his or her fellow human beings. In the process, an element of creativity that is difficult to explain in words intervenes. The entrepreneur helps transform resources into goods, services, and technologies. Thanks to the competitive nature of entrepreneurship, everyone benefits: producers, consumers, and future generations. Kings and feudal lords could not even dream of the kinds of things that are available to a blue-collar worker today.

One would think that the overwhelming evidence pointing to the role of the entrepreneur in triggering wealth accumulation and therefore extended prosperity would make it obvious that governments need to eliminate obstacles and provide general security so that people can go about their business with a reasonable expectation that their efforts will not be ransacked by those who exercise authority or by third parties. But this reality is not recognized by many governments in the developing world and is even ignored by many intellectuals, politicians, and businesspeople in the developed world. That is why notions such as "corporate social responsibility" have come to dominate current thinking about the role of the corporation in today's world. Many people fail to understand that an entrepreneur who discovers opportunity and transforms resources into wealth provides the most "social" service possible to the rest of the community, even when that is not the original intention.

Perhaps some of those who think that entrepreneurial activities are not "social" enough should take a look at studies such as the ones we offer in this volume. We all have much to learn from the many developing countries where recent reforms have unleashed a torrent of wealth creation on the part of small and medium-sized businesses, and from the heroes who, in those nations where profound institutional reform has yet to take place, have beaten the odds and created companies that have helped raise the standard of living of thousands of people, pointing the way for the rest of society.

Just over a decade ago, Peter Bauer, perhaps the greatest development economist of the twentieth century, wrote that,

> Poor people can generate or secure sufficient funds to start on the road to progress if they are motivated to improve their material condition and are not inhibited by government policy or lack of public security. . . . What has to be remembered and emphasized is that having capital is the result of successful economic performance, not its precondition. Economic performance depends on personal, cultural, and political factors, on people's aptitudes, attitudes, motivations, and social and political institutions. Where these are favorable, capital will be generated locally or attracted (Bauer, 2000, 45).

The stories you are about to read prove that prosperity is within reach of even the poorest communities of the world, and that entrepreneurship, not Western guilt, is the way to move forward.

NOTE

1. Richard Cantillon is best known for his *Essai sur la Nature du Commerce en Général,* written in French circa 1732 and published anonymously in England two decades later.

REFERENCES

Andreski, Stanislav. 1969. *Parasitism and Subversion: The Case of Latin America.* New York: Schocken Books.

Bauer, Peter. 2000. Foreign Aid: Abiding Issues. In *From Subsistence to Exchange and Other Essays.* Princeton: Princeton University Press.

Baumol, William. 1990. Entrepreneurship: Productive, Unproductive, and Destructive. *Journal of Political Economy* 98, no. 5, part 1 (October): 894, 899.

Central Intelligence Agency (CIA). The World Factbook. Available at https://www.cia.gov/cia/publications/factbook/.

Council on Competitiveness. 2005. *Catalyzing Cross-Border Innovation: The Mexican Life Sciences Initiative.* Phase I Report. December. Available at www.compete.org.

Field, Erica, and Maximo Torero. 2006. *Do Property Titles Increase Credit Access Among the Urban Poor? Evidence from a Nationwide Titling Program.* March. Available at http://www.economics.harvard.edu/faculty/field/papers/FieldTorerocs.pdf.

Magleby, Kirk. 2005. *MicroFranchises as a Solution to Global Poverty.* Available at www.MicroFranchises.org.

Norberg, Johan. 2007. Entrepreneurs Are the Heroes of the World. *Cato's Letter* 5, no. 1 (Winter).

Pipes, Richard. 1999. *Property and Freedom.* New York: Alfred A. Knopf.

Schaefer, Peter F. 2006. The Next Big Thing for Global Business. *TCS Daily,* December 6. Available at http://www.tcsdaily.com/article.aspx?id=111606A.

Vargas Llosa, Alvaro. 2005. *Liberty for Latin America.* New York: Farrar, Straus & Giroux for the Independent Institute.

Vargas Llosa, Alvaro. 2006. In Search of the Gem. Speech given at the Mont Pelerin Society in Guatemala City, November 6.

World Bank. 2006. Doing Business: Benchmarking Business Regulations. Available at http://www.doingbusiness.org/.

1

Amid Hopelessness, Hopeful Investment
The Case of the Añaños Family and Kola Real
DANIEL CÓRDOVA*

SUMMARY

In the late 1980s, the Añaños family made their living from a small farm in the department (province) of Ayacucho, Peru, the cradle of the Maoist terrorist movement known as Sendero Luminoso, or Shining Path. The region's isolation, caused by the civil war, gave the Añaños an opportunity to found Kola Real in 1988. They never imagined that twenty-five years later they would be the main transnational manufacturers of nonalcoholic beverages in Latin America, with subsidiaries in Mexico, Venezuela, Ecuador, four Central American countries, and, soon thereafter, Thailand, placing Big Cola, their regional brand, right behind Coca-Cola, Pepsi, and Sprite, with more than eight million consumers in 2005. Today, the Añaños have fourteen manufacturing plants with a total installed capacity of two billion liters per year; they employ eight thousand workers, they own one hundred distribution centers, and their sales are estimated at US$1 billion. The Añaños case demonstrates that even in the environments most hostile to investment, free enterprise can allow people to achieve unimaginable development goals.

INTRODUCTION

Many in Peru look back on the 1970s and 1980s as the worst decades in recent memory in economic, political, and social terms. They were twenty years of socialist and populist experiments, by the end of which most of the

---

*With the contribution of Ricardo Alania, Guillermo Quiroga, Gonzalo Galdos, and Claudia Sícoli.

companies in the export and public service sectors had been taken over by the state, and a radical agrarian reform had expelled entrepreneurs from the countryside. The predominant public policies of the time included almost all of the components of typical state intervention in Latin America: price controls, prohibitive tariffs, exchange controls, fiscal deficits, a central bank captured by the politicians, and so on. The per capita gross domestic product (GDP) was 60 percent of what it had been in the early 1970s, growing inflation became hyperinflation in the late 1980s, and a social convulsion occurred that was so violent that a terrorist movement of Communist origin, the Shining Path, came to threaten the very center of political power.

The Communist Party of Peru–Shining Path movement made news in the early 1980s when it began to set off bombs in the rural areas of the department (province) of Ayacucho. Less than ten years later, its attacks shook the entire country, and merchants avoided entering Ayacucho for fear of being identified as oppressive capitalists and murdered. The Añaños family, small landowners in the interior of Ayacucho, had their property attacked and sought refuge in the city of Huamanga, the capital of Ayacucho. As reported by writer Mario Vargas Llosa in 2003,

> How could one make a living in that land ravaged by terrorism and counterterrorism, which, from being poor in the 1980s went to miserable, with thousands of jobless and marginal people begging on the streets? The Añaños studied their surroundings and noticed that, because of terrorist actions, Ayacuchans had been left without carbonated beverages. Coca-Cola and Pepsi-Cola trucks from Lima, which went up the central highway, were constantly attacked by the Senderistas or by common criminals who passed themselves off as guerrillas. Sick of the losses they suffered, the respective companies stopped their shipments or cut them back in such a way that the beverages that did arrive were insufficient to satisfy the local demand. One of the five children of Eduardo and Mirta Añaños, Jorge, an engineer and agronomist, devised the formula for a new beverage. The family mortgaged the house, borrowed money everywhere and put together US$30,000. With that sum, the Añaños founded Kola Real in 1988 and began to manufacture soft drinks in the backyard of their home, which they themselves poured into assorted bottles and labeled. (Vargas Llosa, 2003)

Fifteen years after its beginning, the Añaños Group occupied a privileged space in the market of nonalcoholic beverages in Latin America, having used a competitive strategy that broke with the traditional patterns of the soft drink industry. The experience of marketing their own formula—which was exempt from the royalties that the Coca-Cola and Pepsi-Cola bottlers were obligated to pay—to low-income consumers in Ayacucho led the Añaños to bet that they could "democratize" the consumption of carbonated beverages by offering a product similar to the well-known brands but at a very low cost. Their business model was not to take market share away from Coca-Cola and Pepsi but instead to take advantage of a new market, at the base of the "social pyramid"—those who could not typically afford the more expensive brand-name soft drinks. Little by little, they learned about the industry and the market spurned by the traditional producers, and they began to open plants in other provinces of Peru, reaching Lima in 1997.

Based on their experience in Peru, their entrepreneurial intuition, and their ability to reach their target market, the Añaños realized that what they had achieved in Peru could be replicated in the rest of Latin America. To expand internationally, the Añaños gambled on two large markets—Venezuela and Mexico—in addition to smaller markets that could be penetrated rapidly, such as Ecuador, Guatemala, Nicaragua, Costa Rica, and Honduras.

Soon after expanding into the huge Mexican market, where they withstood a dirty war from Coca-Cola distributors, the Añaños were billing more than the sales of Peru's entire soft drink market. As of this writing, the group's sales are approaching US$1 billion, and the Añaños are rapidly making incursions into new, emerging markets, such as energy drinks, sparkling water, and citrus drinks. In addition, they are making forays into the East Asian market through their new investment in Thailand. From the beginning, the Añaños' philosophy has been guided by the market. Their increasingly global perspective is reflected in the name of their sparkling water: Free World.

In this chapter, we look at the Añaños phenomenon from three perspectives. First, we analyze the group's history against the backdrop of recent Peruvian history. Next, we study their expansion into international markets. Finally, we look at the Añaños Group as a business case study, analyzing the factors that have been crucial to the group's competitive success.

THE AÑAÑOS FAMILY'S BEGINNINGS IN PERU

In recent years, the Añaños Group has become Peru's main transnational company. Its impressive growth in sales—which approached US$1 billion in 2002—has been due largely to its expansion into international markets

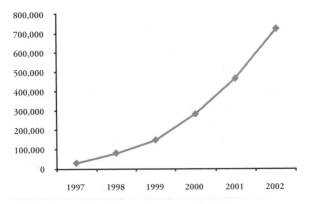

FIGURE 1.1. Añaños Group Sales, 1997–2002 (in thousands of US dollars)

SOURCE: Non-official data—estimated by UPC.

(see Figure 1.1)[1]. Nevertheless, the success of the group's entry into the markets of Mexico, Central America, Venezuela, and Ecuador would not have been possible without its previous growth within the provinces of Peru and eventually Lima.

The history of the Añaños Group and Kola Real, its first and emblematic product, begins in the midst of a civil war unleashed by a messianic far-left group, the Communist Party of Peru–Shining Path, in the late 1980s. Because of the disruption caused by the conflict, other beverage distributors had almost abandoned the market in Ayacucho, leaving room for the launching of Kola Real. However, the emergence of the Añaños Group as a national company did not come until after the military defeat of Shining Path. And it was the company's growth on a national level, beginning with the provinces, that laid the foundation for the Añaños Group's leap from a Peruvian enterprise to a global enterprise.

Peru in the 1980s

Peru in the late 1980s was a country where all the imaginable social ills came together, due to terrorist violence and the consequent social chaos, as well as the worst economic crisis experienced since at least the 1930s.

The Terrorism of Shining Path

In the late 1980s, travel in Peru's interior was almost a suicidal prospect. Shining Path was a threat in practically all the country's provinces. The group's leader, Abimael Guzmán, seeking to impose a Communist revolution, had begun advancing from the countryside to the cities, using the strategy pursued by Stalin and Mao Zedong. Estimates of the casualties related to the attacks and armed confrontations between the terrorists and the police range from 24,000 to 70,000 (Government of Peru, 2003).

In Ayacucho, the department (province) where Kola Real's entrepreneurial adventure began, the estimate of dead and missing people was 25,000.

In 2000, the Peruvian government asked a group of prominent citizens to draw up a report that came to be known as the *Report on Truth and Reconciliation*. The report describes how the Communist Party of Peru–Shining Path (referred to throughout as Shining Path) initiated what it called a people's war against the Peruvian government, with fierce attacks on the civilian population.

Although the report does not state this clearly, the movement's origin was a Marxist intellectual movement at the state university at Huamanga, the capital of Ayacucho. The group of intellectuals who founded Shining Path in the 1970s took advantage of the poverty, ignorance, and weakness of Ayacucho's rural population to begin recruiting "cadres," gradually forming a sizable army. Contrary to the report, Shining Path's origin was due neither to the poverty nor to the inequities that existed and still exist in the region. As Figure 1.2 shows, the per capita GDP in Ayacucho is about 56 percent of the national average. Figure 1.3 shows that 65 percent of the population is poor, with 25 percent living in abject poverty. The existence of similar levels of poverty before and after the Shining Path movement suggests that the incidence of poverty alone does not explain the development of such

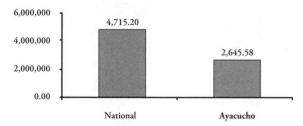

FIGURE 1.2. GDP Per Capita—Year 2001

SOURCE: INEI.

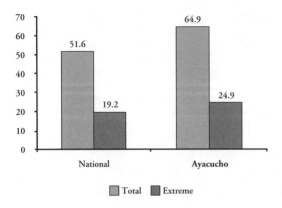

FIGURE 1.3. Poverty Rate—Jan.–Dec. 2004

SOURCE: INEI.

groups. The Marxist Shining Path group was able to exploit these conditions, sparking the emergence of the antigovernment movement.

Shining Path possessed a particularly efficient ideological apparatus that fed on the frustrations of the rural poor, who tend to be of indigenous origin, as opposed to the "Western" population of native-born whites, known as *criollos.* But the origin of Shining Path was neither rural nor indigenous. It was urban and *criollo,* as personified by Abimael Guzmán, the leader whose nom de guerre was President Gonzalo.

According to the commission report, the civil war between the terrorists and the rest of society went through five major periods:

1. The start of the attacks (1980–1982), which the government of Fernando Belaúnde Terry minimized, failing to take appropriate action.
2. The militarization of the conflict (1983–1986), during which the armed forces began a war against the terrorists, but without an adequate system of intelligence. During this period, many innocent civilians received brutal treatment.
3. The spread of violence nationwide (1986–1989), during which Shining Path occupied areas throughout the country, established alliances with drug traffickers, and was complemented by another terrorist movement, the Tupac Amaru movement.[2] The Añaños family founded Kola Real at the end of this period.
4. The extreme crisis (1989–1992), when terrorism reached Lima, generating a sense of fear among many Peruvian citizens that ended abruptly with the capture of Abimael Guzmán, thanks to an intelligence strategy devel-

oped by the national police. Three years after the founding of Kola Real, Peru was nearly peaceful again, and the company could begin to expand.

5. The dismantling of terrorism (beginning in 1992), during the ten-year regime of Alberto Fujimori. Fujimori was criticized for his authoritarian practices and for corruption within the National Intelligence Service, which was led by Fujimori's adviser, Vladimiro Montesinos. During this period, Kola Real succeeded in becoming a transnational enterprise.

The Economic Crisis

The period of terrorist violence during the 1980s coincided with one of the worst economic crises in the history of Peru. The military government of General Juan Velasco Alvarado, in power from 1968 to 1975, had created policies that denied economic freedom and ran counter to the rule of law. A great many of these measures were not reversed until the early 1990s. Some of the most prominent of these included the following:

- The nationalization of a large number of major companies, including mining, fishing, industrial, and service enterprises, to the extent that at one point state-owned companies accounted for 40 percent of the GDP. These companies incurred large deficits that had to be assumed by the state.
- Agrarian reform measures that involved expropriating agricultural property and turning it over to peasants, resulting in the bankruptcy of much of the modern agricultural production. This phenomenon led to the spread of poverty in the rural areas.
- The excessive growth of the state without tax revenues to support it and a very large foreign debt that in the long run accelerated the bankruptcy of public finances.
- The prohibition of many imports and an increase in tariffs and other barriers to trade.
- The rejection of foreign investment.
- The creation of policies that discouraged exports by exerting artificial control over the rates of exchange.

The crises triggered by this social-populist economic model followed one after another from the mid-1970s to the late 1980s. Peru's GDP grew very slightly during both decades (at a slower rate than the population growth, so per capita GDP actually fell), but, as Figure 1.4 shows, it was during the last three years of Alan García's administration that the GDP dropped in real

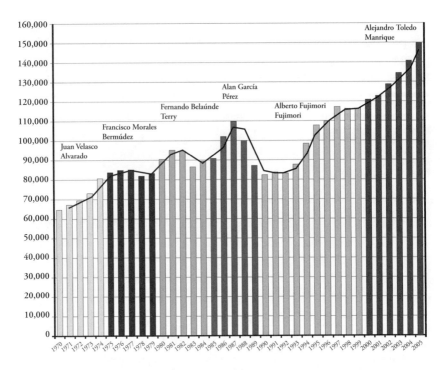

FIGURE 1.4. Evolution of Peruvian GDP in Million of Soles (1970–2005)

SOURCE: INEI.

terms. As can be seen in Figure 1.5, that drop in the GDP was accompanied by a process of hyperinflation that reached 7,650 percent per year in 1990.

Neither the military government of General Francisco Morales Bermúdez (1975–1980), who reestablished democracy, nor the second administration of Fernando Belaúnde Terry (1980–1985), whose first administration had been overthrown by Velasco, changed the populist economic model, which led the Peruvian economy to continue its decline. However, the administration of Alan García (1985–1990) carried the populist model to an extreme. Its policies led to a record-setting fiscal deficit, squandered credit through the state bank, filled the ministries and public enterprises with members of García's party, tightened controls over currency exchange, increased trade barriers, and attempted to nationalize private enterprises, to name only a few. In sum, it created a "perfect storm" that battered the economy and contributed to the spread of poverty. According to Nelson Shack, of Peru's Ministry of Economy and Finance,

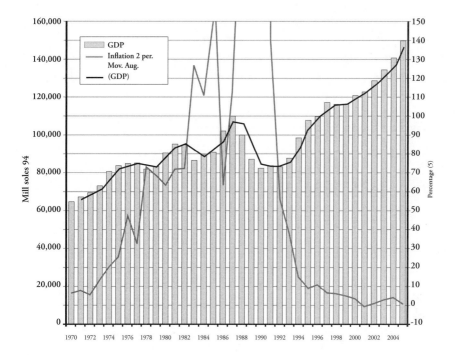

FIGURE 1.5 Peruvian GDP (in Million of Soles) and Inflation (%) (1970–2005)

SOURCE: INEI/Peruvian Central Bank.

Surveys of living standards in metropolitan Lima indicate that in 1991 the population reduced its consumption by 48.5 percent in comparison with 1985. The effects of the economic crisis were felt most strongly in the low-income sectors. Between 1985 and 1991, the poorest decile of the population experienced a contraction in its level of consumption that exceeded 60 percent. . . . Between 1985 and 1991, the percentage of the population in a state of poverty rose from 43 percent to 59 percent nationwide. The increase of poverty was particularly notable in the urban sector, where it rose from 36 percent to 53 percent. Likewise, in the rural sector, the percentage of people in a situation of poverty rose from 55 percent to 80 percent. (Shack, 2004)

In this context, the carbonated beverage industry—in which the two main companies, Coca-Cola and Inca Kola of Peru, currently hold 71.4 percent of the market[3]—fell into a major decline, along with the rest of the nation's industries. The industry recorded its lowest levels of consumption ever. With consumers' purchasing power declining, the prices of carbonated drinks had to be lowered. The idle installed capacity of the traditional beverage manufacturers rose to about 50 percent. There was room for a different type of carbonated beverage company to emerge, one that might succeed in the context of recession and plummeting purchasing power.

The Beginnings of the Añaños Group

It was in the very center of that stage of violence and extreme economic crisis that Kola Real was founded, an enterprise that, fifteen years later, would become one of Peru's most important transnational corporations. Terrorist violence and the economic crisis encouraged the Añaños to come up with a product that was different from the existing soft drinks—one aimed at low-income consumers.

The Environment of Terror in Ayacucho in the 1980s

The department of Ayacucho lies in a broad valley in the south-central mountains of Peru, 2,761 meters above sea level. Industrial production in that department was and is very limited. Most of the manufactured consumer goods come from the coast, particularly from Lima. This was the case for beer—the most popular alcoholic beverage in Peru—and nonalcoholic carbonated drinks in the late 1980s.

During the Shining Path era, distribution of soft drinks in the Peruvian Andes became very difficult. The trucks that distributed mass-consumption goods, particularly the ones owned by leading companies (which the terrorists equated with "exploitive" capitalism) were attacked by the terrorists. In addition, companies' dealers and representatives were intimidated, and some were even murdered.

Pedro Castellano, the current director of the Human Factor Program of the Graduate Studies School of the Peruvian University of Applied Sciences, was at that time sales supervisor for the National Beer Company for the area that included the department of Ayacucho. The company produced, bottled, and sold Pilsen beer, the second-best-selling beer in Peru and the best seller in Ayacucho.

According to Pedro, who was known as "Pilsen" in the area, on one of his many visits to the city of Ayacucho (formerly called Huamanga), he went into a restaurant to eat and—as was his custom—handed out some merchandising trinkets among the customers, a gesture that identified him as a brewery employee. As he did so, a man at a distant table called out to him, and Pedro, always congenial, walked over to his table. In a threatening tone, the man said, "Do you know who's going to die today?" All Pedro could respond was, "I'm here doing my job, so take it easy; calm down. I have nothing against anybody; I just want to have a good time in the company of friends."

At that moment, a light-skinned man stood up from a table and tried to grab Pedro by the neck. Pedro, a former Peruvian Navy cadet, defended himself. A fight broke out, with shouting and gunfire. Pedro thought he was a dead man, but as luck would have it, several plainclothes policemen were present, and they rushed him to the police station as gunshots rang out all around. The policemen had been warned that an attack was going to occur in that restaurant and, dressed like civilian customers, they were ready for it. Pedro remained in the police station, under protection, for four days. Then he was taken to Lima and transferred by the company to another part of the country.

Shortly thereafter, a young, hard-working executive was appointed to replace Pedro. A few months later, he went to the same restaurant for lunch. A man approached him, asked, "So you are Pilsen?" and, without waiting for an answer, fired two shots in the young man's face. A while later, the restaurant owner was also murdered.

Such was daily life in Ayacucho in the late 1980s. Deaths, intimidation, and threats were routine in the lives of people who, despite the danger, had to get up every morning and go to work.

The Añaños' Initiative

The story of the Añaños family has taken on the stature of a legend, and Ayacuchans tell it with pride. It started long before they began their soft drink business, in the province of San Miguel (Ayacucho), where Nivardo Añaños, grandfather of the Añaños Group's founders, owned the Patibamba farm. When agrarian reform was instituted under General Juan Velasco Alvarado (1968–1975), Patibamba was taken away from Nivardo and split up. Nivardo's oldest son, Eduardo, and his wife, Mirta Jeri, a teacher, farmed one of the plots of land while raising their six children. His sister-in-law, Olga Jeri, was married to Amaniel Castro, who started the first bottling company in that area. The story goes that Eduardo became interested in bottling and distributing soft drinks. A while later, in the mid-1980s, pressured by the terrorist violence of Shining Path, he moved to Huamanga, the capital of Ayacucho, where in 1988 the Añaños began to manufacture and store Kola Real in their home.

Huamanga, a small city renowned for having thirty-three churches, was home to three other provincial bottling companies. But the Añaños noticed that the per capita consumption of soft drinks was very limited, restricted to an almost elite group of consumers, and that the leading bottlers made large profits.

The Añaños were middle-income folks whose children had attended public school. Nevertheless, their level of income was sufficient to allow them to send their sons to college in Lima. So before launching the enterprise that would change their lives, the Añaños brothers graduated from universities in the capital. Carlos, who later would be the company's president, studied industrial engineering at Ricardo Palma University. Jorge, who later would head the company's production department, studied agronomic engineering at La Molina Agrarian University, also in Lima.

What led the Añaños, a middle-class family like many other provincial families in Peru in the 1980s, to found a company that later would become the most important Peruvian enterprise? From what we have learned, their entry into the soft drink industry was the result of three circumstances that came together in the right way:

- First, the family—which had been engaged in farming—was forced to leave the countryside. Its property had been attacked. They had emerged unhurt but chose not to live under permanent threat. Instead of moving to Lima, however, like most middle-class Ayacuchans, the Añaños decided to move to the capital of Ayacucho.
- Second, the trucks operated by their competitors—Coca-Cola, Inca Kola, and Pepsi-Cola—were, for obvious reasons, the favorite target of the terrorists. So were beer trucks. Little by little, the trucks stopped coming, leaving the people of Ayacucho without any beverages.
- Third, the children of Eduardo and Mirta Añaños pooled their skills to weigh the situation, and they sensed a tremendous opportunity. The keys to the decision to undertake the manufacture, distribution, and sale of soft drinks were, first, the Jeris' familiarity with the beverage business and, second, the experience gained by Jorge, the oldest son, who, like Pedro Castellano, was a beer distributor.

Thus, as is the case for many successful businesses, first came knowledge of the market (in this case, the local market in Ayacucho), and later came the feeling that something was missing from that market, an intuition that would produce ideas for a new concept of soft drinks—ones priced within reach of the poor. An additional factor was Jorge's knowledge; as an agronomic engineer, he was able to develop a formula that the family could manufacture in their backyard.

On June 23, 1988, while the city was rattled by bomb blasts and threats of subversion, the Añaños, motivated by Eduardo's tenacity and vision and Jorge's experience, founded the Kola Real Company. They had US$8,000 in personal resources and a US$22,000 loan from the Industrial Bank,[4] for which they mortgaged their home. Altogether, their startup capital was US$30,000.

One year later, Eduardo Jr., another brother, began to manage the small bottling plant, and Carlos, the youngest brother, who was studying in Lima, took on the logistics and the supply of raw materials. By 1990, the two other sons, Arturo and Ángel, had joined the company, bringing the entire family into the business of manufacturing and selling a soft drink they named Kola Real.

Setting up the first plant was not a complex process, because the manufacture of carbonated beverages is relatively simple. All that's needed is a concentrate made to specification by a local supplier, to which are added standard products such as sugar, sodium benzoate, caffeine, food coloring, and water. When a company is small, all that's needed is a makeshift plant, with small machinery that can be old (secondhand), hand-operated, and slow.

The Añaños began with a very basic bottling machine that could fill fifty cases per day. The machine still can be found in one of the numerous Kola Real plants in Peru. The success of the initial formula, according to the Añaños, was due mostly to the technical knowledge of the two brothers, both engineers, who created a beverage that was pleasing to the taste of the population with the smallest possible amount of chemicals. Distribution began among the nearby neighbors and then expanded to the neighborhood. Little by little, the drink's fame spread.

Like their first plant, the Añaños' second plant, in Huancayo, was a makeshift operation in the backyard of a house. Their work pattern was not very systematic but was intense in terms of working hours. One of their collaborators said that in Huancayo they would get up at 4 o'clock every morning to unload the sugar from pickup trucks and begin to distribute the product. It was only when they made the leap to production on a larger scale, from seven thousand to twenty thousand cases per month in Huaura in 1993, and particularly when they boosted production to three hundred thousand cases per month in Huachipa in 1996, that the Añaños had to resort to more sophisticated technological systems to manufacture their beverages.

Because of the terrorist presence, the Añaños' ability to distribute their soft drinks to a wider area was limited during their first few years of operation. In order to expand, they would open small plants in other cities, as they did in Huancayo, using small-scale bottling equipment similar to what they had started with. Thus, necessity compelled the Añaños to expand the business in a nontraditional manner. What might have been a weakness— the absence of a distribution network—in time became one of their greatest strengths: a novel system of distribution based on the use of informal networks.

The genius of the Añaños did not lie in the manual production of carbonated drinks, however. Such production was common in the provinces of Peru, with numerous soft drink companies appearing, producing beverages with different brands and flavors, and later disappearing or restricting themselves to small areas of distribution. The key to the Añaños' success lay in the steps that followed and in all the factors that allowed them to grow exponentially and operate on a large scale, nationally and internationally.

During the early years, the Añaños took advantage of the shortage of both beer and soft drinks to make their debut in Ayacucho's small market. Back then, and continuing to this day, the bulk of beer sales in Peru were in returnable glass bottles. Over time, many consumers had built up a stock of bottles in their homes. When the beer and beverage trucks stopped supplying the market, these bottles became useless. The Añaños then began to buy up (for a pittance) all the beer bottles they could find, so they could use them for their product, Kola Real. These were 720-milliliter bottles— known as "family size," an expression that is preferable in Peru to "personal size." The first bottles of Kola Real were distinguishable by their label, a pleasant flavor, their low cost, and their "family" presentation.

Although intuition was an essential component of the growth of the Añaños Group, the family had set a clear strategy from the beginning and, also from the beginning, studied the market in a most professional manner. Carlos Añaños' recollection is, in that sense, revealing:

> A market study we did in Peru revealed that as much as 85 percent of the population could not afford expensive products. The principal actors in the soft drink market were the larger brands, Coca-Cola and Pepsi-Cola, and we asked ourselves why there wasn't another, more economical and quality alternative. (Aldunate Montes, 2003)

From that moment on, the Añaños did all they could to honor the slogan they use, even now, to introduce themselves in the markets of developing countries: "A beverage at a fair price."

What were the strengths that allowed the Añaños to achieve what other entrepreneurial families had attempted without as much success? Undoubtedly, they had the distinctive features of entrepreneurial families: the desire to act, the willingness to make sacrifices to cope with the challenges, and the ability and intuition to expand as they went. These abilities allowed them to deal with their weaknesses one by one, to reduce risks, and to take advantage of the opportunities available in the markets where they positioned themselves. They had scant economic resources, a weak or nonexistent distribution system, and a limited knowledge of marketing. But they had created a product good enough for the market they courted.

They also had gumption and charisma to spare, and they found a way to pool their skills by maintaining familial harmony. Finally, by having the big competitors out of the market temporarily, they could accumulate capital, perfect their product, and learn to improve the stages of production.

The Añaños' period of learning and accumulating start-up capital lasted three years. Their strategy of manufacturing a product similar to Coca-Cola but using their own formula and selling it in 750-milliliter bottles had borne fruit. In 1991, they began to operate a new plant in Huancayo, a larger and more affluent city than Ayacucho, also situated in the heart of the Peruvian Andes.

Huancayo is one of the centers of Andean commerce. It is relatively close to Lima (a six-hour automobile ride), which facilitates trade with the capital. It is also a transit stop between the jungle and the Andes and is surrounded by centers of agricultural and mineral production. The Huancayo plant was small but operated twenty-four hours a day. It had a manual machine that processed two hundred cases per day. Kola Real was immediately successful in Huancayo, allowing the Añaños to grow at a spectacular rate.

The third area of penetration was Andahuaylas, another central location in the Andes, where the Añaños set up a third Kola Real plant. Andahuaylas is smaller than Huancayo and Ayacucho, and, like those two cities, it had been abandoned by the competition because of terrorism. The profile of its consumers was similar: low-income Andean people under no pressure to consume brand-name soft drinks and willing to try something new. As a company representative recalled, "We couldn't go to other areas, other provinces, where the traditional, internationally known brands had a strong presence. It would have been madness for us to come to Lima at that moment. We were aware of our financial and commercial limitations. We had to gain more experience" (Ministry of Labor and Job Promotion, 2003).

Nevertheless, the Añaños gradually moved closer to Lima. Shortly after opening the plant in Andahuaylas, they inaugurated another one in Huacho, north of the capital. This strategy of expansion was described years later by one of the Añaños Group's publicists, with a touch of black humor that played on terrorist terminology: "The Añaños used the strategy of Shining Path, penetrating the nation with their revolution just the way Mao Zedong propounded it—they went from the countryside to the city."

Happily for the country, the Añaños succeeded in their strategy, which led them to expand their activities, and Shining Path was eventually defeated. In addition, the 1990s and the early years of the twenty-first century were years of recovery for the Peruvian economy. Reforms were made that corrected the populist policies of the 1970s and 1980s, allowing the country to open to the process of globalization.

Peru Opens to Globalization

The last three years of the 1980s were particularly chaotic in Peru. An attempt by the government to nationalize the entire financial system triggered a political crisis that matched the ongoing economic crisis. The result was opposition to the government and a proposal for radical change toward a free-market economy. The Freedom Movement, led by writer Mario Vargas Llosa, who ran for president in 1990, proposed a set of reforms that would have reversed the policies instituted by the socialist military government.

Vargas Llosa did not win the election for various reasons, among them the success of a campaign against him that spread fear among the population about the economic adjustment that was needed to get the economy to grow at a realistic pace. The winner of the election was an unknown individual named Alberto Fujimori, the son of Japanese immigrants and a man who for eleven years had concealed his own Japanese nationality. Fujimori advocated not attacking the crisis head-on with the orthodox formulas being recommended by leading economists. After he took office, however, Fujimori had no choice but to apply the economic reforms that were part of Vargas Llosa's proposal. He managed to do so with relative success, although he did not believe in the reforms his administration implemented.

For emerging enterprises, such as the Añaños' business, the reforms made during Fujimori's first term (1990–1995) were crucial. Inflation was curbed because the Central Bank was forbidden to lend money to the state by artificially increasing the monetary supply, and the state managed to balance the fiscal budget. A successful program was implemented to privatize the companies that had been nationalized by General Velasco. Tariffs were reduced considerably, trade policies that emphasized exports were established, and foreign investment was encouraged. At the same time, a series of complementary measures led to an improved economy and substantially broadened economic freedoms. In addition, the government captured Abimael Guzmán, the leader of Shining Path, which eventually led to the defeat of that movement.

The results of these changes began to be felt in 1993. As we saw earlier in Figures 1.4 and 1.5, production recovered and inflation fell until it was no longer a problem. Also, the country's balance of trade gradually reversed, with exports overtaking imports.

During its first fifteen years, Kola Real benefited from many of the economic and political developments discussed here:

- The pacification achieved by the defeat of Shining Path permitted the expansion of Kola Real's business throughout Peru, something that would have been impossible in a country torn by civil war.
- The gradual but sustained growth of the population's purchasing power (see Figure 1.6) and the consequent decline in poverty permitted the reactivation of the soft drink sector (see Figure 1.7). These factors enabled Kola Real to expand its sales within the domestic market.
- The lowering of tariffs (Figures 1.8 and 1.9) and the elimination of controls on exchange allowed the Añaños to gain access to capital goods and consumables at a lower cost.

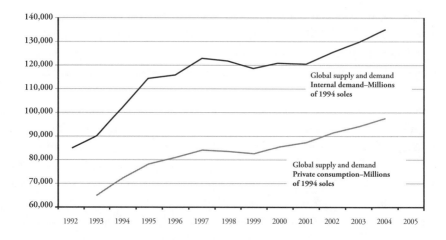

FIGURE I.6. Peru–Evolution of Private Consumption (1992–2005)

SOURCE: Peruvian Central Bank.

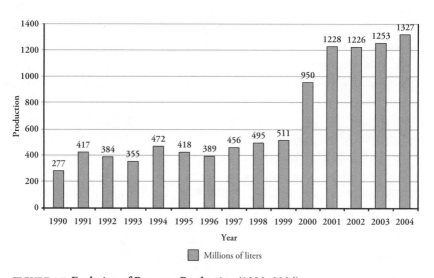

FIGURE 1.7. Evolution of Beverage Production (1990–2004)

SOURCE: Peruvian Ministry of Production.

- The opening of the capital markets allowed the Añaños to invest abroad freely once the period of internationalization began.

Obviously, all the other institutional changes—from the end of inflation to the elimination of price controls—positively affected the development of all

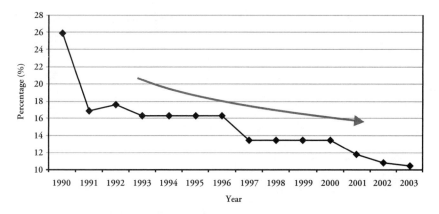

FIGURE 1.8. Average Tariff (1990–2003)

SOURCE: Peruvian Ministry of Economy and Finance.

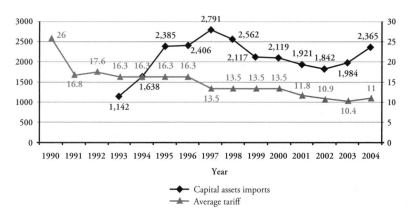

FIGURE 1.9. Average Tariff and Capital Assets Imports in Millions of US Dollars (1990–2004)

SOURCE: Peruvian Ministry of Economy and Finance.

businesses in Peru, including the soft-drink industry. Table 1.1 summarizes the principal measures that changed the institutional environment, helping spur economic growth and improve the business climate in Peru beginning in the early 1990s.

Despite these changes, for Kola Real to keep up the pace of its growth, using the strategy that had proved successful—an alternative beverage at a fair price—the national market would not be sufficient. Peru's opening to

TABLE 1.1: Principal Institutional Economic Reforms in Peru, 1990–199

REFORM	MEASURES	DATE — PERIOD
1. Price Stabilization	–Elimination of price and exchange controls –Autonomy of the Central Reserve Bank –Extreme tax audit measures to reduce the deficit –Reform of tax management, giving effective independence to SUNAT (National Superintendency of Tax Administration	1990 1993 1991
2. Trade Opening	–Elimination of restrictions on external trade (prohibitions of imports, licenses, shares, record requirement) –Elimination of preferential systems, allowances, and artificial prices –Decrease in tariff rates –Elimination of tariff barriers –Creation of Reform Program of the National Customs Superintendency (SUNAD)	1991–1998 1991
3. Capital Market	–Access barriers eliminated from trading activities –Tariff and fees collected by traders were no longer regulated –Banks and financial bodies could trade securities –Use of "privileged information" was standardized –Creation of private systems of risk classification for public offerings of securities –Creation of Public Register of Values and Traders to give investors access to information provided by value issuers. –"Securitization" of assets, investment funds, trade papers and short-term documents	1991 1996
4. Privatization	–Passage of laws regarding international and private investment –Privatization in the communication, energy, industry, and mining sectors –Creation of independent regulatory agencies for public services	1993–1998
5. Private Pension System	–Creation of a system of individual pension accounts, containing the accumulated contributions of the active worker and the return obtained by the investing these resources –Appearance of the Pension Fund Administrators (AFPs)	June 1993
6. Improvement of the Financial Market	–Elimination of interest rates controls –Liberalization of the exchange market –Liquidation of the promotion public banks –New system of regulation managed by the Superintendence of Banks and Insurance	1991–1996

Source: Abusada et al., 2000.

globalization by eliminating capital export controls made possible the next phase of the Añaños Group's expansion: its incursion into foreign markets.

Searching for a National Market

By 1992, the year when the government began to defeat Shining Path, four Kola Real plants were in operation, producing twenty-four hours a day, seven days a week. The group was accumulating experience and had enough capital to continue to expand. With peace returning to the country, the risks of expansion were reduced. But it also was a test, because the competition from traditional companies was bound to return.

In 1993, barely five years after it was founded, Kola Real moved into the Peruvian jungle after creatively evaluating the chances for developing the industry in that market and assessing the favorable climatic conditions (high temperatures) that contribute to consumption of beverages. An additional factor influencing the decision to invest in the jungle (for the purpose of expanding into most of northern Peru) was the special tax code that benefits that area. The government of Peru grants a number of tax benefits to the Amazonian provinces because of the region's lack of integration with the rest of the country, due to geographic and infrastructural disadvantages. As a result, many enterprises choose to invest artificially in those areas so as not to pay the taxes that exist in the rest of the country and then carry out a sort of "domestic smuggling" that is extremely profitable. In that regard, the Añaños were no exception and took advantage of those benefits, among them:

- An exemption from the sales tax on fuels (natural gas, crude oil, and the derivatives of crude oil) that benefits the departments of Loreto, Ucayali, and Madre de Dios, and includes the general sales tax and the selective tax on consumer goods.
- An exemption of the tax on the domestic sale of all goods and services produced in Amazonia, a tax law that is frequently broken by "domestic smuggling," in which a sale is recorded in the tax-exempt region but in fact is made outside that region.
- A special tax credit for companies that settle in the area, which allows a reduction in the amount of taxes paid on taxable transactions (sales outside the region or sales inside the region involving goods manufactured outside the region). The special tax credit amounts to 25 percent (Loreto, Madre de Dios, and Ucayali) or 50 percent (the rest of the region) of the gross monthly taxes, depending on the site in the Amazonian region where the taxpayer is located.
- A refund of the sales tax paid on goods produced outside the area to the merchants in the jungle region.
- A reduction of the income tax to 5 percent or 10 percent (depending on the taxpayer's location), instead of 30 percent, which is the national average.

These tax exemptions have not had a major effect on business development in the regions involved. Most likely, investments like the Añaños' would have been made—although probably elsewhere—even if the exemptions had not existed. But those were the rules of the game, and the Añaños adapted to them, starting from a simple cost-benefit analysis that saved them taxes though caused them to pay higher transportation costs (the "domestic smuggling" to other regions). The result was an operation that was convenient from their private point of view, though certainly not from the point of view of public policy.

The success of the Añaños' incursion into Amazonia was impressive, and soon after its creation the small plant in Bagua could hardly supply the enormous demand generated by the magical combination of quality and price. And for the first time, the Añaños had to confront an aggressive competitor—not one of the big brands but a company with more experience in the same market Kola Real was entering, the northern provinces, where the population had an average income higher than that of the populations of Ayacucho, Andahuaylas, and Huancayo. This was the Concordia Group.

A Battle for the Market in Northern Peru

Concordia was known as a pleasant drink found in the provinces of Peru, particularly in the northern region. Its founder, Victor Rivera, had been a well-known beer distributor and dealer and set up the first Concordia soft drink plant in the city of Barranca, north of Lima, in 1938. That plant began by producing five flavors: cola, strawberry, pineapple, lemon, and soda. With the passing of years and the construction of highways, the company broadened its geographic coverage, gradually acquiring vehicles for distributing its soft drinks. In 1952, the company opened a plant in the city of Chiclayo. Concordia Beverages Inc. became the largest soft drink bottler in northern Peru.

In March 1982, the government enacted the General Law on Industries (Law No. 23407), which sought to promote the creation of industrial enterprises in border and jungle areas, using tax benefits as enticements. To take advantage of these tax benefits, the Concordia Group approved the installation of a plant in the area of Sullana, department of Piura, which began operations in 1986. By the early 1990s, Concordia was the market leader in northern Peru, including the city of Bagua, which it supplied from Sullana. The arrival of the Añaños Group and its flagship beverage, Kola Real, in that city threatened their position.

Concordia's reaction was to initiate a price war in Bagua. The Riveras were convinced that they faced a weak competitor who could not last for long after Concordia cut its prices in half. They were wrong, however. The Añaños Group not only withstood the price war in Bagua but also struck a masterful blow: they set up a plant in Sullana, Concordia's center of production.

One factor that helped Kola Real's expansion in the north and jungles of Peru was Coca-Cola's corporate decision to auction off its factories in Peru. The Añaños did not waste this opportunity and bought some of the equipment at auction. From its Sullana plant, the Añaños Group began to supply the department of Piura and the cities of Chiclayo and Trujillo (principal cities of northern Peru, 800 and 600 kilometers north of Lima, respectively), where Concordia had not reduced the prices of its soft drinks. In the heat of the trade battle, the Añaños brothers said, "You can poison a well but not a whole lake." By this they meant that the price war Concordia had launched in Bagua could not be sustained at a regional level and was therefore doomed in the long run. They were right.

By this time, the Añaños Group's production was considerable. The moment had come to stop using beer containers to bottle their products. It was time to make innovations in the presentation and the containers, and that included the use of larger containers and nonreturnable plastic bottles. It was also time to head toward Peru's principal market, the city of Lima.

As had happened in the north with Concordia, Kola Real's incursion into Lima would shake the very foundations of the market for many years. In Lima, it would have its first confrontation with Coca-Cola and would become a contributing factor in the collapse of the Peruvian company with the best reputation in the industry, J. R. Lindley, manufacturer of one of the most prestigious labels in Peru—the famous Inca Kola.

A Digression: Inca Kola and Its Takeover by Coca-Cola

Peruvians are particularly proud of a soft drink described as having "a national flavor," the emblematic Inca Kola. Practically all Peruvian taste buds—particularly those of middle- and high-income people—have been "educated" to appreciate Inca Kola. The sociological success of Inca Kola has been so great throughout its history that Peru is one of the few countries in which a local product displaced Coca-Cola from first place in the market rankings.

After the Coca-Cola Company bought out Inca Kola in 2002, journalist Lucien O. Chauvin made this comment in an article in *Beverage World* titled "Inca Kola: A Peruvian Treasure Trying to Conquer the World":

If anyone asks any Peruvian what he likes most about his country, he'll hear a list that includes its history, the warmth of its people, its varied food, and Inca Kola. Today, as it begins a partnership with the Coca-Cola Company, Inca Kola is aiming at a successful exportation, worldwide, of its golden treasure. . . . Inca Kola is known in Peru as "the beverage with a national flavor," "the flavor that unites us," and "there's only one Inca Kola and it resembles no other." (Chauvin, 2003)

Johnny Lindley, president of the company and grandson of its founder, José R. Lindley, cites a combination of several elements as the reasons that this sweet, yellow carbonated beverage is one of Peru's most characteristic products. "You cannot identify a single feature that makes Inca Kola so special," he says. "The name refers to our past, the color is reminiscent of gold (for which Peru is famous), and the flavor reminds people of the broad variety of citrus fruits that grow in our country. Combined, these factors identify Inca Kola with Peru." It should also be added that Inca Kola is more a sentiment than a drink, and that sentiment combines perfectly with the slogan "the beverage with a national flavor."

Rolando Arellano, president of the marketing company Consumers and Markets, a Lima firm that studies market trends, says that, to many Peruvians, Inca Kola represents the story of David and Goliath. "Inca Kola is the symbol of the hard-working Peruvian worker, of the small man who confronts the big man and vanquishes him," Arellano says. "That gives the product added value in the local market."

The roots of Kola Peru Inc. go back to 1910, when José R. Lindley, a British immigrant, established his first bottling company in Peru. The company began to produce a wide variety of carbonated beverages with fruit flavors and rapidly became the industry leader. The Inca Kola brand was launched twenty-five years after the company was founded and has been its flagship beverage for almost sixty-five years. Today, the company has a network of bottling plants throughout the country, three of them its own and twelve in franchises that produce 320 million liters per year and employ approximately nine hundred workers. These franchises are in Piura, Chiclayo, Trujillo, Ica, Arequipa, Tacna, Cusco, Juliaca, Sicuani, Puerto Maldonado, Pucallpa, Tarapoto, Bagua, Iquitos, and Lima.

Marketing studies done in Lima in the late 1990s showed that the Inca Kola brand had captured 41.8 percent of the market share for carbonated refreshments.[5] "There are other countries where the flavor of a local beverage is preferred, but I know no instance—other than Inca Kola—of a local beverage that has consistently occupied first place in sales, despite the competition from the most important manufacturers of carbonated refreshments," Johnny Lindley says.

Although food at a McDonald's in Peru can taste the same as in another restaurant in the chain anywhere else in the world, the customers in Peru's ten McDonald's franchises wash down their hamburgers and fries only with Inca Kola. The yellow beverage is also the only drink sold in Bembos, a Peruvian chain with twenty outlets that competes with fast-food franchises such as McDonald's, Kentucky Fried Chicken, and others and holds an important portion of the market.

In 1997, the company began a process of restructuring, during which it increased its exposure to financial debt. Shortly thereafter, the Peruvian economy plunged into a recession and the company was unable to withstand the ensuing price war. Its level of indebtedness was too high. The only solution was to join up with its former competitor by means of an agreement that eventually saved the Inca Kola brand. In 1999, Johnny Lindley and Timothy Haas, executive vice president and president of Coca-Cola's Latin American Group, announced that the Coca-Cola Company would assume control of 50 percent of Inca Kola Peru Corp., owner of the trademark, as well as 20 percent of the José R. Lindley Corp., Inca Kola's bottler. The *Wall Street Journal* reported that the deal amounted to US$200 million (Luhnow and Terhune, 2003).

What caused the disappearance of Inca Kola as an independent company? One theory is that J. R. Lindley operated under the organizational rules of a traditional company such as Coca-Cola, aiming at the same market and borrowing heavily to achieve market share. This excessive debt meant that the company was unable to withstand the price war that erupted in the late 1990s. In contrast, Kola Real was geared to a different market, a lower-income one that required a business model with lower costs.

This was the competitive environment Kola Real faced when it came to Lima in the late 1990s.

Kola Real Enters Lima and Consolidates Its National Standing

By 1997, Kola Real had achieved a promising position in several departments (provinces) of Peru. Its founders then decided to attempt to conquer the market in Lima, by far the nation's largest, and to produce and market in the capital the beverage that had been so successful in the mountains, jungle, and north of the country. They decided to build a plant outside Lima, in Huachipa, at kilometer 8.5 of the central highway, on a large expanse of land with abundant underground water. Two years later, to demonstrate that they had not lost sight of the regional markets, the Añaños set up a new plant in Trujillo, in response to demand that could not be met from the Sullana or Lima plants.

TABLE 1.2. Growth of Kola Real in Peru

1988	Plant startup in Ayacucho
1991	Search for business opportunities in other than the native town. Plant in Huancayo.
1993	Leadership consolidation in the Marañon Northeast region
1994	East region
1996	Opening of plant in the Peruvian north, Sullana Plant
1997	Change of bottle, a Kola Real design Start of support strategy and brand goodwill (investment in advertisement, but always modest) Kola Real introduction into the Lima market. Plant in Lima.
1997	Launch of a new container—PET
1998	Consolidation of leadership in the north of the country

The Lima plant began operations with an installed capacity of 300,000 cases per month, using secondhand machinery. One year later, the weather, surprisingly, came to its aid. The El Niño current, which visits Peru's coastline at least once every decade, generated a particularly intense heat wave and increased the consumption of soft drinks to an extraordinary level. "God is an Ayacuchan," the Añaños commented in jest. They had reached 6.6 percent of the national market (Ministry of Labor and Job Promotion, 2003).

The spectacular reception of Kola Real in Lima prompted the company to expand the capacity of the Huachipa plant. Carlos Añaños traveled to the United States, where he purchased used equipment similar to that employed by the Añaños Group's competitors. Scarcely ten years after they opened their first plant in Ayacucho, the Añaños had nine plants in Peru: Ayacucho, Huancayo, and Andahuaylas, in the central Andes; Huacho, north of Lima; Bagua, Sullana, Cajamarca, and Trujillo in the north and east; and Lima (Huachipa). Table 1.3 lists these plants and their production statistics. In almost all of them, the Añaños had found it necessary to increase their initial production capacity. By that time, the company had created about 1,500 jobs. Table 1.2 summarizes the growth of Kola Real in its first ten years.

TABLE 1.3. Production of Kola Real per Plant, 1998

Plant	Location	Department	Startup year	Initial installed capacity (boxes/month)	Installed capacity, 1998, (boxes/month)
Emb. Asamblea SRL	Ayacucho	Ayacucho	1998	4,000	60,000
Emb. Huancayo SRL	Huancayo	Junin	1991	7,000	90,000
Emb. Andahuaylas SRL	Andahuay-las	Apuimac	1992	7,000	60,000
Emb. San Miguel SRL	Huaura	Lima	1993	20,000	80,000
Emb. del Marañen SRL	Bagua	Amazonas	1993	25,000	60,000
Industrias Gran SA	Sullana	Pura	1994	20,000	700,000
Industrias Añaños SA	Huachipa	Lima	1996	300,000	1,000,000
Emb. Cajamarca	Cajamarca	Cajamarca	1997	30,000	30,000
SRL Industrias Añaños SA	Trujillo	La Liberdad	1998	300,000	450,000

One of the keys to the Añaños Group's rapid development was its handling of human resources, with a philosophy that has always focused on productivity. That is one reason for its accomplishments in terms of quality and price. The wages Kola Real pays its employees are consistent with the average wages in the market and in the soft drink sector, but the company uses methods of variable remuneration that do not exist elsewhere. And although the company has not been immune to labor difficulties, the conflicts have been resolved without strikes or work stoppages.

In May 1999, Kola Real had 17 percent of the soft drink market in metropolitan Lima. At the same time, it had consolidated its position in the provinces, with 19.5 percent of the market in Trujillo, 21.9 percent in Piura, 39 percent in Huancayo and Ayacucho, and 17 percent in Chiclayo. Growth was swift, contributing to the satisfaction of low-income consumers and generating jobs, and it occurred in a sector that had itself grown steadily since 1994.

Figure 1.10 shows the speed of this growth, within the framework of an overall increase in the consumption of beverages nationwide. This general expansion of the market, bringing soft drinks within reach of low-income consumers, helped create the Kola Real phenomenon, both in Peru and later abroad.

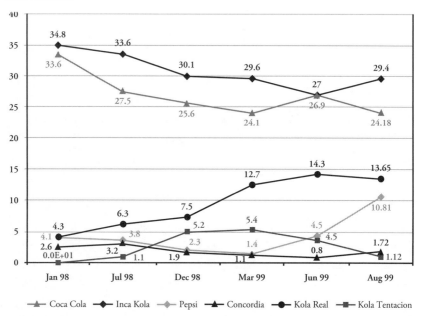

FIGURE 1.10. Kola Real's Market Share in Lima (1998–1999)

SOURCE: Non-official data—estimated by UPC.

This rapid growth came in spite of intense competition. Shortly after it entered the market in Lima, Kola Real found itself entangled in a price war. However, this time the foe was not another regional company, like Concordia. It was the Coca-Cola Company and the traditional national leader, Inca Kola.

From the Price War in Lima to the Decision to Globalize

At the time the Añaños Group entered the Lima market and began to compete with Coca-Cola and Inca Kola, the market's growth was not continuous. A recession from 1998 to 2002, initially "hidden" from the beverage sector because of the phenomenon of El Niño, eventually led the competitors into a nationwide price war that dragged prices down by an average of 20 percent (see Figure 1.11). The new competition from Kola Real also undoubtedly contributed to the price war .

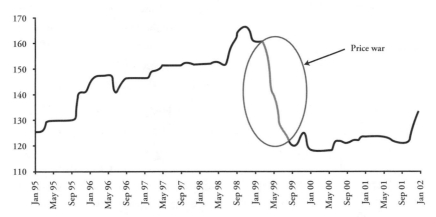

FIGURE 1.11. Soda Drink Price Evolution (1995–2002) (Index 1994 = 100)

SOURCE: INEI. Elaborated by Estudios Economicos del Banco Wiese Sudameris.

The price war unleashed by the rival companies was characterized by major promotional efforts with discounts of as much as 40 percent. It was also accompanied by an extensive campaign against Kola Real, targeting the store shelves and other points of sale. Añaños executives recall that their competitors "tore down our signs at the points of sale themselves, trying to demolish the entire merchandising process we had achieved."

"When we analyzed the situation," says Carlos Añaños, "we faced two logical alternatives. We could begin to invest (maybe disproportionately) to hold on to what we had achieved, or start over from scratch and look for new options" (Ministry of Labor and Job Promotion, 2003). Kola Real then made two wise tactical decisions. First, it would strengthen its relationship with its customers and suppliers by encouraging its more than eight hundred wholesalers to visit one of its plants and by giving guided tours of the same plants to schoolchildren throughout Peru.

The other important decision was to introduce new bottle sizes into the market. Their market share in the 2-liter family format was low, despite the fact that Kola Real was basically aimed at families. Thus emerged the 2.25-liter, 3.0-liter, and 3.25-liter bottles, which made the Añaños industry leaders (in the case of the 3.25-liter format, they were the only producers). At the end of the price war, Kola Real had further consolidated its position, improving its relationships with the distribution channels and reaching the client directly.

Finally, one of the principal keys to success was the consolidation of the distribution system the Añaños had "discovered" spontaneously during the early days in Ayacucho. This aspect is discussed in the section "The Añaños Group as a Business Case Study." The testimony of a distributor for the competition gives an idea of the significance of this factor:

> As we know, Kola Real entered the market with a strategy of low prices that permitted it not only to seize segments of the traditional market but also, and most important, to generate a new market along the base of the pyramid. Simultaneously, in Peru at that time (the country had been closed for decades to automotive imports) there was a growing trade in pickup trucks and second-hand, imported small trucks. That provided a job opportunity to many unemployed drivers who chose to engage in the distribution of Kola Real, a high-turnover product that sold very well. . . .
>
> The owners of these vehicles loaded up in the factory until late at night, due to the disorganization that existed, and were sent to the various districts of Lima. Later, they returned to the factory, turned over their sales receipts and immediately kept their commission. . . .
>
> The demand for the product was such that in a very short time those vehicles were servicing the market throughout Lima, generating sales for both retailers and wholesalers. The latter began to introduce the product, encouraged by the demand arising from the great difference in prices [between Kola Real and] the traditional beverages. It was by this modality that Kola Real made 100 percent of its sales at that time. It was better able to withstand the price war. . . .

At first, the price war led to an increase in per capita consumption of soft drinks, from 34 liters in 1999 to 44 liters in 2000, a jump of 29 percent. But after this considerable increase, and despite the fact that prices have remained low, per capita consumption has remained fairly stable. In 2004, it reached 48.2 liters per person, an 8.6 percent increase in four years. Peru has thus remained one of the smallest markets in Latin America (see Figure 1.12). And the Añaños wanted to continue growing.

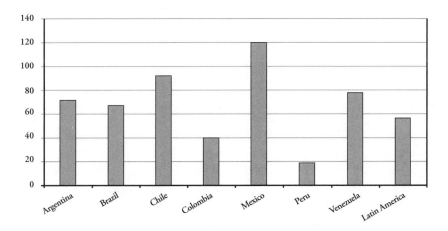

FIGURE 1.12. Soda Drink Consumption per Inhabitant, Latin America Comparison

SOURCE: J.P. Morgan 1998, quoted by M. León, Ipade.

They chose to concentrate on their low-income market niche, making innovations in the presentation of the containers, among other measures, and maintained an 18 percent market share (see Figure 1.13 and Table 1.4). They also decided to gamble on investments abroad, something very few Peruvian enterprises had dared to do.

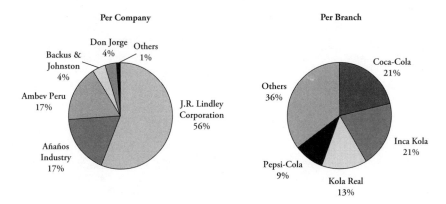

FIGURE 1.13: Market Share per Company and Branch, Year 2005

SOURCE: CCR Peru.

TABLE 1.4. Evolution in the Soda Drink Market in Peru – Total Sales Accumulated, 2001–2005

Description	2001 Annual	2002 Annual	2003 Annual	2004 Annual	2005 Annual
UCP Backhus & Johnston	1.45%	3.39%	4.02%	4.15%	5.55%
Guarana	0.22%	2.28%	2.86%	3.03%	3.57%
Sabore	1.20%	1.11%	1.16%	1.12%	1.03%
Viva	0.02%	0.00%			0.95%
EMB AMBEV Peru	22.17%	16.91%	17.51%	16.85%	14.36%
Chiki	0.29%		0.27%	0.04%	
Concordia	2.94%	2.72%	4.47%	2.68%	1.17%
Evervess	0.02%		0.03%	30,000	30,000
Mirinda	0.68%	0.01%	0.25%	0.02%	
Pepsi-Cola	7.27%	5.30%	5.51%	7.81%	8.08%
Pepsi Light	0.01%		0.05%	0.15%	0.05%
Seven-Up	3.86%	2.68%	2.17%	2.08%	2.80%
Triple Diet	0.36%		0.14%	0.08%	0.03%
Triple Kola	6.63%	5.50%	4.62%	3.99%	2.23%
Twist	0.00%	0.70%			
Kola Tentacion	0.10%				
EMB Coca-Cola	58.86%	59.47%	58.59%	57.84%	59.34%
Crush	1.53%	3.38%	4.51%	3.63%	3.45%
Inca Kola	24.13%	24.72%	21.53%	21.46%	22.34%
Inca Kola Diet	0.53%	0.38%	0.47%	0.39%	0.47%
Canada Dry	0.00%	0.52%	1.11%	0.41%	0.08%
Inca Kola Light					0.00%
Coca-Cola	20.94%	20.10%	19.55%	20.31%	21.77%
Coca-Cola Light	0.38%	0.32%	0.41%	0.38%	0.43%
Fanta	4.64%	4.24%	3.85%	4.06%	3.57%
Kapo			0.06%	0.00%	
Kola Inglesia	0.78%	2.82%	3.75%	3.81%	3.78%
Sprite	2.91%	2.94%	2.83%	3.30%	3.32%
Sprite Zero					0.11%
Schweppes	2.89%	0.06%	−0.14%	0.08%	0.01%
Tai			0.37%	0.02%	
Bimbo Break	0.14%	0.0%			
EMB Kola Real	14.84%	16.08%	16.54%	17.36%	17.13%
Kola Real	12.22%	11.47%	11.33%	11.30%	12.66%
Sabor de Oro	2.40%	3.75%	3.63%	5.38%	4.44%
Plus Cola	0.22%	0.81%	0.02%		
Big Cola		0.05%	1.49%	0.67%	0.04%
Sabor de Oro Light			0.06%	0.00%	
EMB Don Jorge	0.00%	2.95%	3.11%	3.77%	3.58%
Don Isaac	0.00%	2.28%	1.39%	1.28%	1.21%
Peru Cola		0.67%	1.71%	0.23%	2.37%
Other brands	2.69%	1.20%	0.23%	0.02%	0.03%

The Añaños realized that they had found an innovative business model for a market that had not yet been exploited in Latin America. What was the sense of trying to grow in Peru when there were so many other, larger countries with similar characteristics where their model of business was clearly applicable? In the end, the Añaños decided that it was easier, more profitable, and more promising to march—with the same winning strategy they had utilized and consolidated—into foreign markets similar to Peru but with greater per capita consumption.

The Añaños Group decided to maintain its activity in Peru at a level that would allow it to supply 13 to 15 percent of the total market for soft drinks and to initiate operations in other Latin American countries. They then took their first steps into foreign markets, first into Venezuela, in 1999, and then into Mexico, using the product name Big Cola. These two countries far exceed Peru in consumption of carbonated beverages (see Figure 1.12).

THE INTERNATIONALIZATION OF THE AÑAÑOS GROUP

The March 16, 2006, issue of the well-known Latin American magazine *América Economía* included a long article on the emergence of global brands that originate in Latin America. Among the various Brazilian, Chilean, and Argentine brands were two regional brands from Peru: Ebel, a line of cosmetics owned by the Belmont family, with sales behind Avon (United States) but ahead of Carolina Herrera (Spain) and Adidas (Germany) in the Latin American market, and Big Cola, the Añaños Group's star performer in Mexico. (The group is now called Ajegroup, a name crafted from the surnames of the father and mother: Añaños and Jeri.)

TABLE 1.5. Rankings of Soft Drinks Consumed in Latin America

Brand	Country	Consumers and market share		2004 vs. 2005	Ranking
Coca-Cola	EE.UU.	78,722	70.93%	+7.89%	1
Pepsi	EE.UU.	18,890	17.02%	+11.20%	2
Sprite	EE.UU.	13,297	11.98%	+0.77%	3
Big Cola	Peru	8,163	7.35%	+56.32%	7
Brahma-Guaraná	Brazil	3,418	3.08%	-18.93%	13
Inca Kola	Peru	3,079	2.77%	-6.53%	15

With 8 million consumers in 2005, Big Cola places below Coca-Cola, Pepsi, and Sprite in market share but far above Brazil's legendary Brahma-Guaraná and Peru's Inca Kola, which were each consumed by 3 million during that year (see Table 1.5). The trend, however, may soon place Big Cola among the leading regional brands and may even take it to a fight for second place (see Figure 1.14).

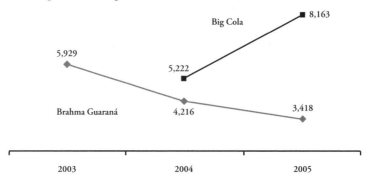

FIGURE 1.14. Soda Drinks: Regional Evolution in the Last Three Years

SOURCE: *América Economía* Magazine N.3, March 16th, 2006.

As of this writing, the company has been in existence for only about twenty years. Seven years ago, it operated only in Peru. By early 2006, the Añaños Group was present in seven Latin American countries and had begun operations in Thailand, taking advantage of the free trade agreement between that country and Peru. The company has fourteen plants and an installed capacity of two billion liters per year. It employs eight thousand workers and owns one hundred distribution centers, and its sales are estimated at US$1 billion.

The business model the Añaños invented in Peru has proven applicable worldwide. Their managerial ability has overcome all obstacles, and they have penetrated the markets with a speed a typical international corporation would find impossible to replicate. In their expansion into other countries, the Añaños have made their decisions based on the potential demand for their beverages, which is a function of the number of middle- and low-income inhabitants, and on the level of per capita consumption. That level depends on various factors, but a warm climate is essential. According to a company representative,

> In 1999, we became aware of the experience we had obtained while opening markets in different geographic areas. That experience

implied the ability to meet people, learn about markets and tastes, to knock on doors and sell. We spent part of 1998 and 1999 developing our strategic profile and preselected countries, like Brazil, Colombia, Venezuela, Ecuador, and Mexico, as investment possibilities. We initially selected Venezuela for its tropical climate and socioeconomic reality, which resembled ours. In Venezuela, we profited from an excellent experience during 1999 and 2000. We secured about 9 percent of the market in one year. We did really well. In 2001, with similar enthusiasm, we decided to begin operations in Ecuador, and, in 2002, in Mexico. (Ministry of Labor and Job Promotion, 2003, 10)

Nobody—least of all industry leader Coca-Cola—imagined that the Añaños would dare enter the gigantic Mexican market. The results were surprising, so much so that in a short while the Añaños found it necessary to move their headquarters to Mexico City, the capital of what is now their principal market.

The First Step: Venezuela

Historically, the Venezuelan soft drink market was dominated by Coca-Cola and Pepsi-Cola. A Mexican group handled the distribution of Coca-Cola, and the Venezuelan Polar Group handled Pepsi. The reasons to invest in Venezuela were clear:

- The market was three times larger than the Peruvian market.
- There was no trademark or independent bottler with national coverage.
- Its climate encouraged beverage consumption, which was almost four times higher than in Peru, even though the prices of beverages were as much as 250 percent higher than in Peru.
- There were cultural similarities, a relative proximity between the two countries and a common language, elements that made the incursion less complicated.

The Añaños saw that the 2-liter product they sold in Peru for US$1.00 sold in Venezuela for US$2.50. In addition, the plastic containers they had introduced in Peru—which were a lot more economical than glass bottles because there were no return costs—did not exist in Venezuela. There was also an unexpected gap in the market at the time because, due to a decision by the Polar Group, which went from bottling Pepsi to bottling Coca-Cola, Pepsi disappeared for a time from Venezuela. The country was also in the midst of an economic crisis, which made the low price—a key element in Kola Real's strategy of penetration—an important factor.

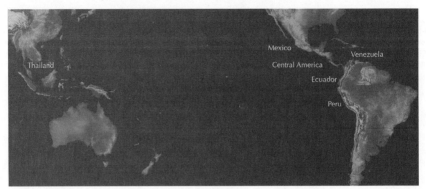

FIGURE 1.15. Kola Real's Geographic Reach.

SOURCE: © maps.com

The factory was installed in the city of Valencia, some 150 kilometers from the nation's capital, Caracas. Valencia had a number of competitive advantages when compared with the capital. Equidistant from Caracas and Maracaibo, the country's second-largest city, Valencia offered good conditions for an operation that covered all of Venezuela. The land was less expensive, and the Añaños obtained direct financing from the seller with very convenient terms.

Investment in a plant like the one in Valencia typically exceeded US$10 million, yet the Añaños managed to keep the investment down to US$5 million by purchasing some of the machines secondhand in the United States. Fifty percent of the financing came from their own capital and the other 50 percent from suppliers, with whom the Añaños had developed an excellent rapport in Peru.

The company entered the Venezuelan market with the Kola Real brand, in black cola flavor (preferred by the Venezuelans) along with orange and pineapple, among others. The novelty for the market was the size of containers—600 milliliters and 1.5 liters—which didn't exist there before. The prices were about half the prices charged for Coca-Cola and Pepsi, and the strategy of distribution replicated the model that had worked in Peru, placing distribution centers and distribution procedures in the hands of independent carriers. Cash sales, along with the suppliers' credit, allowed the company to generate a profit. Advertising was kept to a minimum, as in Peru, and Kola Real's original slogan, "Quality at a fair price," was retained.

The results were positive, despite the economic crisis that wracked Venezuela in the early 2000s. The company gradually won segments of the market, concentrating more on opening markets than on seizing its competitors' market share. The group currently holds a 12 percent market share in Venezuela for its products, which include Kola Real Flavors (pineapple, orange, and lemon in 600-milliliter and 1.7-liter containers), Big Cola (in 355-milliliter, 600-milliliter, 1.7-liter, and 3.1-liter containers), and Agua Cielo sparkling water (in 355-milliliter, 600-milliliter, and 2.6-liter containers) (Suárez, 2004).

The business model used in Venezuela soon was configured for other markets. It was characterized by a strategy of setting the price between 20 percent and 30 percent less than the leaders and by making the product accessible to the largest possible number of consumers. The Añaños later used this model when entering into the markets in Ecuador, Mexico, and Central America (Guatemala, Nicaragua, Costa Rica, and Honduras) and in Chile, with one distributor.

The company's market share in Ecuador is 12 percent (it entered that market in 2001), and it averages 12 percent in Central America. But the group's expansion into the Mexican market—one of the largest in the region, where the company's market share is close to 10 percent—was the most crucial factor in the great leap forward the Añaños Group has made in the recent years.

Mexico: The Big Gamble

The soft drink market in Peru totals US$150 million. In the Mexican market, it's US$1.2 billion. Consequently, achieving 15 percent of that market—something the Añaños viewed as perfectly feasible—would mean making more sales in Mexico than the whole soft drink industry made in Peru (see Figure 1.16). Mexico has the world's highest per capita consumption of soft drinks (150 liters) and the second-largest volume of overall consumption.

The strategy for the Añaños Group's incursion into the Mexican market was similar to the one used in Venezuela, although some innovations were made and the resistance from the competition was more violent. At the time the Añaños Group made its entrance, about two hundred bottlers operated in Mexico. The most important bottlers by far were Coca-Cola's, among them FEMSA, a giant that is present in several Latin American countries, with sales of about US$4 billion.

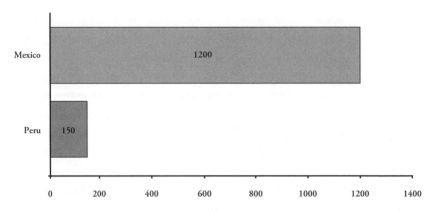

FIGURE 1.16. Market Comparison Between Mexico and Peru (millions of dollars)

SOURCE: Ajeper's data—estimated by UPC.

The Añaños' entry into this gigantic market early in 2002, with the by now famous Big Cola brand in a unique format of 2.6 liters and at a price of US$1 per bottle, took the competition by surprise. This commercial aggressiveness was met with a hostile (and sometimes unfair) response from the giant competitors. Retailers who sold Big Cola were threatened with the loss of their refrigerators; vandals were paid to destroy or damage Big Cola's advertising posters and billboards; thousands of bottles were purchased just so they would disappear from the stores or, in some cases, were adulterated by the introduction of chemicals. A boycott was orchestrated that undeniably generated problems.

But the Añaños Group emerged triumphant from the battle when the Mexican Federal Commission on Fair Trade ruled in favor of Raquel Chávez, a retailer who described the threats she had received from Coca-Cola distributors who wanted her to stop selling Big Cola. The ruling was accompanied by a US$15 million fine imposed on the perpetrators.

In a move similar to the strategy used in Venezuela, the Añaños Group located its first Mexican Big Cola plant in Puebla, a city situated at a prudent distance from the capital, with abundant water, inexpensive land, and access to a highway. Its radius of potential action covered more than 60 million consumers. The initial investment was US$7 million, which allowed the company to install top-quality machinery.

The use of independent companies to handle distribution, already successfully applied in Peru and Venezuela, was also repeated, allowing the Añaños to sell more than 80 percent of their production to grocery stores and small businesses from their 27 distribution centers. Although the advertising was minimal, it earned the loyalty of retailers such as Raquel Chávez, to whom Big Cola delivered profit margins that were higher than those offered by the competition. The Añaños used the concept of "price democratization," conducted door-to-door taste tests, and ran advertising spots that alluded to "the greatest drink in Mexico" and to its "fair price." They also developed an image that emphasized the modernity and cleanliness of their plants and pointed to the jobs that were created in Mexico as a result of their presence there.

In addition, the Añaños gradually began to reach agreements with the large supermarket chains, which, as in all of Latin America, were capturing a growing portion of the retail trade for groceries and beverages. Among them was Wal-Mart, which has more than five hundred stores in Mexico.[6] Within three years, more than 20 percent of the Añaños Group's total beverage sales in Mexico were to supermarkets.

The increase in production capacity and revenues of the Añaños Group as a result of its entry into Mexico has been spectacular. By late 2005 the group had fourteen plants and an installed capacity of 2 billion liters per year. It employed about eight thousand workers and owned one hundred distribution centers. Its estimated sales amounted to US$1 billion.

This capacity will be increased by three new plants in Mexico, one of which will open in the state of Jalisco. Consumption of Big Cola has increased from 870 million liters in 2004 to 1.1 billion liters in 2005. It is the leading regional brand in Latin America, behind Coca-Cola, Pepsi-Cola, and Sprite. And if the trend in sales continues, in only five years Big Cola will be second only to Coca-Cola.

A Global Group: Thailand and the Free World Brand

The Añaños Group is no longer Ayacuchan. It is no longer Peruvian. And it would like to stop being Latin American. Recently, it decided to take its boldest step yet toward globalization, venturing into the Thai market.

Expansion in Latin America will remain the linchpin of the group's revenues, however. It is estimated that the beverage market in Latin America will grow rapidly in the next ten years because free-market economies are being consolidated in democratic environments with increasing stability and rising per capita incomes. With two huge markets—Mexico and Brazil—the Latin American beverage market is expected to reach sales of 150 billion liters, valued at US$120 billion, by the year 2010, a growth of 50 percent since the year 2000.

On March 1, 2006, the Añaños Group announced the installation of a Kola Real manufacturing plant in Thailand. Annual per capita soft drink consumption in Thailand is 48 liters, similar to that in Peru, with a great potential for growth, said Alfredo Paredes, Ajegroup's corporate director for image and communications, when he announced the new venture.

The new plant is to be located in Bangkok, with operations planned to begin in late 2006. It will require a US$10 million investment during the first stage and $15 million by the end of the project. Initial production capacity will be between 15,000 and 20,000 cases a month. Initially, Big Cola will be sold in 3.1-liter bottles. It is expected to account for 10 to 12 percent of the Thai market by the end of 2006. The big challenge is to overcome cultural preferences among Thai consumers for drinks similar to tea. Should they achieve their objective, the Añaños will demonstrate that it is possible for a business from Ayacucho, Peru, to produce a global product.

One of the reasons the Añaños Group chose to invest in Thailand rather than another Asian country is the expectation of a free trade agreement (FTA) between Peru and Thailand (Ministry of Foreign Trade and Tourism, 2005). Negotiations between the two countries have resulted in a framework accord that was ratified by both countries in 2005. This framework defines the parameters of the negotiations for an FTA and it states that the parties agree to promote and facilitate investments between the two countries by improving the transparency of the rules and regulations covering investments, by creating conditions favorable to investors from both countries, and by promoting mutual investments. It also alludes to a previous agreement on the promotion and protection of investments signed on November 15, 1991.

This attention to the FTA with Thailand is another aspect of the Añaños Group's ability to perceive opportunities where others might not cast an eye. Few in Peru have paid much attention to the FTA, even though it represents an undeniable opportunity.

Beyond the group's expansion into international markets for Big Cola, its global vision includes developing products aimed at higher-income consumers, while continuing to follow a strategy of low prices. These products include sparkling water (commonly referred to as "table water") and energy drinks. This new strategy, like all other Añaños Group decisions, is based on a study of market trends.

Based on data from the 75 markets with the highest consumption of beverages, Zenith International estimates that the most significant growth in the industry has been in bottled water, carbonated refreshments, and distilled beverages. As for containers, the study stresses the enormous growth of plastic bottles (or PET, after its chemical name, polyethylene terephthalate). The Añaños, already capitalizing on this trend with the success of Big Cola, plan to launch a bottled water that will be available from all of their plants, under the name Free World.

THE AÑAÑOS GROUP AS A BUSINESS CASE STUDY

The Añaños phenomenon has achieved such magnitude that business schools, specialized magazines, newspapers, and analysts in all professions have turned their attention to it. In 2003, the *Wall Street Journal* sent two reporters to Mexico to learn the story behind Big Cola, an assignment that resulted in a long article. A short time later, writer Mario Vargas Llosa wrote an article about the Añaños that was published in the Spanish newspaper *El País* and distributed throughout much of Latin America. The *Economist* published its own article a few months later. And Professor Alejandro Ruelas-Gossi cited the Añaños as an example in an article in the prestigious *Harvard Business Review* (Ruelas-Gossi, 2004). Ever since, numerous business programs have used the Añaños as a case study in the teaching of business management. The Añaños' intuition and skill have surprised many, and not just because they led to success. They also broke paradigms and rendered obsolete the traditional ways of doing business in the soft drink sector.

The Añaños' experience has had parallels in other sectors, where entrepreneurs gambled on creating quality products aimed at lower-income customers. The success of these projects depended on a business model that emphasized savings all along the value chain, similar to the one used by the Añaños. Such was the case with the Zara chain and the Peruvian clothing company Topy Top, owned by the Flores family (see Chapter 2) .

One of the keys to the competitiveness of the Añaños Group was its ability to find a product and a production process that allowed it to achieve lower costs than its competitors. Another was its ability to overcome the barriers erected by competitors and the environment. Others were the alliances forged with suppliers and clients, the manner in which the company reached the market through novel means of distribution and promotion, and the prudence of its financial management. The final key lay in its ability to continue to create new products.

A New Paradigm of Business to Conquer the "Base of the Pyramid"

The social and economic situation in Peru, as in many developing countries, presents a socioeconomic pyramid in which the majority of the population, at the base of the pyramid, has a monthly income below US$500 (see Figure 1.17). This majority, disdained for many years by the traditional entrepreneurial class, became the objective of an important number of companies that have seen tremendous growth.

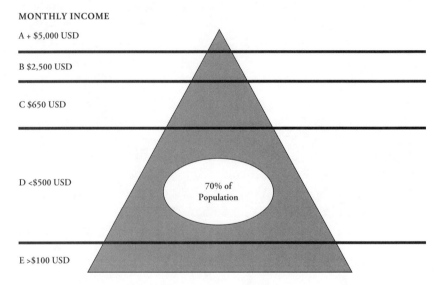

MONTHLY INCOME

A + $5,000 USD

B $2,500 USD

C $650 USD

D <$500 USD

70% of
Population

E >$100 USD

FIGURE 1.17. The Socioeconomic Pyramid in Peru

SOURCE: Apoyo Opinión y Mercado.

In the case of soft drinks in Peru, before the introduction of Kola Real, a great mass of consumers did not have the resources to buy Coca-Cola or Inca Kola. They had to make their own refreshments or buy powdered flavorings in paper packets. The Añaños family aimed at that market, in a move that was a radical change from the business model used by their competitors.

As proposed by Rodríguez, Sabriá, and Sánchez (2004), one of the fundamental reasons for the Añaños to enter the soft drink market was what the authors called "temporary reasons, a set of temporary developments that favor the entry of a company into the BDP market. Normally, these causes are related to the existence of an unstable political and economic situation that leads to a loss of the people's purchasing power."

The global, traditional soft drink brands—such as Coca-Cola and Pepsi-Cola—based their business on marketing and distribution, and achieved worldwide leadership in practically all markets. The local competitors—in the case of Peru, the typical example is Inca Kola—imitated them and saw in them the paradigms, the best practices, and the innovation. That is why the local competitors in many countries normally were satisfied with being followers and capturing the segment of the market left over by the leading brands. Kola Real did not follow that pattern. It competed outside the established rules and outside the established ways of doing business.

TABLE 1.6: Comparison of Strategies Global Drinks – Traditional Brands vs. Kola Real

Product (Benefit)	*Lifestyle*	*Lifestyle (follow the leader)*	*Satisfy a need*
Positioning	*Brand*	*Brand*	*Customer Return*
Bottle Format	*Small*	*Small*	*Big*
Statement	*"That's it," "Move," "Vibe"*	*"Drink it together with everything"*	*Fair price*
Customer	*A.B.C. class*	*A.B.C. class*	*C. and D. class*
Price	*High*	*Follow the leader*	*Low*
Distribution	*Own*	*Own*	*Outsourced*
Promotion	*Towels, turnkeys, t-shirts*	*Towels, turnkeys, t-shirts*	*Glasses, trays (useful things)*
Advertisement	*Very deep*	*Very deep*	*Almost nothing*
Competitive Advantage	*Brand*	*National Brand*	*Costs*
Competitive Strategy	*Commercial pull and push*	*Compete against the leader*	*Create markets*

Table 1.6 compares the strategies followed by Kola Real and the traditional producers of beverages. Unlike the brand names, products like Kola Real and Big Cola do not seek to sell a lifestyle. They aim to satisfy a need at a low cost. That is why their slogan goes right to the point: "A beverage at a fair price." The fair price was determined by making every effort to determine a fair cost at each step in the value chain, breaking paradigms in the process, from the purchases from suppliers to distribution and advertising. This was done not with the traditional intent of becoming a market leader but with the objective of creating a new market at the base of the pyramid.

Low Prices, Great PET Containers, Zero Royalties

> *"We didn't come here to compete with the big ones. We came only to democratize the consumption of refreshments and let the market expand."*

Carlos Añaños, México City
(Ministry of Labor and Job Promotion, 2003)

The Añaños Group's ability to sell Kola Real and Big Cola was based on the strategy of placing an inexpensive product on the market. Rather than gaining market share by wresting part of the trade from the traditional bottlers, the company attracted new consumers—families who didn't normally drink carbonated beverages—and got them to buy them in large plastic bottles. That is why Kola Real currently leads the market in Peru in 1.25-liter, 2-liter, and 3.25-liter bottles (see Figures 1.18 and 1.19).

One of the essential elements of marketing Kola Real as an inexpensive product was having a personal brand, an identity. That placed the Añaños at an advantage in relation to the big-brand bottlers, like Coca-Cola and

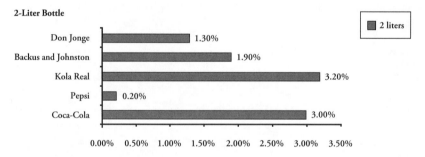

FIGURE 1.18. Kola Real's Market Share in Peru, by Type of Bottle

SOURCE: Non-official data—estimated by UPC.

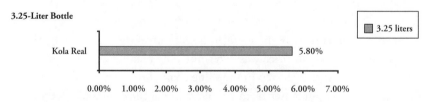

FIGURE 1.19. Kola Real's Market Share in Peru, by Type of Bottle

SOURCE: Non-official data—estimated by UPC.

Pepsi-Cola, which charge the bottler a royalty that is usually quite high. Another factor that helped reduce costs was the use of plastic PET containers. These containers don't require the large initial investment that glass bottles do, and they also have other favorable characteristics, such as simplicity, less risk, less weight, and ease of adaptation to different shapes.

The trend has been, as Carlos Añaños says, toward the "democratization" of the consumption of soft drinks. The range of products has widened and, in all of the markets the group has entered, prices have gone down. In the case of Peru, for example, the Kola Real phenomenon has caused prices to drop by an average of 18 percent in the past five years.

In the case of the Añaños Group, five additional elements of the value chain contribute to the reduction in costs and therefore to the drop in prices: the innovation in distribution, the imaginative austerity in promotion and advertising, the organizational culture, the conservative management of finances, and, more recently, the adaptation to new trends in beverage consumption.

A Key Innovation: Informal Distribution via Direct Self-Sales

A simple yet innovative way of distributing the product made a key competitive difference for Kola Real. Until that time, bottling plants sold directly to grocery stores and wholesalers. In urban areas, the bottlers' trucks delivered directly to retail stores. Authorized wholesalers took care of delivering the product to the stores in areas that were farther away or isolated or that had a low volume of sales. This traditional model requires a series of assets (heavy and light trucks) and specialized personnel (drivers, collectors, route schedulers, etc.) that entail a significant cost. That cost is absorbed by the bottler.

Kola Real did not adopt the traditional system, however. Instead, it used a new system of *autoventas directas* ("direct self-sales"), or direct individual sales, that gave it a very important competitive edge. The direct self-sale system abandoned the direct distribution to the stores and to the exclusive wholesale dealers. This produced cost savings but also eliminated distribution territories and encouraged a distribution process that was more spontaneous and competitive.

The system worked by inviting any person with a vehicle (or without one) to buy Kola Real at the bottling plants or distribution centers. For example, a taxi driver could—as part of his regular job—drive by a plant or distribution center and pick up small quantities of Kola Real to distribute in his neighborhood or within his work radius. Also, an ordinary worker (or an unemployed person) could buy the merchandise in small quantities and distribute it in a specific area.

At first, the distribution system was quite haphazard. However, it became an important mechanism for cost savings and allowed the company to reach into distant areas. Gradually, the system became more formalized, but it continued to be based on the outsourcing of distribution, without its own fleet. The distribution is done from the production plants and the company's own warehouses, always by a fleet driven by third parties or, in the worst case (particularly for the transport of goods from the plant to the warehouses), by leased vehicles.

With this system of self-sales and cash payment, and by turning 93 percent of its distribution over to private contractors, Kola Real began to reach the farthest sites at the lowest cost, carrying out the mission statement made by Carlos Añaños: "To contribute to a significant growth of the whole beverage market, with a quality product that's accessible to most people. To promote and strengthen the development of all the members of the value chain in the organization (suppliers, workers, and clients)."[7]

A key factor in this process was that it took advantage of the available manual labor. In Peru, most of the population is not adequately employed. This means that most people make a living from informal self-employment.

The distribution system developed by the Añaños adapted very well to a country like Peru, where the opening of trade had permitted the importation of an enormous number of secondhand vehicles. This wave of imports led to an expansion of self-employment in public transportation, in the driving of both minibuses and taxis. Seemingly overnight, the formal public transportation system—which had collapsed—was replaced by this informal system.

From the start, this approach allowed a good margin of profit to all participants in the process. In particular, Kola Real offered retailers a profit margin that was 25 percent higher than that for the other brands. The informal method of direct sales also benefited another segment of the Peruvian population that was informally employed: the street vendors and others who sell soft drinks "on the run."

It's interesting to see how the latter sales technique operates. A store, or some business establishment with refrigerators or coolers, becomes the supplier for a group of people who, after picking up their supply of bottles, take over a busy street intersection and offer the drinks to drivers who are waiting for the traffic light to change. Alternatively, the street vendors go to places where crowds are known to congregate and sell beverages in individual-size containers. Incredible though it may seem, these types of sales account for more than 15 percent of the total sales of soft drinks in Lima.

Innovation in Promotion and Advertising

Kola Real was not aimed at the same market targeted by the traditional beverages. Consequently, just as its distribution was adapted to the social reality of a poor country, the way in which Kola Real was promoted differed from the traditional advertising campaigns. Most advertising is done through the mass media—television, radio, and print media—and occasionally by sponsoring special events. It always involves positioning the product as a beverage for consumers with an upscale lifestyle and consumption level.

Thus, the common practice in the promotion of traditional beverages has been to play with the consumer's aspirations: to be successful, live happily, be a famous athlete, and so on. The budgets needed for this type of promotion are always considerable.

In the case of products aimed at the base of the pyramid, this type of advertising strategy was impossible due to its high cost. Additionally, for products like Kola Real, this method is not necessarily the most effective. The target population views the consumption patterns touted by traditional advertising to be far out of their reach. A product can be rejected not only because it's expensive but also simply because it seems expensive.

Before it entered the Lima market, Kola Real broke new ground in terms of advertising, using approaches that brought the product close to low-income consumers. It carefully chose popular events and artists to sponsor and used unusual promotion techniques, such as exchanging Kola Real bottle caps for products that were useful to low-income people, a technique that was remarkably successful in the country's poorer areas.

In areas where the residents demonstrated a preference for Kola Real, the company worked to consolidated its image. In Sullana, it opened the Medical Club for the Kola Real Family, which examined almost a thousand walk-in patients per week at no cost. That club led to two others in Lima. However, the practice had to be dropped because of complications of another nature.

A Quality-Oriented Organizational Culture

The organization of the Añaños Group emerged from the distribution of tasks among brothers. The corporate structure created in the group's Mexico City headquarters adapted the family formula to the type of formal organization required by any enterprise of its size. Little by little, the Añaños have been appointing managers and delegating responsibilities. But, as can be seen in Figure 1.20, all the key decisions are made by the "family board."

The group's organizational force rests on the brothers' cohesion. From the beginning, the manner in which they interacted marked the company's organizational culture. One of the central components of this culture is a tolerance toward mistakes that may be committed. "To err is permitted," Carlos Añaños says. "What's not permitted is doing nothing" (Suárez, 2004). If an employee makes a mistake, it's because he or she has made an effort. It is better to make an effort and err than to do nothing. That is why Carlos Añaños once said, "We're not looking for culprits, we're looking for solutions."

To complement this cult of success, the Añaños promote—through Eduardo and Mirta Añaños—a culture of austerity as a family tradition. The idea that imbues the group's employees is that every possibility to save money must be grasped, as a contribution to reducing the price of the product and consequently to increasing the access of low-income people to soft drinks.

However, many analysts believe that the group will have to work very hard on its corporate management standards so that in the future the corporation can maintain its competitiveness regardless of the presence of the founding family members in its affairs.

The company is dealing with the challenge of professionalization by hiring executives of the highest quality. A Colombian director general and a Mexican director of public relations, among other hirings, give clear signals of that intention. Thus, the Añaños are implementing their own reform of the corporate board by defining and separating the functions of shareholders and managers. The family, who make up the shareholders, retain the authority to look for new business horizons, while the managers are entrusted with the actual running of the business.

However, the group has a long way to go before it achieves the high standards of corporate modernity it seeks. Perhaps the principal challenges the Añaños must face in this regard are to fully delegate the management of some of their subsidiaries and, particularly, to enter the capital market. If

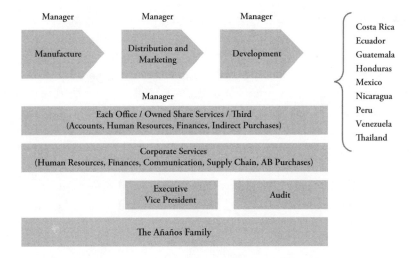

FIGURE 1.20. Añaños Group Business and Organizational Model

SOURCE: Rodríguez, Sabriá and Sánchez, *The Supply Chain at the Base of the Pyramid.*

they gain a place in the stock exchange, the Añaños will have to share their decisions with a different type of management structure, bringing aboard not only managers but also independent directors at the helm of the holding company and the subsidiaries.

Conservative Financial Management and Financing by Suppliers

One of the main characteristics of the Añaños Group's financial management has been their underutilization of bank financing and the consequent reduction of their financial burden. Like most successful family enterprises, the group financed its expansion with its own capital, in this case resorting intensely to financing by suppliers.

When the funds of a company and those of a family are one and the same, prudent financial management represents an aversion to risk. In addition, there is also often an aversion to dealing with banks, which tend to look askance at emerging enterprises and charge them interest rates that are far higher than the average for the market. These factors have influenced the Añaños Group, which has been prudent in its financial management despite its growth.

As in all family businesses, the Añaños Group's financial management has been the product of intuition. It has been guided more by cash flow than accounting balances, giving the company great flexibility to react to crises as well as to opportunities for accelerated growth. In fact, companies with low indebtedness can withstand eventual sales problems—such as a recession—comfortably, without the fear of banks knocking at the door to collect overdue payments, as was the case with J. R. Lindley and Inca Kola, which could not survive the price war in the late 1990s.

Low indebtedness also facilitates a company's access to credit, allowing it to finance an increase in production that might be necessary to meet an unexpected rise in sales. In that sense, another important merit of the company was to gradually establish alliances with its suppliers, who increasingly came to trust the Añaños' sales ability. The suppliers sold their products to the manufacturer on credit and thus became its principal source of outside financing.

Flexibility and the Launching of New Products

One characteristic of the Añaños Group's competitiveness has been its flexibility, which allows it to make decisions swiftly. This flexibility is an advantage every family enterprise potentially has, compared with a corporation with widely dispersed shareholders, such as Coca-Cola, in which major decisions take a long time. An example of this flexibility is the group's launching of Free Light citrus water, which was introduced three weeks before the launch of a similar product by Coca-Cola. The Coca-Cola product had been conceived much earlier, but the company had to go through a much longer process than the Añaños did.

The launching of competitive products for higher-income sectors has marked the Añaños Group's new diversification strategy. Although the target market is not the same, the strategy is similar: to offer a quality product comparable to one launched by a leading company, but at a lower price. That's the case with Agua Cielo, which leads the Peruvian market with a 50 percent share. It's also the case with Sportade, which competes in the sports drink market with Gatorade and holds 45 percent of the market in Peru. Finally, the Añaños Group has gone into the pulp-juice market, where it has gained 30 percent of the market with only one product, only four months after launching it.

Thus, the Añaños' latest venture is to diversify the market segments they sell to while retaining their strategy of offering products of a quality comparable to that of global market leaders, but at a lower price.

CONCLUSION

It should be clear from this analysis of the Añaños Group and from other instances of entrepreneurial success in emerging countries that the theories that oppose globalization and free trade, claiming that nascent industries must be protected, have become downright obsolete.

It is true that the Añaños' success was helped by an extraordinary circumstance—the absence of traditional competitors in Ayacucho, Peru, during the era of terrorism. That circumstance motivated them to create their first product. But the essential stage of their growth came when the group was able to grow and enter markets dominated by competition that they didn't have in their early days.

The key to their success, then, was their ability to compete in these markets, first in the Peruvian provinces, later in Lima, and eventually internationally. For that national and international growth to be possible, there had to be a minimum environment of security and free enterprise. Terrorism had to be defeated, the Peruvian economy had to open, and foreign investment had to be accepted in Mexico, Venezuela, and the other countries where the Añaños made incursions. In that sense, the Añaños phenomenon is a triumph of the free market.

Essential to the Añaños' success has been their identification of a potential market not served by the traditional companies—low-income consumers—and their ability to offer that market a quality product at a low price.

How could the Añaños identify that market? Because they were very close to it. The Añaños come from Ayacucho. The market on which they based the expansion of their business is composed of the people with whom they coexisted. It was a population that wanted to enjoy a cola drink but didn't have the money to buy Coca-Cola, Pepsi-Cola, or Inca Kola. What the Añaños were not aware of at first was that the same market was all around them, in Latin America particularly, but also in Asia and Africa.

That market was not served by the traditional brands, which engaged in an unnecessary, dirty war with the Añaños in Mexico. It was a new market. The Añaños are not interested in being market leaders in any of the countries in which they sell. Their vision is global. Their story is also a triumph of globalization.

How did the Añaños come up with a quality product for such a low price? It was a matter of their entrepreneurial ability and their desire to adapt to the reality of the low-income market in emerging countries. The entrepreneurial story of the Añaños is far from over. In less than twenty years, they have achieved more than anyone, themselves included, might have imagined in 1988. They began in the garage of their home, just as Bill Gates, the founder of Microsoft, did. Unlike Gates, however, the Añaños lived in a poor country that was undergoing an unprecedented economic crisis, and they were at the very center of a civil war.

Their story suggests that entrepreneurship is a much more effective way of combating poverty than the more traditional, government-led efforts that seek to use various mechanisms, from targeted incentives to massive redistribution and protection, to generate the economic activity necessary to raise the standard of living in developing societies. What is particularly interesting in this case is that the Añaños did not benefit from the kinds of reforms that in other countries have spurred entrepreneurial activity, such as the strengthening of the rule of law, the lowering of barriers to entry, the simplification and reduction of taxation, and, generally, the elimination of mercantilist privilege. In their case, the family succeeded in spite of the environment, exploiting the opportunities they were able to identify, even under adverse circumstances. Not every would-be entrepreneur is able to do this in countries where the wrong kind of institutional environment prevails.

In that sense, the success of the Añaños raises the question of how many other successful ventures would generate substantial wealth in a country like Peru if engaging in an entrepreneurial activity were not an act of civic heroism but a more normal activity. There is nothing to suggest that the Añaños' example cannot be echoed in many other areas of the economy, or that many other Peruvians could not generate wealth through successful entrepreneurial activity. Of course, it is very difficult, under the prevailing circumstances, for this example to multiply itself, because the disincentives of the system are enough to prevent many people from following through with the entrepreneurial ideas they might entertain. But the hidden message of the Añaños is that the potential is there. All that needs to happen for this potential to translate into effective wealth creation is a set of institutions that facilitate rather than hinder the initiatives of the would-be Añaños of Peru.

NOTES

1. Vargas Llosa, Mario. 2003. The Añaños. *Daily El País*, Madrid, November 16. The company's financial information is confidential. Table 1 is taken from a report from Ministry of Labor and Job Promotion, 2004, 28.

2. In 1996 this terrorist group attracted worldwide notoriety when one of the last groups to join it held hostage a large number of authorities and prominent figures who had been invited to the residence of the ambassador of Japan in Lima to celebrate Emperor Akihito's birthday.

3. According to data from the National Institute of Statistics and Information of Peru (INEI) and the Corporation of Research Consultants, Lima, Peru.

4. According to information provided by the company.

5. Source: Corporation of Research Companies, Lima, Peru, 2000.

6. It is worth noting that one of the advantages of free trade is the introduction into the local economy of international firms that are not beholden to the local power structure and that abide by international standards rather than some of the shady local practices associated with a closed economy (and that usually occur under some form of official tolerance or complicity).

7. In a speech to National Association of Industries during the Celebration of Quality Week.

REFERENCES

Abusada, Roberto, Fritz Du Bois, Eduardo Morón, and José Valderrama. 2000. *La Reforma Incompleta: Rescatando los Noventa*. Lima: University of the Pacific.

Abusada, Roberto, Javier Illescas, and Sara Taboada. 2001. *Integrating Peru into the World*. Lima: Peruvian Institute of the Economy and Research Center of the University of the Pacific.

Aldunate Montes, F. 2003. Article in *Revista América Economía*, June.

Apoyo Consultants. 2003. *Analysis of the Tax Exemptions and Incentives and a Proposed Strategy for Their Elimination*. Lima: Ministry of the Economy and Finance.

Chauvin, Lucien. 2003. Cinderella Story in Peru. *Beverage World en Español* 122 (March): section 3.

Ferré, Miguel, and Gabriel Natividad. 2003. *Document for Discussion: Kola Real (A)*. PAD—School of Management, University of Piura.

Government of Peru. 2003. *Report from the Commission on Truth and Reconciliation*. Available at http://www.cverdad.org.pe.

Luhnow, David, and Chad Terhune. 2003. A Low-Budget Cola Shakes Up Markets South of the Border. *Wall Street Journal*, October 27.

Ministry of Labor and Job Promotion. 2003. Beverages: Problems Are Opportunities. In *Starting a Business: How Successful Entrepreneurs Got Started*. Lima.

Ministry of Foreign Trade and Tourism. 2005. *Protocol Between the Republic of Peru and the Kingdom of Thailand to Accelerate the Liberalization of Trade and the Facilitation of Commerce.* Available at http://www.mincetur.gob.pe/COMERCIO/OTROS/tlc_tailandia.

Rodríguez, M.A., F. Sabriá, and P. Sánchez. 2004. *The Supply Chain at the Base of the Pyramid.* Navarra, Spain: IESE Business School, University of Navarra.

Ruelas-Gossi, A. 2004. Innovating in Emerging Markets: The Big T Paradigm. *Harvard Business Review,* February.

Shack, N. 2004. The Strategy of the Fight Against Poverty. In *The Incomplete Reform,* ed. R. Abusada, F. Du Bois, E. Morón, and J. Valderrama. Lima: IPE—University of the Pacific.

Suárez, David. 2004. *Peruvian Success—Kola Real Group Expands Successfully in Four Countries.* Available at http://www.gestiopolis.com/canales7/mkt/marketing-estrategico-del-grupo-koala-y-su-expansion.htm.

Vargas Llosa, Mario. 2003. The Añaños. *Daily El País,* Madrid, November 16.

2

Defeating Poverty Doing Business
The Case of the Flores Family and Topy Top

DANIEL CÓRDOVA*

SUMMARY

Aquilino Flores got started washing cars, without any capital, forty years ago. Today, he is the most important textile businessman in Peru, leading a company with annual sales of more than US$100 million. He has about five thousand direct employees and exports of about US$85 million. He also owns thirty-five department stores in Peru and three in Venezuela and has delved into the financial industry through consumer credit cards. The case of the Flores family and Topy Top is one of tenacity, determination, and intuition.

INTRODUCTION

As with most countries in Latin America, the economic history of Peru has been marked by a contrast between the evolution of the official economy—a space for interactions between politicians and mercantilist entrepreneurs—and the stories of thousands of enterprising citizens who carried on in the margins of power and the traditional elites. As De Soto (1986) states,

> As in today's Peru, in the days of European mercantilism the possibility of entering into formal entrepreneurship was the privilege of only a few. At first, the entrepreneur always needed an express authorization from the government, which, for major entrepreneurs, took the form of a letter of privilege. . . . Consequently, access to the

---

*With the contribution of Liliana Alvarado, Pedro Castellano, Gonzalo Galdos, and Claudia Sícoli.

world of business was limited to those persons or groups that had political links and could reward their government for the privilege of operating a legal enterprise.

The instances of success in Peru, which once was the center of the Spanish colony in South America, have not been sufficient to generate a cycle of wealth generation, as has happened in many countries in eastern Asia. But there are enough remarkable achievements to demonstrate that, despite the existing barriers, the excessive operating costs, and the multiple difficulties encountered by small businesspeople, it is possible to overcome poverty by entering the market economy. The case of the Flores family and their business, Topy Top, is further proof that enterprise is the way to overcome poverty in an effective and lasting manner.

In the mid-1960s, Aquilino Flores was performing a job that's still very popular among young people eking out a living in greater Lima: he washed cars. By chance, he took up the street sale of cotton T-shirts in the same place where he washed cars, Lima's emblematic Central Market. From then on, Aquilino developed what may be his main skill: to place himself at the service of the market—to investigate, with the intuition typical of the born entrepreneur, just what the market demands and what the consumer prefers, so that he can produce it and start a chain of production.

Thus began a story of capital accumulation that turned the Flores family into the owner of one of the country's largest companies, creating five thousand jobs in a country where less than half the population has any formal employment, and becoming the principal exporter of textiles and garments. By the end of 2005, Peruvian exports of textiles and garments totaled US$1.3 billion. Most of that production was sent to the United States market, mainly to the principal manufacturers of sportswear, such as GAP, Old Navy, and Nike. Topy Top, the company owned by the Flores family, is now at the top of the Peruvian ranking, with exports worth US$85 million.

Unlike most of the traditional companies in Peru's textile and garment industry that have turned to exporting, however, Topy Top has not slighted the domestic market or similar markets in Latin America. Before Topy Top developed its export trade on a grand scale, it entered the retail market through department stores nationwide, something uncommon in a market that is so centralized in Lima. Proximity to the consumer, in this case the low-income consumer at the base of the pyramid, has been key to the business's expansion to the provinces of Peru. The retail business has allowed the Flores family to discover the financial business behind the retail trade and offer credit cards to consumers, allowing them to take their purchases home and pay later, with interest.

Through its retail chain, Topy Top also sells products imported from China, such as plain fabrics, perfumes, and home appliances. It even sells insurance. From the start, the Flores family's movements have been guided by the market, always advancing with both caution and boldness.

Finally, not satisfied with its export market and its retail business in Peru, Topy Top has taken its first steps toward internationalizing its activities, by opening two stores in Venezuela, a country with a relatively high income and little competition in the textiles and apparel trade. Faithful to their style, the Floreses have entered Venezuela cautiously, using the brand name Pima Express and targeting the low-income market. The next step will be Mexico, in the regional steps of another company that has experienced swift success: the Añaños family, manufacturers of carbonated soft drinks (see Chapter 1.)

How has this entrepreneurial performance been achieved, starting from nothing in terms of capital in an environment that is unfavorable to private initiative? Entrepreneurial achievement of this type is not easy to explain. However, an observation of the performance of this company, an analysis of its strategies, and the testimony of the leading players can give us some clue to the keys to that success.

This chapter begins with a description of Topy Top today. It reviews some figures to illustrate the levels of production, export, and job generation the company has reached. Then it describes some of the characteristics of the company's activities. It highlights the Flores family's ability to move the business forward, from the street sale of T-shirts to their manufacture and commercialization on a grand scale.

This chapter also describes the integration of production, the quantitative leap that resulted when the company began to export its products, the conservative nature of its financial activities, its flexibility in negotiations, and its recent step toward professionalization. Finally, it examines the global vision found in the company's strategic plan.

The second part of this report reconstructs the entrepreneurial history of the Flores family within the framework of the evolution of Peru's economy. Throughout this story, we shall find a series of elements that keep repeating themselves in different forms: the family's ability to take advantage of opportunities; their knowledge of the customer as a key feature of their entrepreneurial success; their ability to overcome the obstacles around them, first working in the informal economy and then in markets that are generally poor, such as those in the provinces; and their efforts to penetrate the markets of developed countries, which are often protected. Topy Top's current success results from venturing into the United States and European markets. The company has diversified, and the family has gradually relinquished its hold on managing the business, leading to the professionalization of its procedures.

The third part of this report presents Topy Top as a business case study. It is always interesting to observe how the successful entrepreneurial performance of a family whose members, with no formal education, developed their business on the basis of intuition is studied to enhance the theories of business participation.

Topy Top has been studied by the University of Navarra, Spain, as an example of development that benefits the base of the socioeconomic pyramid. It is said that the keys to this development are proximity to the market and operational efficiency. Accordingly, we establish a parallel with the business model followed by the famous Zara clothing chain (which has also been studied in detail as a business case) to show how Topy Top has managed to maximize efficiency along the value chain by means of diversity and speed of production at low cost, achieving similar and enviable standards of quality. This comparison reveals hidden profits in the Topy Top strategy.

Finally, the report describes the organizational culture of Topy Top, a high-pressure culture imbued with optimism and effort. This section looks at how some of Topy Top's strategies have run into barriers that are typical in the developed markets, such as labor regulations established by some clients forbidding suppliers to hire women who work at home, or regulations that entail issuing visas to workers who labor in the export trade. We then review Topy Top's strategy today, in terms of strengths, opportunities, weaknesses, and threats.

TOPY TOP TODAY

The Peruvian business world became aware of Topy Top's existence in the late 1990s, when the export statistics published monthly by the Foreign

Trade Association of Peru (Comexperu) began to show the company's continuous rise in the rankings (see Figure 2.1).

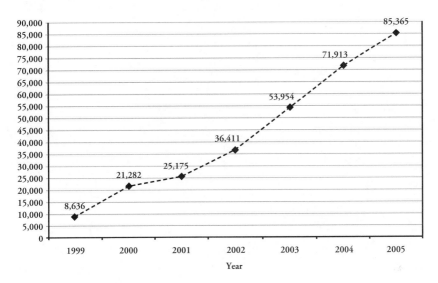

FIGURE 2.1. Evolution of Topy Top Exports

SOURCE: Topy Top.

In 1999, Topy Top exported US$8.6 million per year, and it began to appear in a ranking of leading exporters, which included Nettalco, a former transnational, and San Cristóbal Textiles, a traditional factory reconverted for export trade, both of which exported about US$40 million. Three years later, in 2002, Topy Top was fourth in this ranking, with US$37 million in exports.

In 2004, Topy Top was the second-largest Peruvian exporter of textiles and apparel, with US$71 million, competing closely with Textimax, another company with a great tradition. It reached first place in 2005, with US$85.3 million in exports (see Table 1). By then, Topy Top had built up an excellent reputation in the textile sector in Peru, which had tossed away the mercantilist banners and was successfully embracing globalization.

Topy Top's leap to being a flagship Peruvian company was made when the company accelerated its commercial activities in the provinces and arrived at Lima's most important shopping center, the Jockey Plaza. Positioning itself as the only competitor funded with Peruvian capital in Lima's department stores (where two Chilean-owned chains, Ripley and Falabella,

TABLE 2.1. Ranking of Textile Exporters

	Company	2005	2004	Growth
1	TOPY TOP S.A.	85,364.92	71,913.70	18.70
2	CONFECCIONES TEXTIMAX S.A.	85,123.04	83,535.11	1.90
3	DEVNLAY PERU S.A.C.	81,848.20	38,415.33	113.06
4	DISENO Y COLOR S.A.	78,925.12	65,715.67	20.10
5	TEXTIL SAN CRISTOBAL S.A.	46,236.42	42,197.00	9.57
6	SUDAMERICANA DE FIBRAS S.A.	42,477.05	44,169.65	(3.83)
7	INDUSTRIAS NETTALCO S.A.	41,191.78	40,862.51	0.81
8	TEXTIL DEL VALLE S.A.	36,894.69	34,922.97	5.65
9	CIA.IND. TEXTIL CREDISA-TRUTEX S.A.A.	34,462.15	33,386.68	3.22
10	COTTON KNIT S.A.C.	29,403.87	27,582.17	6.60
11	MICHELL Y CIA S.A.	26,914.18	27,415.13	(1.83)
12	SOUTHERN TEXTIL NETWORK S.A.C.	24,110.01	21,035.62	14.62
13	TEXTILES CAMONES S.A.	21,076.69	8,336.61	152.82
14	HILANDERIA DE ALGODON PERUANO S.A.	20,491.34	15,692.27	30.58
15	INCALPACA TEXTILES PERUANOS DE EXPORT S.A.	19,782.89	20,685.79	(4.36)
16	INDUSTRIA TEXTIL DEL PACIFICO S.A.	17,808.77	17,041.49	4.50
17	CORPORACION TEXPOP S.A.	17,584.86	22,374.99	(21.41)
18	PERU FASHIONS S.A.C.	15,727.10	16,754.44	(6.13)
19	TEXTIL LA MAR S.A.C.	15,327.04	17,955.97	(14.64)
20	CORPORACION FABRIL DE CONFECCIONES S.A.	15,123.24	12,731.58	18.79
21	TEXTILES SAN SEBASTIAN S.A.	15,110.58	14,559.73	3.78
22	INCA TOPS S.A.	13,297.05	9,971.47	33.35
23	FRANKY Y RICKY S.A.	12,236.69	10,677.57	14.60
24	COPERTEX INDUSTRIAL S.A.C.	12,069.51	642.02	1,779.93
25	CONMPANIA UNIVERSAL TEXTIL S.A.	12,041.86	7,453.88	61.55
26	INDUSTRIA TEXTIL PIURA S.A.	11,939.61	13,171.49	(9.35)
27	LIMATEX SOCIEDAD ANONIMA	9,607.63	7,761.16	23.79
28	AVENTURA S.A.C.	9,202.62	9,293.56	(0.98)
29	CIA HITEPIMA S.A.	7,885.12	5,748.29	37.17
30	LIVES S.A.C.	7,693.25	6,361.30	20.94
31	PRODUCTOS DEL SUR S.A.	7,540.02	6,322.78	19.25
32	CIA. INDUSTRIAL NUEVO MUNDO S.A.	7,171.56	8,027.87	(10.67)
33	DEAFRANI S.A.C.	7,156.16	5,113.91	39.94
34	GLOBAL KNITS S.A.C.	6,712.64	4,233.40	58.56
35	APPAREL PRO S.A.C.	6,374.35	4,433.89	43.76
36	CORPORACION CALEX S.A.	6,060.05	5,188.82	16.79
37	EXPORT E IMPORT MUNDO FASHION S.A.C.	6,049.19		
38	SUMIT S.A.C.	5,861.24	5,436.65	7.81
39	GARMENT INDUSTRIES S.A.C.	5,525.99	4,384.19	26.04
40	TEJIDOS SAN JACINTO S.A.	5,502.89	3,812.81	44.33
41	NEGOCIACION LANERA DEL PERU S.A.	5,330.67	6,415.06	(16.90)

42	CORPORACION EL PILAR S.A.C.	5,131.22	3,208.40	59.93
43	CONTEMPO MEGASTORE S.A.C.	4,973.47	2,375.50	109.37
44	FIBRAS INDUSTRIALES S.A.	4,794.77	5,793.51	(17.24)
45	FABRICA DE TEJIDOS ALGODONERA LIMENA S.A.	4,781.09	3,679.46	29.94
46	SERVITEJO S.A.	4,623.28	9,477.38	(51.22)
47	COATS CADENA S.A.	4,408.83	3,222.99	36.79
48	GAITEX S.A.	4,381.46	1,794.50	144.16
49	CORPORACION SANTA MARIA S.A.	4,224.79	3,123.66	35.25
50	FIBRAS MARINAS S.A.	4,199.18	3,674.80	14.27
		977,760.13	838,084.73	16.67
		1,274,892.79	1,093,482.16	16.59

SOURCE: Superintendencia de Administración Tributaria

are present), Topy Top became an obligatory point of reference for the Peruvian consumer.

Although Topy Top has about 4,500 employees, 4,000 of whom work in the various production lines and 500 of whom work in its retail stores, this number does not include indirect employment, including the many small companies and people who provide services to the company. If we take into account the 1,500 to 2,000 apparel manufacturers working as subcontractors, the employment generated by Topy Top climbs to more than 6,000 direct and indirect employees.

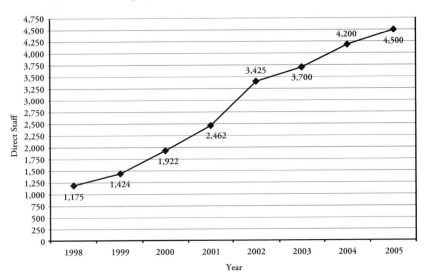

FIGURE 2.2. Evolution of Topy Top Direct Staff

SOURCE: Topy Top.

An entire social circuit, essentially made up of young women (70 percent of the labor force), makes a living from Topy Top, identifying with the company and hoping to climb a career ladder that begins with the simplest machine operators and rises to jobs as line supervisor, floor supervisor, shift boss, and so forth. The rate of growth of the manual labor employed by Topy Top, shown in Figure 2.2, has a direct and clear correlation with the development of the group's export business.

One peculiarity of Topy Top, compared with the other textile-export companies in Peru, is the relative importance it places on the domestic market. It currently owns thirty-five stores in Peru and five in Venezuela. Its incursion into the retail business, initially conceived to sell its own line of garments, has opened the door to other types of business: the sale of imported clothing, perfumes, and domestic appliances, many of them imported from China, and the sale of financial services through a credit card issued in conjunction with Banco Wiese Sudameris, one of Peru's largest banks. Thus, Topy Top has become a global enterprise through three mechanisms: as an exporter, as an importer, and as a foreign investor.

The retail business promises to be extremely important to Topy Top's future development. In fact, department stores have just begun to appear in Peru, as in much of Latin America, and in recent years modern companies have begun targeting the mass-consumption sectors composed of lower-income consumers. Traditionally, such stores in countries like Peru have marketed primarily to high-income consumers, a particularly small segment. In the past several years, both the supermarkets (the case of the Wongs, a Peruvian family of Chinese origin, is emblematic in Peru) and the clothing and appliance stores have begun to penetrate the formerly marginal neighborhoods of Lima, particularly in the booming Northern Cone. The same has happened in the heretofore forgotten provinces of Peru, a country where one-third of the population and almost half of the gross domestic product are located in Lima.

The market for clothing and durable goods has been energized in Peru by the Chilean-owned chains Falabella and Ripley. Nevertheless, it was in Peru, not Chile, where the Ripley chain began to target the low-income markets in Lima, an experience Ripley now seeks to replicate in Chile.

In the case of the provinces, the EFE chain (owned by the Ferreyros family and specializing in domestic appliances) has decided not to compete in Lima, where Peruvian chains like Hiraoka and foreign chains like Curacao have set up shop. Instead, EFE chose to expand only in the provinces, where it has seen sales grow to US$40 million in less than four years. This expansion illustrates how the development of foreign trade (in this case, of imports) has been the basis for the growth of businesses that have helped improve the well-being of a population that traditionally has been ignored.

It was in this context that Topy Top developed its retail business. It competes with stores like Ripley and Falabella in Lima and in some provinces, both in clothing and durable goods, and it is making plans to compete with the EFE chain in the provinces, but only in domestic appliances. It will be interesting to see how it applies its well-known competitive strategy to the appliance sector, and to see whether the Floreses can develop in a sector where they lack know-how.

Until a few years ago, the retail business was based exclusively on the sale of products in stores. Today it has shifted toward consumer credit associated with the purchases made in those stores, a financial business that grows at an increasing rate once the clients' trust has been secured. The Floreses understood this and quickly launched their Topy Top Visa credit card in conjunction with Banco Wiese Sudameris, which was recently acquired by Canada's ScotiaBank. The introduction of the credit card gave Topy Top a presence in three lines of business: textiles and apparel, the retail trade, and consumer credit.

A Visit to Topy Top's Factory and a Store

Entering the headquarters of Topy Top in the populous district of Zárate, northeast of Lima, is an interesting experience. It is only after we enter the factory and drive to the offices that we become aware of the size of the operation. If it weren't for the information and communications that emanate from loudspeakers, a visitor might think he or she was on a street rather than in a factory.

We find ourselves, then, in a small city. The source of income for thousands of families, this city manufactures more than 35 million garments each year, 25 million of which are exported and 10 million of which are sold in Peru's domestic market.

The view from the offices is impressive. From the second floor, we can see much of the garment manufacturing process. Before our eyes are hundreds of people working on assembly lines, workers who appear not to coordinate among themselves but who are participating in a flexible and sophisticated process to meet the demands of quality and delivery stated in their production goals.

The simplicity of the company's founder, Aquilino Flores, remains intact as time goes by. The millions of dollars he has made in almost forty years of activity in the garment industry have not altered his deference. Starting as a car washer at Lima's Central Market, he became a simple street vendor, along with his brothers, at the market. He continued to develop as a small businessman in the garment trade until he became a major industrialist. But he still greets people with the simplicity of a humble person.

He behaves like just any worker, giving no hint of the fact that he is a rich man who manages about five thousand workers who produce more wealth every day. We were two unknown academicians who visited him to ask questions that were often personal, yet he welcomed us courteously, despite the low profile he usually maintains, no doubt for reasons of security. In a poor country like Peru, being rich is not looked well upon, especially if one has risen from the lower social ranks. He comes across as a humble man, one who does not forget his origins, although he is conscious of the success he has enjoyed, expressing an authentic and justified pride in his accomplishments.

Aquilino welcomed us to his offices, a suitcase at his side. He had come directly from the airport, returning from one of his many trips. In the division of labor within the family, Aquilino, the most important man in the company, handles the sales, marketing, and product conception and makes sure that what the company produces will be accepted by the market. This preoccupation with the market was, and continues to be, the key to the company's success, which is why Aquilino spends as much time outside Peru as he does inside the country.

Aquilino never worked alone, however. The story of Topy Top is the story of all the Flores brothers, he stresses. And that collaboration remains intact. Aquilino and his siblings form a unit, a solid and functional team, in the words of Estevan Danieluc, the general manager they hired some years ago to reorganize the company and professionalize its operations. Manuel Flores is in charge of the productive processes. His expertise is technological; his objective, productivity. He is always looking for ideas and new ways to reduce costs. Carlos supervises accounting, while Marcos and Armando, who have no specialty, work full time performing specific assignments.

The austerity of the offices and the simplicity of the people who welcome us are reflective of an organizational culture directed toward profitability. The optimism of R. Benavides, a young man who has just completed his MBA (he was first in his class) with the backing of the company and who "is being groomed for manager," in the words of Estevan Danieluc, gives us an idea of the company's future, a future that will depend in part on whether or not a new government will change the rules of the game and restrict economic freedoms.

We came to Topy Top because we knew Estevan Danieluc, the company's general manager. Previously, Danieluc was a shareholder and managing director of Nettalco Industries, a company he founded and later sold to the transnational company La Fabril (Bunge & Born). Years after retiring from Nettalco, Danieluc was hired by another important company in the industry, San Cristóbal Textiles, as a general manager to reorganize the company and direct it toward the export market. The company was deeply in debt, and Danieluc pulled it out of its predicament.

A native of Uruguay who resettled in Peru, Danieluc shows a particular admiration and appreciation for the accomplishments of the Flores family. His testimony is particularly valuable because he views the business from two perspectives: that of a professional who has had wide experience in the traditional corporate sector of the industry, and that of a newly appointed general manager of a family enterprise that has grown in an explosive manner, breaking the usual patterns of the industry.

Intuition has been pivotal to Topy Top, Danieluc tells us. In meeting the challenge of delivering quality products on time, the Flores family applied the usual textbook strategies. However, other aspects of the family's methods of decision-making, involving efficiency and competitiveness, appeared in no textbook at all. These innovations will be studied by academicians, conceptualized, and converted into new paradigms for the industry.

Danieluc suggested that intuition, in this case, has worked. But he immediately cautioned us that the company's growth means increased systematization of its processes, the formalization of the decision-making process, and involvement with the financial world and the capital market. Growth that is too rapid can lead to inefficiency, he maintains. One learns to correct inefficiencies on the go, each time making improvements that bring profitability.

Some of the innovation achieved by the Flores family is evidenced by the Topy Top department stores, particularly regarding the types of products they offer in Peru. We walk through the store at the Jockey Plaza Shopping Center and buy some garments. In this center, Lima's most exclusive, there are many big-name stores. Topy Top is next to Tommy Hilfiger and is near Calvin Klein, Lacoste, Hush Puppies, and others. In addition, the Chilean-owned chains Falabella and Ripley offer a broad range of quality clothes at moderate prices. The primary difference between these stores and Topy Top is the prices.

Like all Topy Top stores, this one is very well located. Attention to the customer is optimal. Promotions are everywhere. The styles change every week. The custom of changing stock slowly, by season, is not observed. In that sense, Topy Top has followed the new paradigm set by Zara, the Spanish chain. Merchandise that does not sell within a certain period goes into baskets and is marked down for final sale. This ability to rotate the items and generate new styles requires a constant design effort, which Aquilino Flores supervises directly, in consultation with the store managers. The need to meet short production deadlines demands continuous improvements in the operation.

Characteristics of the Topy Top Approach

This discussion highlights five characteristics of Topy Top's approach: the integrated nature of production, the predominance of exports, the conservative financial approach, its flexibility, and the move toward professionalism.

Vertical Integration of Production

Topy Top's final product consists of knit apparel made of 100 percent cotton. But the present factory, founded in 1997, does not simply produce garments. This factory uses a vertically integrated production process that goes from knitting to finishing, including dyeing, cutting, sewing, printing, embroidery, and laundering. The factory uses large and very sophisticated machines to perform the operations prior to sewing. In the sewing, and of course in the finishing, an army of workers looks after every detail. Figures 2.3 and 2.4 compare Topy Top's original production process to the one it uses today. The process of vertical integration involved gradually internal-

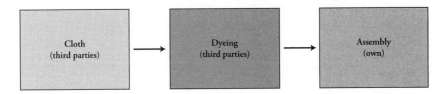

FIGURE 2.3. Topy Top's Original Production

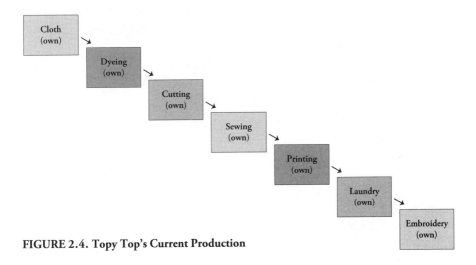

FIGURE 2.4. Topy Top's Current Production

izing each step of the production process. The Floreses began as informal merchants; later they went into sewing, and much later they subcontracted the other processes, such as dyeing and printing. The change in process was possible thanks to the growth in sales and the consequent availability of resources to hire the best technicians they could find. In that sense, an advantage well utilized by the Flores family was the fact that they coexisted with a sizable group of textile enterprises with several decades' experience in the business.

As we saw in the rankings of exporters, Topy Top is among dozens of Peruvian garment manufacturers that have turned to exports. It therefore has many competitors. Nevertheless, the rivalry among them is relative. In fact, to the degree that they face a global demand, the possibility of cooperation between companies or individuals in the same sector has grown. This interaction with other companies has allowed Topy Top to learn and innovate, for example, through the hiring of technical personnel and, more recently, of higher-level executives.

An example of the importance Topy Top places on its environment has been the recent opening of a plant in Chincha, 250 kilometers south of Lima. This is a small city where, sometime in the 1980s, several garment manufacturing companies opened for business, among them San Cristóbal Textiles. Gradually, a labor force knowledgeable about the textile trade was created in the area. When the time came to increase its production capacity, Topy Top decided to settle in a place that contained a labor force with specialized know-how.

Topy Top's competitiveness depends increasingly on specialized labor, rather than on low-cost manual labor. The industrial complex at Zárate and the plant at Chincha have state-of-the-art machinery and personnel especially trained to ensure the timely delivery of its products at competitive prices. The company's growing capital investment has allowed it to cut costs while generating an increasing number of jobs. In that sense, the vertical integration of the different areas of the production process and the reduction in production time have been key elements in the company's success.

Predominance of Exports

Topy Top's critical growth occurred as a result of the company's incursion into the export market in recent years. It couldn't be otherwise. The Peruvian market is very small in comparison with the markets of North America and Europe. Left behind were the theories that entrepreneurs like the Flores family could not become successful exporters of manufactured goods without resorting to government protection. Also left behind were the theories that the export of manufactured goods from the Third World were possible only on the basis of cheap labor.

Although it is true that the relatively low wages in Peru are a competitive advantage to Topy Top, it is not the most important factor. The real key to Topy Top's success as an exporter is its vertical integration of intensive capital processes with intensive manual-labor processes, in addition to its high standards of quality and speed.

Statistics for 2004 showed a production of almost 35 million garments per year, of which 26 million were intended for export (see Table 2.2). In dollar terms, Topy Top in 2005 had sales of about US$107 million. About

US$87 million of these sales, or 80 percent of the total, were exported. Ninety-five percent of the export volume went to the North American market. The Venezuelan market (under the brand Pima Express) was just getting started during that year. The remaining 20 percent of production was sold nationwide through Topy Top's chain of retail stores, under the brand Trading Fashion.

TABLE 2.2. Evolution of Topy Top Garment Production

Garment Production	2002	2003	Var %	2004	Var %
Plant	6,720,447	7,473,395	11.20	9,857,183	31.90
Services	6,906,472	10,650,347	54.21	15,981,366	49.96
Export	13,626,919	18,123,742	33.00	25,828,549	42.51
Serv. INKANIT	2,586,992	2,217,967	14.26	2,984,612	34.57
Services	3,625,332	2,043,715	43.63	5,585,178	73.29
Domestic Market	6,212,324	4,261,682	31.40	8,569,790	101.09
Garment Total Production	19,839,243	22,385,424	12.83	34,398,339	53.66

SOURCE: Topy Top Annual Report

In 2005 the value of imports, mostly from China and intended for sale in Topy Tops' thirty-five department stores, was US$20 million. Imports from China are garments such as jeans, which are not produced by Topy Top and therefore do not compete with its products. All cotton knit garments sold in Topy Top stores are produced exclusively by Topy Top.

Exports to the North American market are made directly through specialized brokers. Many of these brokers are Peruvian entrepreneurs who have devoted themselves to linking Peruvian textile manufacturers with the demand in the United States and Europe. Some brokers began as managers of textile companies. Others created their companies in association with partners abroad.

Topy Top's success in exports, therefore, has followed the logic established when the company was founded. That logic seeks to:

- Generate value by serving the client (Villaorduña, 2005,10).
- Develop the product as a function of demand, trying to stay ahead of what the client wants. The company is particularly demanding in terms of quality, to which end Topy Top is implementing an ISO 9000 system.[1]

- Develop a culture of cost reduction at all levels of the organization (Villaorduña, 2005).

Topy Top is planning to expand into other markets with its own brands, designed and produced at the local level. Its first effort in this area has been to create the Pima Express brand for the Venezuelan market, as a test for the type of expansion it envisions, which is unquestionably more risky but has a greater potential for profitability in the Latin American market.

Conservative Financial Approach

One of the main characteristics of Topy Top's financial approach is its conservative management, which is reflected in its patrimonial solidity. Like most other successful family enterprises, Topy Top has financed its expansion with the family's own capital. The family has resorted very cautiously to bank credit. When we visited the company, early in 2006, its indebtedness was very low for a company with sales of more than US$100 million. Its long-range liabilities amounted to US$4 million and total bank indebtedness was US$11 million, but the accounts receivable totaled US$18 million.

TABLE 2.3. Topy Top General Balance (in US$)

	2002	2003	2004	2005
Current Assets	22,435,590	21,868,133	33,881,415	38,771,646
Machinery and Equipment	19,596,722	23,769,735	30,521,490	30,287,371
Subsidiary Companies	1,236,517	1,638,831	793,629	392,090
Leasing	1,171,277	1,246,759	1,280,451	1,295,893
Leasing Interests	605,003	643,992	488,696	407,998
Other Current Assets	263,593	324,066	344,794	363,858
Total Assets	45,308,702	49,491,518	67,310,475	71,518,856
Current Liabilities	23,479,193	18,699,933	29,287,795	26,757,506
Non-current Liabilities	4,527,103	4,244,479	4,474,160	3,475,547
Total Liabilities	28,006,296	22,944,412	33,761,955	30,233,053
Deferred Gains	2,343,649	2,588,848	2,585,303	2,448,594
Equity	14,958,756	23,958,258	30,963,217	38,837,209
Total Equities and Liabilities	45,308,701	49,491,518	67,310,475	71,518,856

SOURCE: Topy Top Annual Report

Topy Top's strength has been to maintain that prudent financial management, despite its growth and despite the evident desire on the part of

Peruvian banks to lend money to the company. A similar phenomenon can be seen in Topy Top's principal competitor in exports, Textimax Garments. The Isola family, which owns Textimax, has also maintained a low profile and financial prudence, resulting in an enviable solvency and greater profits. As can be appreciated in Topy Top's general balance sheet, shown in Table 2.3, its long-term indebtedness is practically nil. The liabilities are essentially composed of short-term financing, which is standard pre-export financing for the export trade. The assets easily cover the company's total liabilities, something very infrequent in companies of this nature.

The contrast between the performance of these family-owned firms and the performance of the companies in the traditional economic groups, which are indebted to the banks, is significant. So are the results. In fact, San Cristóbal Textiles, a company with ties to the Raffo Group (former shareholders in Peru's largest bank) operated while burdened by bank debt, which reduced its chances for investment and growth.

As in all other areas of Topy Top's business, its financial management has been a product of intuition. That management has been based on the cash flow recorded by the company, which allowed it to maintain a low level of indebtedness, permitting the company to respond better to reduced sales caused, for example, by a recession. On the other hand, low indebtedness facilitates the company's access to credit, in case it needs it to finance a sudden increase in production to accommodate new orders.

Flexibility as an Imperative

Topy Top's whole approach is aimed at achieving the flexibility it needs to win the competitive battle. For instance, one of the most important results of its improvements in the production process has been a reduction in the time it takes to produce garments, from receipt of the order for a specific design to the delivery at the port of destination. Until recently, the general manager says, delivery time was 120 days, from receipt of order to delivery. Today, the same process takes place in 45 days. Simply imagining the number of steps needed to produce the 2 million garments Topy Top manufactures each year for Old Navy is a difficult task. The process requires a complex organization that not only must respond in time but also must maintain a margin of error below 5 percent and a minimum of surplus or shortage.

How has this organization established itself from a garment workshop set up by a group of brothers who educated themselves as their enterprise grew? Intuition was and continues to be a key factor in the company's approach. However, part of that intuition eventually led them to abandon spontaneity and adopt an organizational structure that looks increasingly like a corporation.

Toward a Formal Corporate Organization

It's no secret that Topy Top, initially known as Flores Creations, at first carried out much of its activity in informal commerce. This was true particularly in the first years of its activity, when 100 percent of its sales were made in the local market or were exported through informal merchants to Bolivia and Ecuador in particular. Nevertheless, over time, formalization became necessary, due to three inextricable factors:

- The company's growth, which turned it into one of the country's principal taxpayers.
- The reorganization of the tax codes in the early 1990s, which created the Superintendence of Tax Administration (SUNAT), replacing the disastrous General Tax Directorate, which reduced tax revenues to 5 percent of gross domestic product despite the sky-high taxes imposed by the administration of the populist Alan García. The SUNAT made it difficult for companies of a certain size to avoid paying taxes.
- The beginning of formal exports in 1995, which facilitated the collection of the tax on sales and the partial collection of tariffs on consumable goods.

The tax imperative became an important incentive for carrying out the overall formalization of the company. But it wasn't the only incentive, and it wasn't the only aspect of the company that needed to be formalized. More important still was the formalization of the business and operations, the gradual professionalization of the company, as the Flores brothers realized they couldn't manage the entire company by themselves. It became necessary to learn from technicians with experience in other companies, and to create executives who could be day-to-day administrators.

In that sense, perhaps the most important step was to hire a professional general manager, an industry specialist whose mission was to help the business grow, emphasizing exports and professionalizing the entire organization.

For Topy Top, professionalization has been a consequence of growth. Entrepreneurial growth tends to generate organizational problems and potential inefficiencies. The only solution is to systematize and depersonalize the decision-making process. Until a few years ago, Topy Top had no managers. The only people holding that title were the shareholders, who were also the only directors—the members of the Flores family. Today, the managers are professionals.

Thus, in addition to the general manager, Estevan Danieluc, we find other managers who are not members of the Flores family: César Vargas del Pino, administration and finance manager; Nicélida Códova, commercial manager; Gustavo López, systems and planning manager; and Mario Minaya, comptroller. The board of directors, however, has not brought in independent directors who are not shareholders and remains exclusively controlled by the Flores brothers—Manuel Flores, president; Aquilino Flores, general director; Rosaura Flores; Florentino Flores; and Armando Flores.

What's the outlook for a company of Topy Top's size that, although becoming professionalized, retains a family approach? Aquilino Flores is working on a successor. His sons have studied at the best universities and are beginning to take on responsibilities in the company. Aquilino wants his daughter to develop the credit card business. He continues to work twelve hours a day. His ambition is expressed in one word: growth.

But Aquilino is aware that in order to continue to grow beyond the current levels of sales he will have to conceive investment projects that are larger in scope than those he has devised previously. For this to occur, he will need to enter the capital market. It is probable, then, that we shall soon see Topy Top issue long-term bonds or trade on the Lima Stock Exchange or even on the New York Stock Exchange. Such a change will require a more integral reform in the organization, something the Floreses will surely implement with the combination of prudence and aggressiveness they have previously used to grow.

A Vision of the Future

A natural result of the process of formalization at Topy Top has been the formulation of a strategic plan, drawn up in November 2005. The plan reflects clearly how the day-to-day intuitive management has been replaced by clear short-term objectives (one year in the future) and scenarios for the long term (ten years ahead) by identifying strengths, opportunities, weaknesses, and threats.

The Mission

Topy Top's mission today is conceived globally: "To dress the world with fashion clothes that are casual and of high quality." Among its principles are respect for the legal framework, for the environment, and for the community. The Floreses commit themselves to ethical behavior with honesty and transparency. Their foremost principle is the client's satisfaction, on the basis of quality and service. They are aware that the development of human resources is the foundation of their organization, so they make it a priority, along with a permanent search for flexibility and innovation.

The Objectives

The objectives contained in Topy Top's strategic plan reflect a consistency between its mission and its business goals. It commits to:

- Sustained growth in the sale of clothing with high profitability.
- Increasing the company's specialization in the manufacture of styles with added value, for the production of high-quality exports.
- Continuously improving the processes of production and administration, so as to improve productivity and reduce costs.
- Efficiently directing innovation and the continuous development of designs and a variety of products with greater added value.
- Developing human resources as a fundamental part of the company's competitiveness.

A Global, Long-Term Outlook

The most impressive aspect of Topy Top's strategic plan is its vision for the next ten years, a vision characterized by its global vocation. How does this Peruvian company, formed by a family from one of the poorest provinces in Peru, analyze the evolution of the world apparel market? It sees it as a market that inevitably tends to grow, as the barriers to free trade are eliminated.

The analysis made by the Flores family and its team of the various scenarios possible until 2014 began with a look at what the apparel market has been since 1980 and what it can be in the future. Figure 2.5 demonstrates the repression of the garment market during the era of the Multifiber Arrangement, also known as the Multifiber Accord or Agreement. These accords were the mechanism by which the industrialized countries imposed

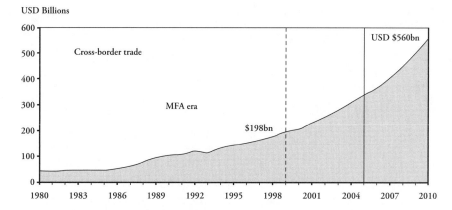

FIGURE 2.5. Global Apparel Is Expected to Expand Significantly by Lifting of Trade Barriers

SOURCE: J.P. Morgan.

import quotas for the purpose of protecting their textile industry. This was the era of the GATT, the General Agreement on Tariffs and Trade, which became the World Trade Organization, or WTO, during the so-called Uruguay Round. During that round, many barriers to trade—such as the Multifiber Accord—were eliminated.[2]

Not surprisingly, beginning in the late 1990s, after the Multifiber Arrangement was removed, growth in the garment trade accelerated worldwide. Factories began to multiply in Asia, Central America, and the Far East, further demonstrating that the elimination of obstacles to international trade favors production and employment in the poorest countries.

In its projection of both optimistic and pessimistic scenarios to 2014, it is clear that Topy Top sees its greatest opportunities in freedom and in the least intervention by the state, whereas it is more pessimistic about the obstacles to commerce and the possibility of populist politics in Peru.

- The company views the increase in per-capita consumption by export-oriented countries such as China, India, and Pakistan as an opportunity. At no time are these countries mentioned as a threat to the company's development. Furthermore, it considers the importation of plain fabrics from China, for instance, as a business opportunity to the extent that those imports do not compete with Topy Top products and complement Topy Top's sales of knitwear at retail stores.

- With regard to the prices of products, Topy Top's pessimistic scenario mentions subsidies in the competing countries. Its optimistic scenario stresses freedom of price and an increase in sales as a result of the demand for better-quality garments.
- As to new competitors, the optimistic scenario states that "they have always existed and always will exist, but the company must and can respond to the challenge with better products, offers, and service."
- Regarding the role of the WTO, the optimistic scenario hopes that it will safeguard the environment and respect labor laws worldwide.
- The company believes that an evolution of the Free Trade Agreement of the Americas (FTAA) would be favorable to the integration of commerce at the continental level.
- Regarding the national situation in Peru, Topy Top's directors are eloquent in their optimistic scenario, which states that competitiveness will not be the result of government action, that the rate of exchange must be realistic, and that the Central Bank must perform its stabilizing task (this scenario contains a criticism of the exchange-rate delay defended by the Peruvian Central Bank). Their pessimistic outlook alludes to the possibility of a fresh outbreak of terrorism, to the insecurity felt by citizens, to piracy and smuggling, to the high costs of the infrastructure, to a controlled rate of exchange and to a Central Bank that "does not meet its obligations." Economic freedom, low transaction costs, and the rule of law add up to the best scenario, in Topy Top's view.
- As to labor legislation, Topy Top's directors indicated that "the company has survived several political scenarios and will continue to do so." Their pessimistic scenario is presented in the framework of "populist governments, a strong tax pressure on the formal economy, an increase in labor costs, and an increase in corruption."
- Finally, with regard to the environment, Topy Top's pessimistic scenario envisions "a greater rigidity in environmental controls, which would increase costs in the textile industry." However, they consider it proper to invest in measures to comply with the current and future standards.

This vision of the future, held by the Flores family and its management team, is the product of their experience. They know that one doesn't always emerge from poverty because of the kindness of the state. They have lived through periods of lesser economic restriction and periods of open trade and greater liberalization of the markets. They progressed the most during times of greater economic freedom, when they opened their eyes to globalization. They have lived through periods of political uncertainty, of insecurity in the streets, and of terrorism. They know that the cost of not having a rule of law is high.

Let us take a closer look at the story of the rise of this entrepreneurial family, which managed to clear dozens of obstacles before going from poverty to wealth.

THE STORY OF TOPY TOP IN THE HISTORY OF PERU

The Flores family comes from Huancavelica, one of the poorest provinces of Peru. As shown in Figure 2.6, the per capita gross domestic product (GDP) of this province, in the southern Andes of Peru, is equal to half the per capita GDP of all of Peru, which at present is US$2,763 (International Monetary Fund, 2005). According to the current poverty statistics, 84.4 percent of the population of Huancavelica is considered to be poor; 60 percent live in abject poverty (see Figure 2.7).

The situation was not very different in the 1960s, when Aquilino Flores

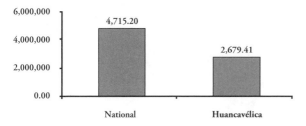

FIGURE 2.6. GDP Per Capita in Constant Soles—Year 2001

SOURCE: INEI.

decided to move to Lima to make a future for himself. The per capita GDP in Peru in 2005 was similar to the GDP in 1966, the year the Floreses began selling clothing on the streets. In fact, the 1970s and 1980s were decades of economic regression in Peru, as shown in Figure 2.8.

The first years of Topy Top's entrepreneurial experience took place in a difficult economic environment. The socialist reforms of dictator Juan Velasco Alvarado (1968–1975) had created rules of the game that discour-

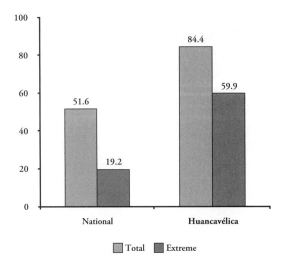

FIGURE 2.7. Poverty Rate—Jan/Dec 2004

SOURCE: INEI.

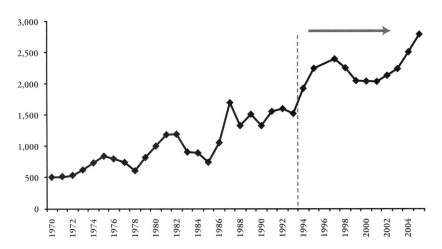

FIGURE 2.8. GDP Per Capita of Peru (1970–2005) in US dollars

SOURCE: BCRP, Apoyo.

aged competitive business development. Those decades were characterized by state seizure of businesses, price controls, high and differentiated tariffs, import bans and import quotas, exchange-rate controls, a state-run banking system, and so on.

The notorious populist paraphernalia that had done so much to hamper development in Latin America were imposed in a particularly radical manner in Peru. Despite it all, the Flores family consolidated its apparel business during this time, overcoming obstacles and adapting to the opportunities offered by the market.

The big leap for Topy Top, which was founded in 1978, came in the late 1990s with the development of exports. The rules of the game had changed in Peru. In the early 1990s, the liberal wave that swept the world and the economic disaster that the populist President Alan García (1985–1990) brought upon Peru, permitted the implementation of a set of reforms that broadened economic freedoms and allowed the resurrection of the Peruvian economy.

Some of the companies Velasco had nationalized were privatized during this time. Price controls and exchange-rate controls were eliminated. Tariffs were lowered, state-run banking was eliminated, and the Central Bank was forbidden to artificially increase the supply of currency. The new context of open markets generated economic growth that in the last few years has been based on an unexpected increase in exports of both raw materials (mainly minerals and fish) and manufactured goods (see Figure 2.9). Among the latter, exports of apparel developed the most. If these liberal reforms had not occurred, the story of Topy Top would not have been the same.

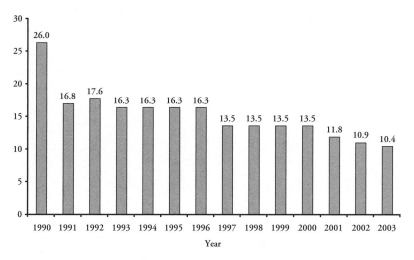

FIGURE 2.9. Average Tariff (1990–2003)

SOURCE: Peruvian Ministry of Economy and Finance.

The Beginning: A Young Car Washer Becomes a Street Vendor

The entrepreneurial history of the Flores family goes back forty years, when the father and breadwinner died. As a result of this tragedy, the oldest son, Aquilino, decided to move to the capital, Lima. The city already was becoming a refuge for thousands of Peruvians from the provinces who had been displaced by poverty and the scarcity of job opportunities in their marginalized regions.

The migration of Peruvians from the Andean region to the coast of Peru, and particularly to Lima, has been the most important characteristic of the nation's demographic evolution, beginning in the mid-twentieth century, as the birth rate increased. The city expanded to the south and the north as squatters occupied land that has never been adequately defined and formalized.

Little by little, the bulk of Lima's population settled in what is now known as the Southern Cone and the Northern Cone of the capital. The Northern Cone is the center of the expansion of the new consumer market and the emergence of entrepreneurs from the provinces.

At the time Aquilino Flores arrived in Lima, however, the bulk of the informal retail trade was conducted around the Central Market. Aquilino arrived—as Peruvians say about someone who has no money—"with one hand covering his front, the other his rear." The only resources he had to make a living were his work and his imagination. He was only 12 years old. He decided to take up a job that is still popular in Lima today: car washing.

Car washers in Lima usually take over areas where cars are parked for a long time. They generate regular clients, whom they charge the equivalent of US$1 per wash. They have the ability to find water nearby. They fill a bucket and take great care in leaving the car shining clean. Car washers near the Central Market in the 1960s included neighborhood businessmen among their clients. This was the first "market" the young Aquilino Flores dealt with. And knowing his inborn ability to sell, a skill he would exploit in the future, we must assume that he quickly developed an empathy with his clients.

One of those clients, a clothing merchant, befriended the young man. He must have seen in Aquilino a particular ability to sell, a sharpness, charm, and politeness, because one day he told the boy that he should try to sell T-shirts instead of washing cars. Aquilino asked him for twenty T-shirts and a two-day trial period. The scene is not hard to imagine. The businessman smiled and told him wryly that twenty was a big number, but he gave them to him and added, "Take as long as you need, but do it." That was on a Wednesday. On Friday, the boy showed up with the money and no T-shirts; he had sold them all. The businessman was surprised by the boy's efficiency and continued to supply him with T-shirts. Thus began Aquilino Flores' clothing business.

Aquilino sold more and more T-shirts. He developed a relationship with the street vendors at the Central Market. He worried when sales took too long or failed. Today, more than forty years later, he remembers how he pestered the vendors to whom he distributed the T-shirts. He repeatedly asked them what the customers liked, what they said when they purchased the shirts, and what they said when they didn't buy.

"Why do you ask so many questions, kid?" the vendors asked. Aquilino understood that, to be successful in business, he had to sell what people wanted. Without realizing it, intuition led him to discover the importance of the customer. That knowledge—of the need to understand what the customer wants and to supply that product in the best manner and as soon as possible—laid the foundation for the enormous success of Topy Top. From that time on, young Aquilino began to suggest changes in the styles and colors of the T-shirts.

Two months after placing his first order with his friend the businessman, young Aquilino showed up with a surprise request: "Bring me more T-shirts, but make sure they have pictures on the front." The businessman, who didn't manufacture them that way, refused to oblige. Aquilino found a solution. He accepted the blank T-shirts from his friend and subcontracted the printing of pictures, which at the time were popular among the consumers. Thus he began to add value to the garments as a response to the demand and, not coincidentally, to earn more money.

Aquilino's adventure soon attracted his siblings. Over time, they too left Huancavelica and moved to Lima to find a different future. Meanwhile, Aquilino had developed know-how in the business of garment sales. The Flores brothers went into the street sale of garments in Lima's marketplaces.

The work was particularly hard. The Floreses recall that, in order to find the best spots at the marketplaces, they had to be there at 4 a.m. They knew that the right location and display were key elements of retail sales. They began by staying close to the customer, and they still believe in this principle.

From Street Sales to Manufacturing Goods for Border Areas

According to a recent study on the Topy Top business model, done by the University of Navarra, the model "did not emerge from market research but originated gradually, as the founder of the business learned about the clothing market. Aquilino's experience—first as a street vendor and later as a businessman—helped him identify the needs of the low-income segment of the population. Later, he gradually developed a model of business that allowed him to offer a wide and constant variety of good-quality clothing at affordable prices" (IESE, 2004).

The Difference Between the Floreses and Gamarra Street

Unlike most emerging entrepreneurs in the garment trade in Peru, the Flores brothers did not take part in the commercial emporium on Gamarra Street, in the populous district of La Victoria. Although they are frequently described as having been involved in that garment center, the Floreses indicated that their evolution was parallel to the evolution of Gamarra but not part of it. The big difference between the Floreses and most small businesses on Gamarra Street is that the latter aimed mostly at high profit margins while the Floreses bet from the beginning on production and on-time delivery.

Gamarra had its origins in the sale of fabric remainders sold by the major manufacturers to informal merchants on a cash-only basis. These sales allowed manufacturers to close their stocks and avoid paying the mandatory taxes. For their part, the small merchants were able to start a business that could become prosperous. Most of these enterprises have remained small in scale and continue to address the domestic market. Those firms that have become formal businesses have done so mostly by going into exports, either directly or indirectly. But none has attained the dimension of Topy Top.

A visit to Gamarra today is impressive. It has 120 commercial galleries in a space of forty city blocks. Fourteen thousand stores engage in the selling and/ or manufacture of garments and fabrics. The center provides employment to more than sixty thousand people and mobilizes about 60 percent of the textile and apparel sector devoted to domestic sales, with almost eight thousand dressmaking shops that have an average of five machines each. It is estimated that more than US$800 million circulates through Gamarra every year.

Visiting Gamarra is like entering a country in eastern Asia. Part of the reason is that, in recent years, large numbers of South Koreans, attracted by an environment they know, have come to Peru to set up dressmaking shops. But it is also because the thousands of small shops and stores, side by side, give a feeling of overcrowding. The variety of stores and sidewalk vendors—either producing or selling garments and fabrics—creates a feeling that's almost asphyxiating.

But the businesses prosper, which explains why people say that 1 square meter of real estate in this zone is the most expensive square meter in Lima—more expensive even than the same space in Lima's most exclusive residential areas.

The Gamarra emporium is a productive cluster. And like every productive cluster, its formation and evolution have been spontaneous. Producers of the same goods cooperate by exchanging information, by forming partnerships to fill orders, and by supplying each other. But they also compete aggressively.

The shopping galleries in Gamarra have been built by businessmen who have no professional training or postgraduate education. Most of them are migrants from the provinces who arrived in Lima with the dream of progress and today proudly display their commercial buildings. Although no official figures or statistics exist, it is estimated that, on average, 1 percent of these businessmen speak English, fewer than 10 percent read the business pages of the major newspapers at least three times a week, fewer than 5 percent have read a book about management in the past year, and fewer than 15 percent attended a class in managerial development in the past year or sent their workers away for training or have a computer in their establishments. Of the latter, fewer than 10 percent know how to use a computer and fewer than 5 percent make use of the Internet. Fewer than 20 percent have intermediate managers between themselves and their working personnel. Fewer than 10 percent of Gamarra's personnel have a high school education.

The galleries' swift development, which led to the presence of more than three thousand street vendors and dealers in smuggled and under-priced merchandise, was mainly due to tax evasion. Of the street vendors who made a fortune working at Gamarra, we should mention the Guizado brothers and the well-known Diógenes Alva, the wealthiest businessman in Gamarra today.

However, the Gamarra businessmen have taken longer than the Floreses and others to move toward modernity. We believe that this is due to two interrelated factors. First, the informal trade continues to be a profitable business, in view of the high taxes every formal business owner in Peru must pay (50 percent in payroll taxes and deductions and 19 percent in sales taxes, not to mention the nontaxable transaction costs). Second, they have not turned to the export business. And "what formalizes a company in this industry is exportation," says Estevan Danieluc.

Business leaders in the Gamarra area have recently staged protest marches, demanding protection against the importation of garments from China. Therein lies the difference between these vendors and garment exporters like the Floreses, who concentrate their efforts on being more competitive on a worldwide level and want nothing more than free trade with countries like the United States.

The Floreses have gone beyond their counterparts in Gamarra. As Danieluc says, "As a family and businesspeople, the Floreses are more like the Rodríguez Bandas and the Añaños than the Guizados, for example" (*El Comercio,* 2004). The Rodríguez Bandas are a family of entrepreneurs who have achieved fame as dairy merchants. In Peru, they have beaten Nestlé with their brand of milk, Gloria, the bestseller in Peru, where, for reasons of storage, people consume a lot of canned evaporated milk. The Añaños own the most successful emerging transnational soft drink company in Peru (see Chapter 1).

Danieluc is referring to the leap toward formality and professionalization made by the Flores family in the late 1990s. Before that came more than two decades of learning and capital accumulation.

Early Days as Clothing Designers

In 1996, the Flores family set up its first clothes store, Flores Creations, so they could wear the clothes they made and then respond more exactly to what the customers demanded. They began with only one sewing machine, then grew to two, then three, and ten. Along the way, they began to abandon street vending and became clothing designers. Actual sales were left to a solid network of street contacts and small stores in midtown Lima. Flores Creations grew thanks to the immense satisfaction of their clients. Aquilino recalls that the clients—retail merchants and gradually more wholesalers— "went away but always returned, because they found what they were looking for: novel clothes, good price, and quality."

Flores Creations' first major sale totaled US$10,000 and was intended for indirect, informal export to South America's southern cone, passing through Bolivia. It was placed by a client who began to buy garments and take them to Desaguadero, a city that owes its existence to informal commerce, on the border between Peru and Bolivia.

The trade that goes through Desaguadero consists, even now, mostly of smuggled goods. The city is a crossroads for merchandise coming from Bolivia, Brazil, Paraguay, and Argentina, as well as Peru, Ecuador, and Chile. At present, the commercial networks associated with Desaguadero have assumed an industrial dimension that is much superior to the time when Flores Creations received its first major order. The police cannot deal with the smugglers—or won't. Most often, they benefit from the trade, allowing merchandise to go through in exchange for a bribe, or "fee." From time to time, news programs on TV tell about seizures and police operations that give an appearance of order that really doesn't exist.

The famous $10,000 order covered a very large number of T-shirts, an amount far above what Flores Creations could produce. Rather than give up the opportunity, the Floreses took advantage of their contacts at the Central Market and enlisted every workshop they could to fill the order. Once more, the market opened a door to growth and they walked right through it. And it was no ordinary door. It was an opportunity that enabled them to find markets outside Lima and even outside Peru, markets that they were in a position to enter.

The border markets gradually became an essential part of the Floreses' business. The market at Huaquillas, on the border with Ecuador, allowed them to reach—indirectly—the markets in the northern part of South America, such as Colombia and Venezuela. They reached consumers in Argentina and Paraguay through Desaguadero.

Once they discovered the possibility of filling large orders directed toward the border markets, the Floreses consolidated their efforts to expand their production capacity. They decided to open a second workshop in Zárate, the same district where, more than twenty years later, they would open a factory whose size they themselves couldn't foresee.

Zárate is a district near the center of Lima. Its nearness to the center of the capital made it an adequate site, both because wholesale merchants were situated in the center and because the demographic density provided access to manual labor with sufficient ability to handle the fast-paced work required.

During the 1970s, Flores Creations continued to grow. Within ten years, it had managed to expand its production capacity to five small factories working at 100 percent capacity. Business grew as a consequence of the attention paid to orders, which came from merchants everywhere in Peru, but particularly from those who did business in border areas. It couldn't be otherwise. Between the time of the Flores family's beginnings as street salesmen and the expansion of the company's production capacity, the Peruvian economy had experienced a change that was anything but favorable.

On October 3, 1968, Gen. Velasco Alvarado had led a coup d'état with the support of the armed forces for the purpose of imposing a socialist revolution in Peru. Gradually, the legal environment became hostile toward legitimate businessmen, thereby promoting an informal market.

The high barriers to the importation of fabrics and garments harmed buyers who imported these goods legally. The traditional textile industry, much of which was in the hands of second-generation Italian entrepreneurs and others of Palestinian or Jewish origin, struggled between selling merchandise legally in the domestic market and engaging in informal practices. The restrictions on the development of private enterprise finally ended, turning the sector into a hotbed of "unbilled" production and trade—that is, without invoices that might require the payment of taxes.

The state's administrative inability to enforce the formal rules of the game, which were so restrictive, enabled the development of emerging enterprises, including Flores Creations. The possibility of smuggling across the borders was, for the moment, its best source of growth.

The step from trade to production, and then from small-scale production to a larger scale, involved constant learning, particularly in terms of improving the technology used and developing efficient processes. At this stage, the Floreses realized that the whole world could open to them. They began to travel to the United States and Europe to buy secondhand machinery that would allow them to compete to best advantage.

During those trips, they were careful to assimilate even the slightest industry detail that might allow them to improve their competitiveness. Not surprisingly, during a trip to Germany, they were inspired to drop the antiquated and traditional name Flores Creations (in Peru at the time there were hundreds of garment manufacturers, especially humble workshops, that carried the name of the designer accompanied by the generic word "Creations"). They decided to adopt the name Topy Top.

As the Flores brothers tell the story of the name, while in Germany, a machinery supplier was trying to impress them with the quality of his products. Repeatedly, the salesman insisted on the need to use leading-edge technology. "This is the top of the top," he kept saying to them. And the

Floreses, whose English was still rudimentary, joked among themselves about the German's expression. Every time they referred to a product, they called it "top of the top," eventually mangling it into "top y top," Spanish for "top and top." So the name stuck—Topy Top.

It was 1978. General Velasco's foray into a socialist revolution had failed, leaving the country devastated by an agrarian reform based on the expropriation of agroindustrial companies and large farms. The result: a huge number of state-owned companies that had been nationalized, a tendency toward inflation that later would become hyperinflation, and a commercial structure that was closed to the world.

Although the Floreses could have continued to grow moderately from the proceeds of the domestic market and the informal border exports, passive growth was never enough for them. They perceived that their business could be more profitable as long as the products continued to be attractive and low in price. So to lower their costs and improve the designs of their clothing, they decided to delve into the early stages of production, beginning with the knitting of the fabrics and continuing with the dyeing.

Toward the Integration of Production

The leading merchants in Huaquillas and Desaguadero were Topy Top's biggest clients, buying large quantities of clothing every month. As the size of the orders grew, maintaining and improving the quality of the garments with purchased fabric became more difficult. The color and quality of the fabric was, naturally, an essential aspect of the garments' appearance.

That is why the Flores family decided to direct their efforts toward the vertical integration of their production process. They started by buying undyed fabric from third parties and subcontracting the dyeing process, both of which were expensive. And although a textile tradition existed in Peru, meaning that fabrics and dyes were readily available, the suppliers did not match the Floreses' competitive pace.

To understand the process of garment production in Peru, and in particular its origins, we must go back to the early twentieth century, when cotton was planted all along the coast, essentially for export purposes. The crop became so important that Peruvian entrepreneurs involved in the industry devoted huge sums to genetic research. One of them, Fermín Tangüis, in the 1920s developed a cotton that was resistant to a fungus that had begun to plague the crops.

Tangüis's cotton became one of the flagship products of Peruvian agro-exports, and it formed the basis of the Peruvian textile industry. Little by little, the industry became more diversified, and ancillary professions, like dyers, arose.

By the early 1980s, the cotton farms and the exportation of cotton had disappeared. Velasco's agrarian reforms had ruined the production of the crop. In 1980 President Fernando Belaúnde, who had been deposed by the military dictator Velasco, was elected again by an overwhelming majority. His economic team made a timid attempt at opening the economy but did not have the vision to implement reforms that would revoke the socialist structures inherited from the military government. It left intact the state-run enterprises, continued to enforce agrarian reform, permitted the acceleration of inflation, and did little to halt the incipient terrorism of Sendero Luminoso—Shining Path—in Peru's southern sierra.

A short time later, Belaúnde's administration disavowed its desire to open the economy and set the stage for the return of the most disastrous populist government Peru ever had. The government of the traditional Aprista Party, headed by a 35-year-old politician named Alan García, led Peru to chaos, hyperinflation, and recession between 1985 and 1990. Between 1987 and 1990, annual production dropped by 25 percent and annualized inflation skyrocketed from 100 percent to 7,000 percent.

During the years of populism within the framework of democratically elected administrations, the textile sector, protected from international competition, became one of the most mercantilist sectors of Peru's entrepreneurial world. Sheltered by the National Association of Industries, the traditional industries embraced the theories of Raúl Prebisch and the Economic Commission for Latin America (ECLA, or CEPAL from its Spanish name).

According to these theories, public policies should aim to avoid imports and develop the domestic market. Thus, certain industries were selectively protected. The movement, grouped in CEPAL and led by Prebisch, was very popular in Latin America in the mid-twentieth century, and many populist-leaning governments heeded its recommendations (Prebisch, 1962). The Peruvian government was among these. Prebisch's analysis stated that the Latin American countries (countries in "the periphery") were condemned to underdevelopment because they exported raw materials and imported manufactured goods from the developed countries (countries in "the center"). Prebisch also maintained that the prices of raw materials tend to drop, while the prices of industrial goods tend to rise, and that industry uses more manual labor. The solution then became to give artificial incentives to industry to replace the imports that came from the center. That way, Prebisch said, industries would be born in Latin American countries and could be developed.

These policies failed for various reasons. On one hand, macroeconomic imbalances occurred because of the policies that complemented the protection, such as monetary expansion (Prebisch and his school were confirmed Keynesians), which generated inflation. On the other, exports were given no incentives, which created a trade imbalance. In reality, domestic goods could never replace imports, because the industries called upon to do that task became importers of consumer and capital goods that were not produced in the countries in the periphery. Finally, many of the protected industrial firms ended up resting on their laurels. Having no incentive to enter worldwide competition, their ability to attain adequate levels of efficiency was limited. It is not surprising, then, that entrepreneurs with competitive aspirations, such as the Floreses, did not find among their suppliers the dynamism they needed to grow.

The fact that they could not find dependable suppliers compelled the Floreses to take the steps that followed. Their suppliers did not meet delivery deadlines, asked for excessive production time, delivered inferior products, and were not accurate in their execution of orders. In 1982, Topy Top stopped buying fabrics and started buying thread to manufacture its own. To do this, it imported five circular knitting machines. In 1984, the Floreses decided to set up a dye plant. The chief of the dye shop where Topy Top had sent thousands of meters of fabric for dyeing encouraged them. He told them that the money they were spending on so much dyeing would be better spent on a dye plant of their own, and that they would soon recoup their investment. He also pointed out that they themselves would be able to control the quality of the dyeing process, choose the colors, and tighten the deadlines. Impressed by the man's integrity and knowledge, the Floreses offered him a job as director of their dye plant, at a very high salary—even though they risked being unable to pay him.

He was the first top-level executive the Floreses hired. Until then they had managed the whole operation, working at salaries below those of the managers of traditional companies. However, none of them knew the textile dyeing business. This began what would become a constant in the Floreses' successful growth: their belief in the importance of hiring of top-notch technicians and paying them what the market demanded.

The dye plant developed swiftly. Once installed, the Floreses achieved a production rate of eight thousand garments per day, a productivity far higher than that of their traditional suppliers. In 1985, thanks to the success achieved with the dye plant, the Floreses bought another plot of land in Zárate, 5,000 square meters, and established Peru Color Star Inc., which became the largest dye plant in the nation.

The increase in production led to a quest for new markets. Aquilino began to investigate the market he was reaching indirectly through the border dealers and began to travel frequently to Brazil, undoubtedly the largest market in Latin America and little explored because of the language barrier: the native language there is Portuguese, not Spanish.

To Aquilino, the language difference wasn't an impossible obstacle. He toured Brazil, visiting department stores and markets to collect samples of the clothes being sold, items that Topy Top did not yet produce. He returned to Lima filled with ideas and loaded with samples that might inspire new styles. He had realized that political and cultural borders are artificial barriers in terms of the trade in sophisticated apparel. Thus, Aquilino became a citizen of the world and was about to become a global entrepreneur.

Topy Top enjoyed sustained growth during the 1980s, although it was a decade of stagnation and declining industrial production in Peru. The only explanation for Topy Top's growth during this time was its ability to gain increased market share because of its increasing productivity, due to the process of vertical integration. The increase in textile production and dyeing was accompanied by an improvement in the mechanical processes, which led in turn to lower costs and better quality, elements on which Topy Top based its gains in competitiveness. These gains allowed the company to edge competitors out of the market.

By 1990, Topy Top was in a position to produce 10 million pieces of apparel yearly, an amount greater than the orders it received. In addition, the company manufactured, stamped, dyed, and even embroidered faster than its competitors. It had put together a complete process of production, but it had excess production capacity.

The Peruvian market was in a recession. Production had fallen for three consecutive years. Hyperinflation had soared to 7,000 percent in one year.

Shining Path continued to expand the radius of its terrorist activities.

Mercantilism was the survival tool most often used by entrepreneurs. They sought the necessary contacts to obtain a special license, a kind of preferential exchange to get cheaper dollars from the Central Bank, a credit subsidized by the state bank (staffed by officials of the party in power), and engaged in other practices that destroyed value rather than creating it.

In this context of economic, political, and social chaos, the Floreses' business bogged down, as did most of the Peruvian economy. New breezes had to blow, new rules of the economic game and a new political context had to be established before they could take advantage of new opportunities and begin their real takeoff—represented by a boom in the export of Peruvian textiles and apparel.

Retail Trade and Exports

The last three years of the 1980s were particularly chaotic in Peru. President García had attempted a populist solution to the economic crisis. As might have been expected, the cure was worse than the illness. García's attempt to bring the entire financial system under state control had generated a radical opposition to the government and an outcry in favor of a radical change to a free-market economy.

Elected in 1990, Alberto Fujimori applied economic reforms that tended to reverse the effects of the policies implemented by the socialist military government. And he did so with relative success, despite his controversial "self-coup" and the constitutional reform he managed to impose by resorting to a nationwide referendum.

From Topy Top's perspective, the reforms made during Fujimori's first term (1990–1995) were crucial. Inflation was defeated after the Central Bank was forbidden to lend money to the state by issuing currency (which had artificially boosted the monetary supply), while the state managed to balance the fiscal budget. The companies that had been nationalized by General Velasco were successfully privatized. Tariffs were lowered considerably, and exports became a priority in trade policies.

It also should be noted that a private pension system was instituted, inspired by the Chilean model of individual retirement accounts. This led to a fairer and more transparent retirement system and generated a local capital market. By mid-2006, the money held by pension funds represented more than half of the liquidity in soles and more than one-third of the total liquidity in the Peruvian monetary system (Central Reserve Bank of Peru, 2006).

The basic elements of these new rules of the game were encapsulated in the Constitution of 1993, which—although it was the result of a breakdown in the democratic constitutional order established by the previous Constitution of 1979—contained a far superior economic chapter and favored the development of a market economy in Peru.

Finally, the leader of the Maoist terrorist group Shining Path, Abimael Guzmán, was arrested, an accomplishment that eventually led to the defeat of that movement. Thus, on one hand, the conditions of stability and security were set so the domestic market could integrate (trade between Lima and the provinces had been threatened by the terrorists' attacks) and, on the other hand, the economy opened to globalization, generating opportunities in international trade.

Effects of Foreign-Trade Reform on the Apparel Industry

Of the reforms mentioned in the previous section, the one that undoubtedly had the greatest effect on the apparel industry was the reform in commercial regulation. This reform involved two major factors. First, tariffs were significantly reduced, along with tariff dispersion (see Figure 2.9). Also, a system of simplified reimbursement of tariffs (called a "drawback") was instituted for exporters, allowing companies like Topy Top to get a tariff refund equal to 5 percent of the value of their exports. This reduced the cost of importing consumables and machinery and made exports more profitable.

Second, the commercial accords signed in the 1970s and '80s were updated, with the goal of expanding Peru's commercial ties with economies with greater growth (Apoyo, 2003). This change liberalized tariffs for the United States and Europe, allowing firms like Topy Top to venture with unexpected success into exportation.

Trade reform began with the reduction and simplification of tariffs. In September 1990, the number of tariff rates was reduced from twenty-four levels to three: 15 percent, 25 percent, and 50 percent. The average tariff dropped from 46.5 percent to 38.1 percent. Tariff reduction continued in the following years until it reached 13.5 percent in the late 1990s and 10.4 percent in 2003 (see Table 2.4).

In addition to tariff reduction, the liberalization of trade in the 1990s managed to eliminate a great many of the nontariff restrictions (mainly the prior import licenses). Tariff reform also extended to the standards of sanitary control in the sectors of agriculture and health. At the same time, the processes of sanitary control for the importation of products in the sectors of agriculture and health were simplified. Finally, with Customs reform, the paperwork needed for foreign trade was simplified.

TABLE 2.4. Tariff Evolution (1990–1998)

Date	Amount of Tariff	Tariff Sample Average	Standard Deviation /1	Variability Coefficient
Jul-90	39	46.5	25.7	55.3
Aug-90	24	38.1	12.4	32.5
Sep-90	3	26.3	13.3	50.6
Jan-91	4	26.3	13.3	50.6
Mar-91	3	16.8	3.9	23.2
Mar-92	2	17.6	4.4	25.0
Jul-92	2	17.6	4.4	25.0
Jun-93	2	16.3	3.4	20.9
Apr-97	4	13.5	3.5	25.9
Jan-98	4	13.5	3.5	25.9
Mar-98	4	13.5	3.5	25.9

Note: /1 According to the average tariff
SOURCE: Abusada et al. (2001)

On another front, the need for trade with the more developed economies grew stronger and led to a long effort to negotiate a free trade agreement with the United States. The process of change in Peru's trade relations with the United States, which are of singular importance to companies like Topy Top, can be summarized as follows:

- In 1991, the Andean Trade Preference Act (ATPA) was enacted. This exceptional measure was granted unilaterally by the United States to Peru, Bolivia, Colombia, and Ecuador to support those nations' struggle against illicit drug activity.
- In 1993, Peru was deemed eligible for the ATPA. The trade accord excluded the export of fabrics and apparel, footwear, canned tuna, crude oil and derivatives, and so on. However, Peru's other exports to the U.S. market grew for several years. In fact, Peru was the country that utilized the ATPA the most.

- The ATPA expired in 2001, but in 2002, after more than three years of effort coordinated by the public and private sectors, the U.S. Congress approved a new act that renewed and broadened the benefits of the ATPA. That legislation, called the Andean Trade Promotion and Drug Eradication Act (ATPDEA, 2002), reactivated the ATPA's tariff preferences and added new products, such as apparel. From that moment on, a boom began in the export of Peruvian apparel to the United States, with Topy Top leading the charge.
- In 2004, the first round of the negotiation of a free trade agreement between the United States and Colombia, Peru, and Ecuador was accomplished.
- Early in 2006, President Alejandro Toledo of Peru signed a trade promotion agreement (TPA) with the United States. It was expected to be approved by the congresses of both nations before the end of the year, when the ATPDEA expires.

In contrast to the characteristics of the utopian policy of commercial integration espoused by the ATPA, which dominated the scene in the 1970s and '80s, preferential access to the U.S. and European markets has created new levels of trade based on industries such as modern agroindustry and apparel.

At first, open trade was seen as a threat by the Peruvian industrialists, who were accustomed to state protection and fearful of competing on a worldwide scale. Nevertheless, they very quickly became aware of the possibility of accomplishing more by exploring foreign markets.

It is not surprising that the reduction in tariffs on apparel coincided with an increase in imports that has benefited the Peruvian consumer by generating a remarkable improvement in general attire in the past fifteen years. That increase, however, was much smaller than the increase in exports (see Figure 2.10). The figures speak for themselves.

In 1982, Peru exported US$20 million worth of textile products. By 2004, that figure exceeded US$1 billion. Traditional businessmen who defended the protectionist theories began to change their minds when they saw the chance to compete on a worldwide scale, with greater access to imported consumables and machinery. This growth in exports began in the mid-1990s. A major boost came in 2003, when the United States reduced tariffs unilaterally through the ATPA and, later, the AT-

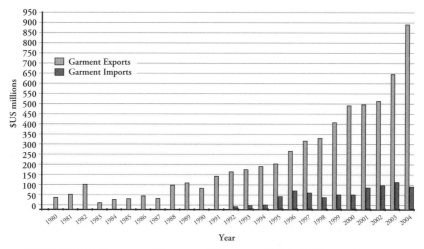

FIGURE 2.10. Exports and Imports of Garments (1980–2004)

SOURCE: INEI.

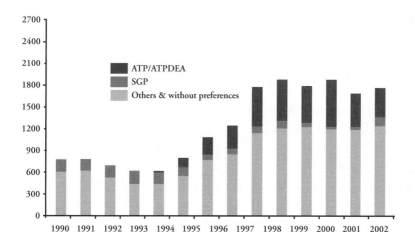

FIGURE 2.11. Exports to United States

SOURCE: USITC.

PDEA (see Figure 2.11). Topy Top was one of the companies that took full advantage of this situation.

Another factor that has redirected the textile and apparel business toward exports has been the reorganization of the industry toward the manufacture of apparel, both wovens and knitwear, at the expense of plain fabrics.

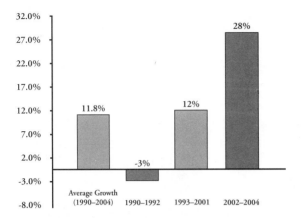

FIGURE 2.12. Annual Growth of Peruvian Exports to U.S.

SOURCE: Agencia de Promoción de Exportaciones (Prompex).

In other words, the trend has gone from exporting less-elaborate apparel to more-elaborate garments. The development of Peru's textile exports is a dramatic example of the impact of the restructuring of the industry in the 1990s, which resulted in a substantial decline or disappearance of certain industrial segments, while many others showed a dynamic performance.

As Figure 2.12 shows, Peruvian exports to the United States increased substantially beginning in the mid-1990s and accelerated tremendously in the mid-2000s—so much so that beginning in 2000, Peru developed a significant surplus in its trade with the United States.

In the context of open trade and a greater connection with the more developed economies, the Flores family began to think about expanding its market, both in the country's interior and abroad. First came the market in Lima and the provinces; then came the market in developed countries. The former came about through the widening of their activities in the retail trade; the latter, through their efforts to secure orders from the big brands worldwide.

Topy Top's Expansion into Retail Trade

As has been the case throughout the Floreses' history, luck and the utilization of opportunities characterized the family's entry into formal exportation and the official retail trade in the Peruvian market. Everything started with a friend in Canada who knew the business the Floreses were in and

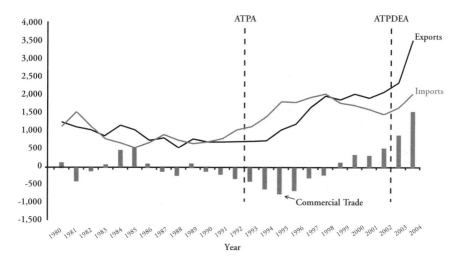

FIGURE 2.13. Exports and Imports of Garments (1980–2004)

SOURCE: Superintendencia de Administración Tributaria (SUNAT).

encouraged them to export to a developed market, such as Canada, which he had observed. It had room for Topy Top's products, he told them.

Convinced by his friend, Aquilino traveled to Canada to assess the market. He managed to contact some clients and bring back some orders, and he began to export to the Canadian market on a regular basis. This effort was not without difficulty, because Topy Top continued to manufacture goods in different workshops in Zárate, and the widely spread operation was hard to control. In about 1996, the Floreses bought 20,000 square meters of land in Zárate for the purpose of centralizing their operations, which they did one year later.

The transition to formal exports was not easy, however. And it didn't evolve from a perfectly conceived plan. Just when exports to Canada seemed to be going smoothly, a major setback occurred. An order of 50,000 T-shirts for children, in various sizes, was rejected because of a minor flaw and was sent back to the port of Callao. Without missing a beat, the Floreses decided to dispose of the stock at home. Not to do so would have meant accepting a loss they couldn't afford.

So they decided to convert one of their workshops, at the intersection of Junín and Huanuco streets in Lima, into a small retail store where they sold only the T-shirts that had been returned from Canada. They first printed the shirts with images that would attract children and then labeled them "super sale" and displayed them in large baskets. In that manner, they sold all their goods in a store without frills, without counters or shelves and with salespeople who wore no uniform. The only asset in their first store was good-quality apparel at low prices.

In addition to enabling the Flores brothers to get rid of 50,000 T-shirts in record time, the experience helped them realize that selling directly to the public was profitable. They had made $1 per garment more than if they had exported them. In other words, the goods rejected by Canada had brought them approximately US$50,000 in net profit.

The Floreses then began to take seriously the retail sale of their products. At first, they sold only the leftovers from their export trade, and for that purpose they leased the former Bon Marché store in the center of Lima, with 700 square meters of space. The store sold T-shirts for consumers of various ages. Soon thereafter, the logic of selling leftovers from their export production took a turn: Topy Top began to devote part of its production solely to the domestic market, and the idea was born to establish a Topy Top retail chain.

When the time came to decide how to handle the provincial market, the Floreses faced a difficult decision. The market surveys they had done were not favorable, and the decision to abandon their network of distributors and sell directly to the consumer was risky. But they took the risk. Their first store in the provinces was in Huancayo, a busy commercial city in the center of the Peruvian Andes, in the department of Junín. The Floreses' distributors in Huancayo ceased to be their allies when they entered the Huancayo market directly, however. Learning that the Floreses would cease to be their suppliers and become their competitors, the merchants in Huancayo refused to pay their debts. The Floreses absorbed the blow and eventually settled in as retail merchants in Huancayo.

Other big cities followed, such as Arequipa, Cuzco, Trujillo, Huaraz, and Chiclayo. Later, they opened stores in smaller cities, such as Iquitos in the Peruvian jungle. There, Topy Top was all by itself, because these cities were too small to justify an investment by larger corporations like Ripley and Falabella. But they were big enough for Topy Top, which became a point of reference for quality casual clothing at low prices.

Thus did Topy Top break the paradigm of the traditional textile manufacturers, who felt that "you can reach the public only through wholesalers." The Floreses had begun their business by taking the pulse of the client, placing themselves next to the client and staying there to ensure the continuity of success. After dominating the production process, they returned to their roots, rediscovering the retail trade.

The Topy Top chain continued to develop until it had thirty-five stores throughout the country, including one in Lima's most exclusive shopping center, the Jockey Plaza in the exclusive district of Surco. There, Topy Top competes directly with the best department stores and big-brand retail stores. Its domestic market can be divided into two large segments: inexpensive casual apparel for adults and special clothing for children, from lines they expanded by licensing popular characters like Sponge Bob and Goku, among others.

By acquiring those licenses and expanding its retail business, Topy Top broadened its line of imports for children, buying from China complementary products, such as backpacks, school bags, puzzles, and towels. The Floreses' incursion into the Far East resulted in the acquisition of a wealth of novelty items bearing the images of the licensed characters, which turned their new business into an unprecedented success.

Sixty-five percent of the stock in Topy Top's department stores consists of the company's own garments, under the label Trading Fashion. The rest comes from imports and the local purchase of products that Topy Top does not manufacture, such as jeans. The retail business has thus surpassed its initial intention of selling surplus items and has become a way to increase sales. Synergy has also allowed the Floreses to become active in the importation of plain-fabric products from eastern Asia.

Finally, the Floreses observed that the big department stores opened by Chilean investors in Peru offered credit cards that gave customers special discounts and allowed them to pay on the installment plan. Very soon, they discovered the key to the large-scale retail trade: the financial business, a business that in countries like Peru was becoming the retail chains' main source of profit.

Topy Top decided to move boldly into this business and made 60,000 credit cards available. As of this writing, it's too soon to evaluate the outcome, but the results of sales in the retail chain—which have exceeded US$20 million—reveal considerable potential.

Betting on Large-Scale Exportation

The development of Topy Top's retail market nationwide went hand in hand with its leap into large-scale exportation. Shortly after his first experience with Canada, Aquilino Flores traveled to the United States in search of new clients. Some traditional factories in Lima, such as Nettalco, Textimax, and San Cristóbal Textiles, had begun to produce high-quality garments for big-brand companies like Gap. Flores was aware of this and felt that Topy Top was capable of entering that niche successfully. But he also knew that the conditions for becoming a supplier were extremely harsh in terms of standards of quality and swift delivery time.

Topy Top received its first order of this kind from the Gap chain in 1998, for US$8 million. The company had had the vision to hire a commercial manager who had worked for a competitor and had already serviced a contract of this type. The manager knew the market, had the necessary contacts, and knew he could depend on Topy Top to fulfill the order. After that first order came dizzying growth, from US$9 million in exports in 1999 to US$36 million in 2002 and US$85 million in 2005 (see Table 2.5).

TABLE 2.5. Yearly Exports of Topy Top, 1999–2005 (in US$ million)

Year	Exports
1999	8.636
2000	21.282
2001	25.175
2002	36.411
2003	53.954
2004	71.913
2005	85.365

Source: ADEX – Prepared by ADEX Manufacturing Area

The export business became the company's main source of income and therefore the object of Aquilino Flores' strongest efforts. He quickly realized the need to create a sales and marketing department that dealt exclusively with the export business. Product chiefs—brand managers who perform like account executives—were assigned clients that they had to attend to, down to their smallest requirements.

Although Topy Top's most important market was the United States (its main client remains Old Navy, for whom the company manufactures about 2 million garments per year), one of its main goals had been to expand into other markets, such as Europe. One such market was Spain, and Topy Top soon gained the Zara store chain as its main client in that country. Other clients in Spain were the well-known chains Corte Fiel and El Corte Inglés.

Gradually, Aquilino Flores and the commercial segment he continues to lead developed different strategies to satisfy the foreign client. Every manufacturer of casual attire has its own culture and procedures, to which one has to adapt. For example, Gap, Old Navy, Abercrombie, Hollister, and others send their own designs to Topy Top so it can give them quotes on a specific format that includes number of pieces, sizes, material, colors, delivery date, and so on. As soon as possible, the marketing department sends the buyer samples and price quotes. The items may have slight modifications, but they follow the original design.

For companies like Zara or El Corte Inglés, the process is different. Topy Top must deliver to them samples in different colors and finishes. Normally, the samples must be inspired by fashion apparel designed by international brands, such as Hollister, Abercrombie, Gap, and other popular brands with a proven record of acceptance in the market.

Zara's strategy is known worldwide for its innovation.[3] The chain seeks its inspiration in the market of high-fashion casuals, and it is known for the speed with which it goes from initial design to placement of the garments in its stores, at very low prices. It also has challenged the practice of seasonal rotation of styles, changing the clothing available in its stores much more frequently. Meeting the deadlines and the quality demanded by Zara has been an exceptional achievement for Topy Top.

Topy Top's marketing team is unflagging in its efforts to find out what the public wants—just as young Aquilino did through the street vendors at the Central Market, whom he insistently quizzed about the customers' preferences. Now it occurs through the purchasing executives of the largest vendors of casual attire. Although the environment is different, the logic is the same. The key to the big leap into the export business was to attack the competitive factors one at a time, using the mystique of hard work, imaginative innovation, and intuition, always looking for the most efficient way to gain in the market economy.

TOPY TOP AS A BUSINESS CASE STUDY

As might be expected, Topy Top has drawn the attention of business schools. And, as often happens, the intuitive manner in which the Floreses developed their business has contributed to the creation of concepts on which academicians will develop elaborate theories.

The concepts of management based on competitiveness are developed by observing enterprises that have broken the mold in terms of their experience and the intuitive innovation with which they deal with market challenges. Few companies have seen such rapid growth within a short time without first achieving an important innovation in the production process, developing a novel way to satisfy a need, or inventing products that create new needs.

In the case of the apparel industry, it might seem at first that the great innovations can come only via quality (advantages in design, manufacture, and materials) and prices. These are the basic or direct factors of competitiveness. The secret of growth based on achievements in quality and price is to adopt a strategy that permits the market's expansion, which is possible only by addressing the base of the social pyramid, as opposed to haute couture, which is rather a niche market.

Nevertheless, when one examines the industry in more detail, one runs into hidden, indirect factors of competitiveness that are indispensable for a business to make great leaps in the mass market. Those factors have allowed Topy Top, as well as the Zara chain, to achieve its competitive gains.

The hidden factors involve key aspects of the value chain, such as variety, speed of delivery, low inventory, and filling orders with a minimum of flaws. All these permit manufacturers to sell more in a shorter period of time, creating greater profitability.

Topy Top's direct competitiveness and its optimization of the value chain were achieved partly by the creation of an entrepreneurial culture that emerged from the Flores family itself and became more formal over time. This culture involved doing business while maintaining a vision of the future, one that became increasingly ambitious as the firm's entrepreneurial consolidation proceeded.

Success at the Base of the Pyramid[4]

The case of Topy Top is already being cited in business schools as a success story. The University of Navarra uses it as an example, along with very large companies that began as small enterprises, such as the Mexican giant Cemex. According to this study, the common keys to the success of these companies were the following:

- A constant commitment to the project on the part of top management. In the case of Topy Top, the synergy between the Flores brothers, who, according to the general manager, work "as a unit," was crucial to the company's entry into the mass market.
- Market research, the practice of "knowing in depth the consumers, their habits of consumption, their needs and aspirations." As we have seen, this factor was vital in Aquilino Flores' entrepreneurial intuition.
- A medium- and long-range vision, because the results of a business directed at mass consumption are not usually immediate. In the case of Topy Top, the absence of bank financing—involuntary at first and voluntary later—led to growth based on the full reinvestment of profits. The results we know today were obtained only after decades of activity.
- The development of the business based on competition within the economic and social milieu. For Topy Top, this factor was seen in the flexible relations it developed with chains of suppliers and local clients.
- A concentration on the functionality of the production process more than on the product itself, seeking to gain efficiency along the entire value chain.

The academicians at the University of Navarra believe that the Flores family intuitively developed its business model for the base of the pyramid. The principal components of this model have been the diversity of styles, the constant (weekly) introduction of new styles, the good quality of the apparel, the affordable prices, and excellent service. The vertical integration of the production processes (producing and dyeing fabric) allowed Topy Top to control the quality and variety of the clothes it could offer. By investing in top-quality machinery, it has managed to achieve ever lower costs.

On the other hand, the academicians point out that selling in two sets of markets with different logistics—the export market and the domestic market—allowed the Floreses to diversify and grow more than their competitors. For the export market the company needed longer and more rigid productive processes. It handled contracts for at least two thousand garments. The domestic market, which is handled through the retail chain, is more flexible and varied.

One of the principal reasons for the Floreses' entry into the retail chain was the slow rotation of styles in the stores they were selling to. Their clients did not do promotions to get rid of the stock; instead, they preferred to wait, so as not to sacrifice their profit margins. In contrast, Topy Top's strategy is intensive rotation. The Floreses discovered early on that speeding up the sales enabled them to use their capital better and obtain greater profits, even if they reduced their margin per garment. Intuitively, they began to unveil what Bovet and Martha (2000) call the "hidden profits."

In Search of Hidden Profits

Spanish process consultant Carlos Herreros analyzed Zara's impressive case as the breaking of a paradigm in the generation of value. Quoting Bovet and Martha, who also analyzed that case and the Cemex case, Herreros (2000) wrote:

> The standard chain of supply cannot furnish personalized products rapidly and dependably. Even using the "just-in-time" systems, it can only provide standard products and services like those of wholesalers, at the lowest cost possible. In a value network, the customers' preferences are transmitted to all the associated suppliers, who work to furnish their components just like the company, another supplier, or sometimes the customer demands. At the center of the network is the company (in this case, Zara), which coordinates all these activities, continuously updating all the participants. For its efforts, the company captures and seizes part of the value created.
>
> Zara, a Spanish clothing retailer, produces "fashions for the masses" of urban and modern youths. It is organized so that in less than two weeks it can turn designs into products hanging from the store racks. The result of this high-speed operation is that the clients form long lines at the stores on the days new merchandise arrives.
>
> Value networks also contribute to create powerful brands. Concrete is just concrete, but the Mexican company Cemex offers something even more valuable. Cemex has optimized its network of plants and concrete-mixing trucks and has connected them via satellite. The company guarantees the delivery of concrete in less than 20 minutes from the time the order is placed, a guarantee so infrequent in the sector that it has turned Cemex into a major brand. Even products as indifferent as concrete can delight clients if they are adapted to the clients' preferences and if delivery is fast, dependable, and easy.

The hidden profits are achieved only in the presence of five conditions, all of which are present in the Zara case (according to Herreros) and, in our opinion, in the Topy Top case:

1. Clients must be offered the greatest diversity of intelligent options. In that sense, the folks at Topy Top are constantly trying to be creative and innovative. That innovative perfectionism can be seen in their quote process, in which, upon receiving an order, they offer a range of alternatives that are different from the order. This allows the client to select from options that may be better than their own original idea. The product may be more expensive than a similar product produced elsewhere in the world, but, by eliminating imperceptible details from the garments and adding bright and colorful—but inexpensive—details, the clients can charge higher prices. In the case of Zara, Herreros contrasts the agility in their bids—an aspect also applicable to Topy Top—with the bids from "mature markets," pointing out the dilemma between variety and efficiency. Zara and Topy Top appear to have solved this dilemma by offering variety without losing efficiency (see Figure 2.14).

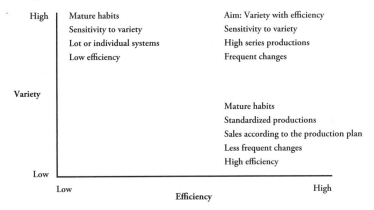

FIGURE 2.14. Variety with Efficiency: A Challenge to the Mature Thinking

SOURCE: Carlos Herreros, HCF Consultores.

2. Faster is better, as long as the client pays for the speed. One result of the optimization of Topy Top's production chain has been a reduction in the time between order and shipment. This, obviously, is a worldwide trend. Delivery times were reduced from 120 days to 45 days, and suppliers continue to speed up the process. At Zara, delivery time has been reduced to 15 days, although with smaller volumes. One of the characteristics of

Topy Top is its constant search for ways to reduce production steps, so the process can be made cheaper and faster. Herreros (2000) made the same comparison with mature markets, showing that Zara and Topy Top provided fast response to orders at a lower cost (see Figure 2.15).

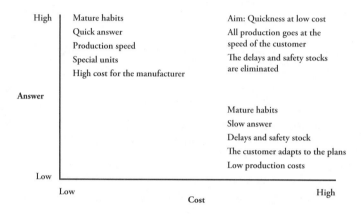

FIGURE 2.15. Speed and Costs: A Challenge to the Mature Thinking

SOURCE: Carlos Herreros, HCF Consultores.

3. It is possible to do the right thing without doing everything. Despite Topy Top's tendency to vertical integration, from the beginning the company resorted to subcontractors to fill its orders. Its current installed capacity allows it to manufacture most of its production, but the company still keeps a network of approximately 1,500 dressmakers who work at their own shops or at home. The challenge is to get these outside workers to meet the deadlines and the quality standards the process requires. In other words, the gains in productivity due to outsourcing should not be at the expense of a loss of quality. Figure 2.16 compares Zara's innovation with that of Topy Top and shows how high standards of quality can be achieved despite an increase in the production of garments.

4. The suppliers must be treated like partners. The secret of Topy Top's relationship with its suppliers is based on its knowledge of the client, its closeness to the client (normally, the samples are delivered in person by the product chiefs, so the needed modifications can be made at once and the deal can be closed), and unconditional support (the company is always ready to help the client in an emergency and to assume risks involving special garments).

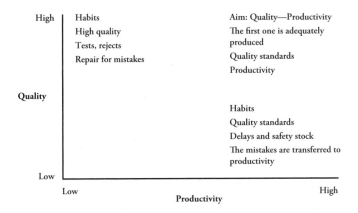

FIGURE 2.16. Quality and Productivity: A Challenge to the Mature Thinking

SOURCE: Carlos Herreros, HCF Consultores.

5. The goals are "super service" and "perfect orders." This is a kind of obsession among Topy Top's managers. The commitment to creativity is a commitment to quality: give the client the best of the best, no matter what it takes. At Topy Top shops, no deviation from the approved design is permitted. Once the design has been approved, the garments are produced in strict compliance. The company makes use of its creativity and experience to deliver what the client requested. No garment made outside specifications is tolerated. Topy Top's commitment to "super service" includes the constant perfecting of the designs it receives from its clients and the development of alternative methods. Collaboration and alliances with suppliers and clients are paramount.

Topy Top's perfectionism is not limited to the broadening of its industrial production and its venture into the retail trade. At a certain level, innovation has become the principal source of its competitiveness. Topy Top's technicians develop logistical, commercial, and productive processes that generate value incrementally, bringing to light hidden profits. The key to this trend has been the handling of human resources, starting from the founding of a very private entrepreneurial culture.

The Entrepreneurial Culture

Like its founders, Topy Top has made intuitive decision-making one of its strengths, complementing it with technology and acquired knowledge. However, it has not overlooked the dictates of the heart, which finds wisdom in its empirical interaction with reality. This austere and intuitive way of leading the company is reflected in its handling of human resources. Despite the company's growth in terms of labor force and the importance of coordinating the various processes, it wasn't until Topy Top's personnel reached eight hundred that management hired an executive to head the human resources department.

The management of human resources at Topy Top is based more on productivity than on cheap manual labor. The remunerative system consists of a basic wage equivalent to the legal minimum wage (earned by an apprentice and the equivalent of US$200 a month) plus a bonus for productivity.

Although the bonus system was fairly informal at the start of business, at present the company has a computerized system that measures productivity over time and automatically calculates the bonuses for each worker and work group. Also, the Floreses, and now the new management, have always sought to keep their employees and minimize personnel turnover. For this reason, in addition to the bonus incentive, they have incorporated a system of promotions based on merit.

At Topy Top, as in every organization that seeks to compete successfully in the world market, there is a kind of urgency to create products and gain new clients. At Topy Top's workshops, one senses a frenzied but optimistic rhythm, fed by the desire to be the best in the industry. A chat with Topy Top workers elicits statements that demonstrate an attitude of enthusiasm and optimism. The workers are certain that they will be successful in whatever they do. They know that their well-being depends on their productivity. No challenge is too great. They have outperformed competitors of all sizes, have attracted customers with all kinds of specialized needs, and have penetrated markets that were previously reserved for the big, traditional companies. Once they have accepted a challenge, they won't give up until they achieve their objective.

Optimism and Drive

Topy Top's philosophy has a constructivist basis. The overwhelming optimism felt by its managers is expressed in the belief that they can get anything they want. They don't try to depend on the situation, or on labor negotiations, or on aid from the government. If a market closes, they look for room elsewhere; if they need workers with special skills, they find them in the labor market or train them as needed. What permeates the organization is the spirit of the Flores brothers, who started the business without resources or special training.

The work ethic is alive in the culture promoted by the Flores brothers. It harks back to the days when they rose at 4 A.M. to find the best spots at the Central Market. That love of labor today drives the Flores brothers to work twelve to fourteen hours a day.

Although the presence of managers is increasingly indispensable, the Flores brothers continue to make all decisions within their board of directors, interacting with the team leaders. According to Estevan Danieluc, "Aquilino, Carlos, and Manuel are a unit. The three think in complementary fashion and always try for a consensus. If there is disagreement, the project is abandoned."

One of Danieluc's tasks is to take advantage of this original wealth while eliminating the inefficiencies that may result from a centralized decision-making process in an organization that continues to grow. For that reason, new managerial positions are being created that didn't exist before. More and more activities are being delegated to professionals unrelated to the family. Inevitably, labor relations are being regulated by written rules, rather than the workers' direct relation with the bosses.

An Efficiency That Looks Like Chaos

If you were to examine the productive process at Topy Top, you would perceive a kind of organizational chaos. But once you understood the modus operandi, you would realize that it's a productive chaos, something like the order of the disorderly alluded to in the Coca-Cola commercial: "You are not disorganized; you're only organized differently."

Chatting with the executives, you would discover that each area has a different organizational structure. In effect, beyond the organizational chart, the members of the organization cooperate informally among themselves. Some of the people we interviewed said things like, "I have my own organizational chart." What's essential, they told us, was to know who can help you in the performance of any task, or who has the resources to facilitate the completion of any objective. Once you know "who's who" you can take advantage of this type of informal support.

Although those in authority abide by the company's formally adopted policies, the Floreses have always taken advantage of the potential of workers with new ideas, and they reward—with sudden promotions—those who somehow contribute to the innovation of processes or to an improvement in the implementation of a project. There have been many instances in which bold employees managed to establish direct relations with the Floreses in order to propose a project to improve the business.

Thus, the Floreses have managed to impose an organizational system with enough flexibility to enable the professional development of their employees based on their ability to visualize and carry out opportunities for improvement, whether it involved entering a new market or creating a new system of production. This apparent productive chaos does not clash with the company's formal organization; it complements it and frees it from the rigid thinking that discourages the pursuit of productivity.

Above all, the same rule applies to everyone: "super service" to the clients, who do not see what goes on within the company but celebrate the quality and low price of its products. If a flaw occurs, everyone rushes to fix it and nobody asks who the culprit is. What's important is to correct the problem and go on to meet the demands of the order. Anyone who visits Topy Top's facilities can sense this spirit.

The Fight Against Stress

The regime of "productive chaos" that runs parallel to the formal bureaucracy generates an environment of great pressure, stress, and uncertainty that leads workers to say that they labor under "a lot of adrenaline, a lot of pressure." Topy Top's style of business no doubt generates a tiring and even exhausting work experience. Employees work two eight-hour shifts, back to back. Many workers find it hard to get used to this, to the point that some literally burst into tears as a result of the pressure.

This organizational culture, which demands boldness and a profound commitment, with a policy based on knowledge and innovative leadership, asks its workers to resist stress. It asks them to be strong and resist exhaustion, to understand the complexities and tolerate ambiguities—at the very least, to place their trust in their directors and leaders.

To Topy Top's leaders, the challenge is to find ways to respond creatively to this pressure so that any unnecessary suffering can be avoided and a sustainably humane working environment can be provided to all its employees. Gradually, the company has organized activities to support the workers beyond providing cash wages, so as to reward their efficiency and commitment. Yearly olympiads, Christmas baskets (75 percent of the cost of which is paid by the company), and adequate dining facilities are some of the ways the company alleviates the pressure of work and supplements cash wages. It should also be noted that, according to Peruvian law, the workers share 10 percent of the company's profits at the end of every year, plus 1 percent for their productivity.

Nevertheless, much remains to be done at Topy Top to meet the labor and organizational standards that are proper for a company of its size. Along with the professionalization of the company, the working conditions of its personnel are improving. Also, those aspects of flexibility that led to a certain informality in the organizational operation are disappearing. In the long run, the organizational demands of a corporation will require the company to abandon many of the characteristics of family management, and labor relations will become depersonalized. Little by little, direct contact with the owners to solve conflicts will have to be replaced by the hierarchical relations that inevitably rule every corporation.

International Labor Standards and Problems with Visas

Many important buyers in the international textile market, such as Adidas and Reebok, were harshly criticized by the international media in the 1990s because their suppliers, particularly in Asia, utilized child labor, treated their workers poorly, and engaged in methods of production that were banned in the Western world.

To avoid the resulting loss of prestige, the buyers for these large brands opted to impose standards that their suppliers had to implement through new policies and practices. In some cases they went to extremes, demanding that companies such as Topy Top maintain standards that not only failed to contribute to their workers' well-being but also harmed them.

One group of workers harmed by these standards and certifications consists of poor women who are not able to travel to a factory and work full time. Many poor communities enthusiastically embraced the garment factories' practice of subcontracting out specialized work that required intensive manual labor. Women who could not leave their homes because they had children to care for were able to do this work at home. For a while, training was given to women by the Mothers Clubs and the Popular Dining Halls (groups formed by neighbors in low-income communities to save money on the purchase and preparation of food, child care, and so on) so they could embroider and sew appliqués and thus gain employment they couldn't find elsewhere.

However, many of the standards imposed by American and European clients expressly prohibit removing the garments from the factories and taking them to someone's home to be embroidered or appliquéd. This rule, created to protect the workers, ended up disqualifying mothers who urgently need the income and the on-the-job training.

Although this situation does not prevent Topy Top from proceeding with its production, the company's employees and executives resent the fact that they are prevented from continuing a practice that was a true social service and was perceived as valuable by the neediest people.

Another factor involved in working with firms in developed countries that hampers the development of companies in the process of internationalization, such as Topy Top, is the restricted access to international travel. As we have seen, Topy Top has developed a strategy that includes visits to and direct dealings with its international clients. This practice gives excellent results by building closer relations that enable Topy Top to fine-tune its strategies of products and services.

Lamentably, it has become increasingly difficult for Topy Top to hire the personnel it needs for international travel because it must take into consideration the restrictions in the issuance of visas. Most workers have never traveled abroad, and obtaining a visa without a previous record of departure and return has become increasingly difficult. An indirect consequence of this policy by the rich countries is that the people who can obtain visas with the greatest ease are young people from wealthy families, because they can give proof of parental support, frequent trips abroad, and so on. This creates a growing exclusion of the poor and a wider social rift.

The restrictions on freedom in the developed world are an additional hurdle to entrepreneurial development in countries like Peru, which require that development to emerge from poverty.

STRENGTHS, WEAKNESSES, OPPORTUNITIES, THREATS—AND STRATEGY

As we have seen, part of the process of professionalization at Topy Top has been the formalization of its decision-making process. The development of a strategic plan is an example of this transition. The SWOT analysis (FODA in Spanish, for strengths, opportunities, weaknesses, and threats) contained in that plan allows us to learn how the company sees itself over the long term. The strategy resulting from that analysis reflects Topy Top's plan for dealing with business in the face of an uncertain future.

The SWOT Analysis

According to Topy Top's self-evaluation, the company sees its future in terms of the following positive and negative elements.

- The strengths the company is aware of are: knowledge of the market in general and the capacity for retail trade in the local market, the development of exclusive styles and the trademark, constant technological innovation, product quality, flexibility, and versatility. The owners also know they are in good standing in terms of service and have service-oriented human resources.
- The weaknesses the company has identified are: excessive dependence on the American market and client Old Navy; a commercial structure that's still insufficient, and design and product development that are still insufficient. The organization and processes lack structure. In need of improvement are cost overruns, shortages and surpluses of materials, and quality of products. The management and supervision structure is weak. An integral plan for the development and training of human resources is missing.
- The opportunities are: the unsatisfied demand from the local and regional retail markets; the possibility of establishing more strategic alliances with clients and suppliers; the existence of unexplored markets in Europe, the United States, and the rest of the Americas; the possibility of a trade promotion agreement with the United States and other countries, which would lower or eliminate tariffs; the existence of financing sources with low interest rates; and the potential for wide development of the credit card business.
- In that regard, a fundamental issue that Topy Top's management has been discussing with the labor unions has been a reduction in labor costs. In fact, Peruvian legislation already envisions lower payroll taxes for small and medium-sized businesses. Topy Top sees this as an opportunity for the government to extend this tax structure to all companies, which would reduce the cost of manual labor by 24 percent without altering the workers' wages. Also, Topy Top is part of a group of companies that advocate a reduction in tariffs to reduce the cost of woven fabrics.

- The threats perceived are: the withdrawal of the main client, for whatever reason; the persistence of informality and smuggling in the local market; competition from Asia and the big chains; the dismantling of tariff preferences (in the event that the TPA with the United States is not signed); the lack of raw materials; and a return of populism. A free trade agreement with the United States is seen as critical because Chile, Jordan, Israel, Morocco, Australia, Central American, and Caribbean countries already have one.

The Strategy

Topy Top's strategy, looking ahead to 2014, involves the entire corporation and can be summarized as follows:

- Regarding the clients:
  - The Floreses intend to develop the retail business at a regional level, focusing on casual fashions, with lines made of materials other than cotton, and to develop other segments with a view to diversification. To that end, by the year 2010, they hope to have a chain of one hundred fully owned or franchised stores with sales of about US$100 million.
  - They will seek to diversify their international exports. They are already in the process of consolidating the European market, seeking to eliminate the risk of concentrating their sales on a few big clients.
  - They will look for new channels of distribution and sale, via the Internet and catalogs.
  - They will give new impetus to the development of fashions, with an eye to creating products in different materials that are ahead of the trends.
- Regarding the price of their products, the Floreses will foster synergy between their trademark apparel, the retail trade, and sales through Topy Top Visa credit cards. On one hand, the reengineering of their processes is helping the company achieve full automation of its operations, adapt to ISO standards, and continue to work toward speedy fulfillment of clients' orders. On the other, they are considering establishing an independent financial business, linked to the retail trade.
- Regarding competition, the Floreses' strategy will be aimed at developing and manufacturing fashion products with greater value and differ-

entiation. They will also try to reach the final consumer directly in the local and foreign markets. That relationship has already begun through a sales strategy that hinges not on shipments but on the personal presence of Topy Top salesmen at the markets to which they deliver samples, in an effort to gain time and maintain accuracy. In that regard, they are opening an office in New York to tend to the U.S. market and another one in Barcelona, Spain, to serve the European market.

- The Floreses are also trying to achieve a financial structure that will permit them to finance 40 percent of their activities through the capital market now and 70 percent in the future. This is being done for the purpose of achieving sales in excess of US$150 million, with a minimum profit margin of 10 percent. The effort will entail a reform in the company's corporate government, leading to a formal organizational structure. All of this will require, among other aspects, continued improvements in the area of human resources.

- Regarding the national situation, the Floreses will do whatever is necessary to protect themselves from the ups and downs of currency exchange rates, will seek to reduce risks in the face of threats such as an outbreak of terrorism, and will participate in campaigns against smuggling and piracy. Also, they will work to promote adequate legislation aimed at labor flexibility, gradually increasing the outsourcing of their activities.

- Finally, the Floreses will try to adapt as best they can to international standards on environmental protection, using the best technology available, and will try to obtain the certification demanded by their international clients. This task is not easy. In fact, according to management, the company has had to make significant adjustments to its systems of production and logistics to comply with the demands of the current certification. New exigencies will continue to develop in the near future.

This strategy is not new, of course. What is new is its explicit formulation, the fact that the Floreses have put it down in black and white, ending the reign of intuition. The size of the company demands this. However, there is a risk that the something will be lost in the process, that natural mystique that turned a car washer into the most important textile businessman in Peru.

CONCLUSIONS

What enabled this entrepreneurial effort to emerge from nothing (in terms of capital) in a poor country like Peru? Let us review the answers we've discussed in this chapter.

- First, the Flores family took advantage of the opportunities provided by the environment, always guided by the market and the innovation of their productive and logistical processes. That ability began when young Aquilino Flores seized the opportunity to sell twenty T-shirts in two days at Lima's Central Market. It is repeated when he fills a sophisticated order for thousands of garments from the Zara chain of stores in Europe. Another constant feature in the company's history is the ability to turn serious problems, such as the rejection of large quantities of merchandise, into business opportunities.
- Topy Top entered the retail sales business by accident, which led the group to take a serious look at the concomitant financial business. The opening of international trade that occurred in Peru in the early 1990s gave the company an opportunity to export. This opening has not prevented Topy Top from becoming an importer, particularly of Chinese products, to help develop its retail business. These imports have complemented its sales of knitwear.
- Topy Top's competitive strategy has always been based on market analysis, beginning with an intuitive analysis that turned into systematic analysis as the company grew. In particular, this analysis hinged on closeness to the client and on taking advantage of the hidden profits found in variety, speed, diversity, and quality. An integral part of this success was based on the organizational culture of Topy Top, one that is innovative and flexible and that encourages workers' commitment to the company.
- The Flores family was able to go from being a mere trader in purchased clothing to one of the key companies in the production of garments in a very few years. This required permanent training.

Topy Top's vertical integration of the production processes began as a response to the need to guarantee the quality of the orders they received from third parties. Their first step was to buy the thread needed to manufacture their own fabrics. Later, they decided to set up their own dye plant, at which time they began to define the quality and colors of their garments and to increase the productivity of the dyeing process.

Another important step was to locate their plants in areas with a long tradition in the textile industry, so they could benefit from an experienced labor force, hire high-level technicians, and invest in technology and specialized machinery. This vertical integration generated big gains in productivity that translated into quality production at low cost.

As before, Topy Top's growth was the result of taking advantage of an opportunity. This opportunity was provided by Peru's opening to globalization and, more recently, by the elimination of tariffs in the United States and Europe. Finally, Topy Top's internationalization continues with its first exports to Venezuela and, perhaps, to Mexico, always accompanied by the opening of retail stores where the company can sell its own products.

In sum, the Topy Top case affords us an optimistic look into the possibilities of wealth creation originating in situations of poverty, even in countries with weak institutions, like Peru. Its history refutes the belief that the war on poverty in these countries is a matter of state intervention. The story of the Flores family is one of development without state participation, of an entrepreneurial evolution that overcame hurdles that many intellectuals or managers trained in elite universities would have considered impossible. It is therefore a story that shows us that it is possible to emerge from poverty on the strength of human action vis-à-vis the market, action that was made possible by a reduction in state intervention, excessive taxation, and bureaucratic fees, both in Peru and in its foreign markets.

NOTES

1. ISO 9000 has become an international reference for the requirements of management quality in business-to-business affairs. The ISO 9000 standards refer specifically to "management quality." This means that the organization must comply with (a) the consumer's requirements for quality, and (b) the requirements of the regulations applicable to the sector, while (c) seeking to augment customer satisfaction and (d) achieving a continuous improvement of its performance in the search for these objectives (ISO, 2006).

2. The GATT's standards were deficient in many respects. In the sector of textiles and clothing, an exception to the GATT was negotiated in the 1960s and early 1970s that made room for the Multifiber Arrangement, among other accords. Even the institutional structure of the GATT and its system of problem-solving were causes for concern. This ended with the Uruguay Round and the creation of the WTO in 1994.

3. Zara is an exceptional case that has broken the pattern of retail sales worldwide. With sales of $2 billion and more than a thousand stores in thirty countries, it represents an impressive entrepreneurial accomplishment—in one generation.

4. This section is based on a study by IESE Business School (2004). The concept of developing businesses at the base of the pyramid has been developed by C. K. Prahalad and Stuart, among others. See Prahalad (2005).

REFERENCES

Abusada, Roberto, Javier Illescas, and Sara Taboada. 2001. *Integrating Peru into the World.* Lima: Peruvian Institute of the Economy and Research Center of the University of the Pacific.

Andean Trade Promotion and Drug Eradication Act (ATPDEA). 2002. Available at http://www.mincetur.gob.pe/COMERCIO/OTROS/Atpdea/procedimientos_aduaneros/normas_origen.htm.

Apoyo Consultants. 2003. *Analysis of Tax Exemptions and Incentives and a Proposed Strategy for Their Elimination.* Lima: Ministry of the Economy and Finance.

Apoyo Consultants. 2004. *The Outlook for the Apparel Sector Aimed at Exports.* Lima: Apoyo Consultants.

Bovet, D., and J. Martha. 2000 *Value Nets: Breaking the Supply Chain to Unlock Hidden Profits.* Hoboken, NJ: John Wiley.

Central Reserve Bank of Peru. 2006. *Weekly Bulletin,* July 21, 1.

Claros, Jesús. 2005. Gamarra: Latin American Capital of Fashions in 2005. Available at http://www.peru.com/articles/2000/01/finanzas/20000113/index.asp.

Danieluc, Estevan. 2003. Andean Woolens Keep the World Warm. In *Starting a Business: How Successful Entrepreneurs Got Started.* Lima: Ministry of Labor and Job Promotion, Consortium of Private Organizations to Promote the Development of Micro and Small Enterprises.

De Soto, Hernando. 1986. *The Other Path.* Lima: El Barranco Publishers.

El Comercio, Dia 1. 2004. Interview with Estevan Danieluc. July 19.

Herreros, Carlos. 2000. *Zara: A Challenge to the Mature Thinking.* Available at http://www.gestiondelconocimiento.com/documentos2/carlos_herreros/caso_zara.htm.

IESE Business School. 2004. Examples of Success at the Base of the Pyramid: The Cases of Hindustan Lever, Cemex, SCH, Topy Top and Tetra Pak. In *The Supply Chain at the Base of the Pyramid,* Rodríguez et al. IESE Business School, University of Navarra, Spain.

International Monetary Fund (IMF). 2005. World Economic Outlook Databases. September 21, 2005. Available at http://www.imf.org/external/pubs/ft/weo/2005/02/data/index.htm.

International Organization for Standardization (ISO). 2006. *Management Standards: Understand the Basics.* Available at www.iso.org/iso/en/is09000–14000/understand/inbrief.html.

Kwan, C. H. 2002. *Overcoming the China Syndrome in Japan.* trans. Jaime González-Torres. Shanghai Academy of Social Sciences. Available at http://www.revistasice.com/Estudios/Documen/ice/807/ICE8070501.PDF.

Limas Garragati, V. 2005. *Topy Top: Unlimited Quality—World-Class Peruvian Garments.* Lima: Centro Publishing Company.

Ministry of Foreign Trade and Tourism. 2006. Protocol Between the Republic of Peru and the Kingdom of Thailand to Accelerate the Liberalization of Trade in Merchandise and the Facilitation of Commerce. Available at http://www.mincetur.gob.pe/COMERCIO/OTROS/tlc_tailandia.

Morón, E., et al, 2005. *Free Trade Agreement with the United States: An Opportunity for Sustained Growth*. Lima: Peruvian Institute of the Economy (IPE), University of the Pacific.

National Institute of Statistics and Information. 2005. *National Survey of Housing and Poverty (ENAHO), 2001–2004*. Available at http://www.inei.gob.pe.

Navarro Rojas, C. 2004. We Hope to Become a Corporation in 10 More Years. *El Comercio, Day One*. July 19.

Peruinforma.com. 2003. Topy Top Received Golden Mercury Award as the Principal Exporter of Manufactured Goods. Available at http://www.peruinforma.com/imwebsite/article.php?=Print&sid=8051.

Pongo, H. 2004. The Mestizo Entrepreneurs. Available at http://www.lafogata.org/04latino/latin05/b01.htm.

Prahalad, C. K. 2005. *Business Opportunity at the Base of the Pyramid*. Columbia: Norma Publishers, 2005.

Prebisch, Raúl. 1962. Latin America's Economic Development and Some of Its Main Problems. *Economic Bulletin for Latin America* 7: 1.

Rodríguez, M. A., F. Sabriá, and P. Sánchez. 2004. *The Supply Chain at the Base of the Pyramid*. IESE Business School, University of Navarra, Spain.

Villaorduña, J. M. 2005. *Topy Top: Unlimited Quality—22nd Anniversary*. Ferrer S.A.

3

Nakumatt: A Kenyan Supermarket

JUNE ARUNGA AND SCOTT BEAULIER

INTRODUCTION

In the Western world, we take supermarkets for granted; many of us are, in fact, highly critical of these institutions. But in extremely poor parts of the world, such as Kenya, one would be hard-pressed to find a more important source of human flourishing. Until recently, Kenyan consumers were limited to a narrow range of locally produced foods and unreliable goods that were sold primarily at kiosks. With the emergence of the supermarket, however, individuals are now able to purchase a wide variety of reputable products at fair market prices. This paper examines the overall retail environment in Kenya. We pay special attention to the case of Nakumatt, Kenya's largest supermarket chain. The story of Nakumatt's emergence and the challenges it continues to face can help us better understand the challenges of entrepreneurship in less developed countries (LDCs).[1]

THE ECONOMIC LAY OF THE LAND

Kenya is a relatively large (582,650 km^2) sub-Saharan African country located in the Horn of Africa. It borders the Indian Ocean to the east. The "failed" or "weak" states of Somalia, Sudan, Ethiopia, Uganda, and Rwanda are all in close proximity to Kenya (*Foreign Policy*, 2005). By the end of 2007, its population will have surpassed 35 million, having grown at a rate of 2.56 percent in 2006 (CIA). The rate of urbanization in Kenya is one of the highest in the world, and the proportion of people living in urban areas was approximately 25 percent in 2005.[2] Even though nearly 80 percent of the population lives outside of the urban areas, agricultural production accounted for only 27 percent of gross domestic product in 2005. Kenya's official unemployment rate is high (40 percent in 2001) when compared to Western standards, but its economy is relatively strong when compared to those of its neighbors. In 2005, Kenya's gross domestic product per capita was $428 (in constant 2000 US dollars). It is classified as a "least developed country" (henceforth LDC) by the World Bank, but its income level is above the average level for that category of $316 per person (in constant 2000 US dollars). Despite its low level of income, Kenya has not received a tremendous amount of foreign aid when compared to other LDCs. In 2004, foreign aid to the country amounted to $19 per capita .

Kenya gained independence from Great Britain in 1963, and Jomo Kenyatta was brought to power as its first independent leader. Kenyatta ruled until his death in 1978. From that time until 1991, Kenya's government was dominated by the Kenya African National Union (KANU). After 1991, numerous opposition groups attempted to grab power from the KANU. Many of these attempts resulted in damage to property, injuries, and allegations of corruption. By the beginning of the twenty-first century, the situation in Kenya had stabilized and improved to the point that an opposition group leader, Mwai Kabaki of the National Rainbow Coalition, was elected president in 2002.

Today, the political environment in Kenya is relatively stable.[3] The government's anticorruption effort has helped attract foreign investment and foreign aid. There is greater awareness of the seriousness of the HIV/AIDS problem that afflicts every African nation. Relations in the region remain tense, with ongoing conflicts in Somalia, Ethiopia, and Sudan, but Kenya has been active in welcoming refugees from several East African countries and brokering peace efforts in Somalia. The typical problems afflicting most African nations—disease, poverty, and corruption—are all present in Kenya; however, it has been fortunate enough to avoid war.

In LDCs such as Kenya, the focus of poverty alleviation programs has been on what the state can do to end poverty, reduce income inequality, increase literacy, and better stabilize the overall economic and political environment. Although there is clearly an important role for government in efforts to alleviate poverty, the role of business and the entrepreneur often gets lost in discussions of what government ought to be doing. It is becoming increasingly apparent that business and entrepreneurship, not government, is the key ingredient in alleviating poverty in LDCs (Easterly 2001, 2006).

When Kenya became an independent nation in 1963, its leadership immediately implemented an economic plan that created incentives for private (including foreign) industrial investment, smallholder agricultural production, and some public investment. Under the new leadership, the economy flourished. In its first ten years, the average annual growth rate was 4.3 percent,[4] and Kenya was touted as an emerging economic leader in Africa. With rapid economic growth, primary school enrollment increased, health care services expanded, and income per capita rose from US$260 to $396. Kenyans believed that their vision of a prosperous, independent nation would soon be reached.

But this was not to be. Government spending as a percentage of gross domestic product (GDP) increased from 11 percent in 1963 to 16 percent by 1973 and 18 percent by 1983. Although these percentages are small when compared to Western governments, the quality of government in Kenya is much worse. Vague regulations and licenses make it extremely costly to run businesses. Inefficiencies in the production of public goods, such as water, electricity, and education, make it necessary for most Kenyans to seek out private alternatives while still paying for costly government services. Taken as a whole, the high level of government intervention, coupled with import substitution industrialization and difficult international conditions, combined to slow the economy. By the early 1980s, Kenya's government had placed a significant strain on the private sector. The resulting instability caused an economic decline, which was exacerbated by worldwide oil shocks in the 1970s and early 1980s.

The oil crisis caused a severe imbalance of payments in Kenya, since most of Kenya's oil is imported. As Kenya increased its borrowing to deal with this imbalance, its growth slowed considerably. In response to the crisis, Kenya's leadership turned inward and began implementing macroeconomic policies based on protectionist ideas. This protectionism led to a devaluation of Kenya's currency and a number of corrupt government practices in which the most protected industries were the ones engaging in the most "rent-seeking" activity.[5] Poor governance, declining levels of investment, and poor service delivery by the government put Kenya on a steady decline during the rest of the 1980s and the early 1990s. Between 1978 and 1994, Kenya's average annual growth in per capita income was 0 percent (World Bank, 2006). As a result, the standard of living of the majority of Kenyans deteriorated and the level of poverty increased at an alarming rate.

In the early 1990s, the economic instability in Kenya led to civil unrest and political instability. In response to this upheaval, the ruling regime sought to buy votes through a financial scheme based on high-level corruption, which led to one of the worst public scandals in the country's history, known as the Goldenberg scandal.[6] Coupled with irresponsible monetary policy, the affair led to double-digit inflation. In trying to mop up excess liquidity, the Central Bank raised interest rates to 30 percent. Many businesses closed. Except for a brief period in the middle of the decade, the 1990s were characterized by utter economic failure.

By the year 2000, the country's GDP was once again at the same level as in 1978. Kenya's economic stagnation was reflected in almost all sectors of the economy, and the level of poverty deepened. World Bank statistics indicated that more than 15 million Kenyans were living on less than a dollar a day. The middle class had almost disappeared, and the gap between the rich and the poor was at new heights. According to Transparency International, Kenya was declared the third most corrupt country in the world in the year 2000; only Nigeria and Cameroon were worse. In response to this corruption, donors cut off aid.

In December 2002, things finally began to change. Kenya's citizens went to the polls and voted out KANU president Daniel Toroitich arap Moi in free and fair elections. The newly elected Rainbow Coalition government, an alliance of opposition parties formed months before the polls, delivered a crushing defeat to KANU. The elections were generally peaceful and drew praise from international observers. They were considered a new beginning for the fledgling republic. On being elected, Kenya's new president, Mwai Kibaki, pledged to end authoritarian rule, tackle high-level corruption, and relieve the country's economic woes.

The general consensus regarding the new Kenyan government under President Mwai Kibaki is that he has been successful in turning things around, albeit slowly. When an International Monetary Fund team traveled to Kenya in October 2005, it released a statement supporting "the Kenya government's expectation of 5 percent economic growth during the fiscal year 2005/6." The economy grew by 2.2 percent in 2004, but barely grew in 2005. Even though Kenya is still struggling to grow, the fact that it is experiencing some positive growth is an encouraging sign. The recent push for economic growth in Kenya has come primarily from agriculture, tourism, and a recovery in the manufacturing sector.[7]

These successes notwithstanding, the new regime is widely perceived to have failed to fulfill many of its anticorruption promises, reform the economy substantially, and create five hundred thousand jobs a year. As a result, the country is a long way from overcoming the legacy of the last few decades. A Human Development Index released in 2004 shows that, in real terms, Kenya has become poorer since 1963. According to the United Nations Development Program, Kenya has an extremely young population—42 percent is under 15 years of age, and only 23 percent is over 65. Other sources state that 65 to 70 percent of the population is under 30. With a president and a vice president who are each over 70 years old and a third of the cabinet being over 65, Kenya is a country of young people ruled by older people.

Even with the new economic surge, the average life expectancy in 2004 was only 48 years. Life expectancy has dropped from an average of 58 years in 1990 to 48 years in 2004, largely because of disease, high infant mortality, and the HIV/AIDS crisis. In 2004, 120 of every 1,000 Kenyan children died before the age of 5. Thirty-seven percent of the population is undernourished. Only 57 percent of Kenyans have access to clean water, and 23 percent live on less than US$1 a day. There are only 14 physicians for every 1,000 people. In 2002, 6.7 percent of the population had HIV/AIDS.

The World Bank statistics do not read any better when it comes to technology and infrastructure. Only 10 out of every 1,000 Kenyans have landline telephones, and 12.5 are Internet users. Of the same 1,000, 25 own TVs, while 223 own radios. There are 1.6 million cellular phone owners in the country.[8] To top it all off, in 2006, Transparency International ranked Kenya 142nd out of 163 countries in terms of perceived corruption (the lower the ranking, the greater the perceived corruption).

Nowhere are the statistics more indicative of the general backwardness of the country than in Nairobi's slums, the capital city. Since independence, Nairobi's population has increased by a factor of eight, from 350,000 to 2,818,000. Even though 45 percent of the country's GDP is produced in Nairobi, only one-tenth of the population of the country lives there. Two-thirds of Nairobians live in slums.

Kibera, the largest slum in Nairobi, and one of the world's poorest slums, houses nearly one million people. Hundreds of thousands of these are unskilled workers attached to local industries. Most of them, at least the ones who have work, earn between US$1.50 and $2 per day. Given the fact that the government has set the minimum wage at US$0.90 per day, these incomes are decent ones for Kenyans living in slums.

Nick Wachira, associate editor of the *Nation* newspaper, the largest daily newspaper in Kenya, recently wrote an extended piece on the country's "comeback" economy:

> In Kibera, the economy is dead. Even as the government continues to revel in the glory of rising fortunes in the country, economic prosperity in Kenya is unlikely to mean much to millions of urban poor in Kenya when it comes to reducing poverty . . . The urban poor are illiterate and lack the basic skills to run a business. Together with tens of thousands of small family-owned businesses in Kenya, the urban poor will continue to be excluded from the mainstream economy, without a fair chance of even scratching at the fringes of material prosperity.

The fact that Kenya has been so poor and so corrupt for such a long period of time makes the story of successful businesses such as Nakumatt even more impressive. This story helps us understand that the entrepreneurial spirit cannot be destroyed, even when governments are providing a weak and perverse institutional environment. By looking closely at the Nakumatt story and making sense out of how it has succeeded, we can gain a better understanding of the inherent challenges of doing business in LDCs and, perhaps, use this case study to make more general claims about poverty alleviation in general.

THE RISE OF THE ENTREPRENEUR IN KENYA

In 2004, the Ford Foundation office in Kenya hosted a series of lectures dealing with issues in law, economics, political science, and sociology. Though many of the lectures had titles that seemed straight out of the scholarly conference circuit, they were generally pessimistic regarding Kenya's future.

After a series of presentations sounding the death knell for the country, to which the audience seemed to respond with masochistic stoicism, leading economist David Ndii of the Kenya Leadership Institute told the audience that there was nothing wrong with the country. All Kenyans needed, he said, was "a government that could leave them alone to run their businesses and their lives."

Ndii's argument was that the sheer ability of Kenyans to survive all of the challenges that had come their way was proof enough. He talked of punitive taxation, a government that was extremely hostile to business, nepotism, rent-seeking, bribery, and exclusive political and economic networks. Ndii used the example of secondhand clothes dealers as a major success story in the face of all these obstacles. He might also have been talking about Nakumatt.

Between the lines drawn up by grim statistics there is a harsh anecdotal tale of survival in Kenya that amounts to a growth in the entrepreneurial spirit of the people. We will focus on Nakumatt's survival later in this chapter, but it is important to note that Nakumatt is not the only example. The 1990s saw the emergence of several 30-something-year-old entrepreneurs who have since made a mark on the country. Joe Gichuki, a financial consultant, accountant, and former general manager of SEPSO, a personal services firm helping out small enterprises, explains,

> When I ran SEPSO, we met lots and lots of aspiring business-people. What we were looking for was what we called the "missing middle," something you don't see a lot of in Africa—that sector that lies between people who make shoes on the roadside and the big companies . . . this was a big problem in the 1990s because these middle industries were simply not there. Apart from industry, there are people doing a whole load of things in the services sector. This "missing middle" is the crux of industrialization. Everywhere in the world this is what makes industrialization. Ninety-nine percent of firms in Japan have 50 workers or less. If you want industrialization, that is the kind of businesses you want in the country.

Gichuki attributes the emergence of a new generation of young entrepreneurs with exciting ideas to the tough 1990s:

> Most people running small, successful enterprises started in the early 1990s. This was both an interesting and possibly the worst time in independent Kenya—a time when people who had not thought of themselves as poor became poor after Goldenberg, the biggest financial scandal in Kenya since independence.

Gichuki also talks of a severe marginalization of the major tribes that were dominant in business by the ruling clique at the time:

Moi started marginalizing the Kikuyus, who were the most populous tribe and the owners of many businesses. They ended up exiting the State. It reached a point when people were no longer relying on the State for anything, from getting your product to the market to infrastructure, licenses, marketing, investing. The Central Province was totally marginalized. State instruments that were used to regulate business became dormant at the time. But this proved a benefit in a sense because people decided—I am going to make money where I can, wherever I can. The early '90s really opened people's eyes.

Nick Wachira, associate editor of the *Nation* newspaper, attributes the explosion of entrepreneurial ideas in the 1990s to an increase in access to information:

People started to know things they didn't know before, and this had a lot to do with the new inflows of information on the Internet. Remember, that's when the first private TV station in Kenya started, and they were not allowed to even broadcast news for three years. Also all the FM stations opened in the 1990s. You had access to information, on how to do things. This is something that people didn't have before. Back in the 1970s, you had a Special Working Party on Public Universities. Now you had private universities coming up. For the first time in Kenya, knowledge and information were becoming accessible. This helped people know "I can do whatever I want."

Another factor in the rise of entrepreneurship was the fact that the financial scandals caused donors to withdraw their support from Kenya. According to Gichuki,

Kenyans also realized that they could function without donors. Not function well . . . but at least survive. Today, we now talk about 5 percent economic growth in Kenya, 7 percent in Uganda, and 6 percent in Tanzania. But both Uganda and Tanzania's growth is fueled by donor funds and is therefore temporary. Fifty percent of the Ugandan budget comes from donor money. Though donors are part of the Kenyan economy, they have been left out of our budget. Kenya's economy is no longer run by one single donor or by a batch of donors. The 1990s gave us a confidence to run our own affairs that had not been there before. This translated into new entrepreneurs coming up. Now Kenyans are not worried about annoying donors. We are thriving even without major donor assistance. Now you have university students running and thinking of businesses. I know a young Kenyan who just started a garbage-collection company.

The gradual liberalization of the economy brought about by the decline of the 1990s also played a role in motivating Kenyans to start businesses. Nick Wachira explains that the government started losing hold of business: "People in the 1990s became smarter than government systems. Cell phones were faster than government information. Space and time closed down faster than the government could realize." There were fewer political risks when the Kibaki government came to power. The common practice of politically connected people forcefully extorting shares from successful businesses largely stopped. "It was very hard to start a business without a godfather," says Wachira. "Nobody was going to give you money just because you had a business plan. Now we even have venture capital firms in the country, and they are giving money for good ideas."

Of course, many obstacles remain, such as slow reform, the legacy of previous decades, and institutional deficiencies. Public relations manager Okoth Obado, who works for Ogilvy and Mather, adds that the lack of protection of ideas is a big problem that stands in the way of entrepreneurship: "There are no mechanisms for the protection of ideas. Many dreams are going down the drain. There is the hijacking of ideas. This hinders some small businesses from growing into great businesses."

For reasons we will discuss later, Nakumatt is one of those entrepreneurial ventures that was able to survive and turn the obstacles into opportunities for growth and wealth creation. The obstacles standing in the way of entrepreneurship were and continue to be numerous, however, and the continued success of Nakumatt in particular and businesses in Kenya in general remains uncertain.

THE INFORMAL ECONOMY IN KENYA

Because of the business impediments mentioned earlier, many entrepreneurs in Kenya are unable to raise the kind of capital that major supermarkets need in order to operate from day to day. As a result, Kenya's retail sector today consists of a mix of kiosks, dukas,[9] self-service stores, convenience stores, medium supermarkets, supermarkets, and hypermarkets. There are currently more than 225 supermarkets in Kenya (Neven et al., 2005), scattered throughout the country. The largest of these supermarkets are chain stores like Uchumi, Ukwala, Nakumatt, Tuskermatt, and Woolmatt. Each has more than three branches located in the main urban centers of Nairobi, Mombasa, Kisumu, Nakuru, and Eldoret. Hybrid supermarkets with stand-alone stores can also be found in major cities and towns. In the informal sector, there are 1.7 million enterprises involved in the wholesale and retail trade. The majority of these (1.2 million) are found in the rural areas.

With a gross product of 129 billion Kenyan shillings (KSh) and double-digit annual growth over the last five years, the retail sector contributes 10 percent to the country's GDP and has an ever-growing share. Supermarkets control only 20 percent of this market.

Although it is difficult to obtain accurate data, there are about 2.6 million informal sector businesses in Kenya, employing about 2.5 million Kenyans and generating about Ksh197 billion—between 20 and 30 percent of Kenya's GDP (African Centre for Economic Growth, 1992). The informal sector operates in all areas of the economy and thus produces a wide range of goods and services. In small-scale manufacturing, it deals with food processing, tailoring, fabrication, carpentry, and repairs and maintenance; prominent commodities produced include textile fibers, with more than 957,000 operators. Other informal sector industries include cork and wood, charcoal, cereals and cereal production, fish and fish preparation, and furniture.

Services in the informal sector are largely unspecified and embrace a wide range of distribution trades, hotels, and restaurants. Retail trading has the largest share of these services at 26.6 percent, while catering and the selling of drinks represent 4.2 percent. Building and construction, transport and communication, and community and personal services such as traditional doctors, repair services, domestic services, and hairdressing, also feature significantly. Educational, medical, dental, and veterinary services constitute only 1.2 percent. Business services, such as artisanship, engineering, accounting, and bookkeeping, account for only 2.1 percent of the informal sector services. Other small-scale activities are stone quarrying and sand harvesting.

The concept of the informal sector was popularized by an International Labor Organization mission in 1972. The mission observed that a majority of Kenyans were working outside the formal economy and needed to be brought into the mainstream. Since then, the authorities have claimed to support the underground economy in terms of job creation, incomes, and development of entrepreneurship. The government's commitment to the sector, however, is lame at best. Besides roadside declarations supporting informal sector businesses, there has been little encouragement for formalization through the removal of the barriers that foster informality. On the other hand, the authorities have also been lax in enforcing regulations because the informal economy is seen as a safety valve for social tension. The only significant step taken by the government with regard to informal businesses was the writing of Sectional Paper No. 2 of 1992 on the small-scale and *jua kali* enterprises and their role in job creation.

Some nongovernmental organizations (NGOs), microfinance institutions, and the Kenya Industrial Estates (KIE) have assisted small-scale enterprises within the informal sector with credit facilities and basic training in business management. The KIE has also constructed many sheds and workshops for business operators in the informal sector. Entrepreneurs operating in the underground economy have formed associations under the umbrella of the Kenya National Federation of Jua Kali Associations to promote their interests.

As in other parts of the world, Kenya's informal economy is faced with unfavorable policy guidelines and a poor regulatory environment made up of abundant and overlapping norms, an inadequate physical infrastructure, lack of information, limited markets for products and services, poor access to capital, and, to some extent, lack of managerial skills.

One of the most unusual retailing phenomena in independent Kenya is the emergence and rise of the secondhand clothes market. It started off in Gikomba, a small-scale clothes market originally founded in the 1970s. The market encouraged the rise of an informal segment in which small traders started dealing in imported secondhand clothes.

In the late 1980s, the secondhand clothing industry grew as the price of textiles plummeted. Thanks to Structural Adjustment Programs (SAPs) that sought to liberalize prices and modernize production, textile prices experienced a rapid drop. Although this liberalization helped to eliminate a number of inefficient textile factories, it also led to a boom in the secondhand clothes market. As the Gikomba market grew, it drew food vendors and quickly became a hub where fresh produce and grains from all over the country changed hands among merchants who would then sell them to retail outlets in the different estates of Nairobi. For a while, the food segment of Gikomba was a key hub in the food trade—in fact, it constituted the second largest wholesale food market after Wakulima in the central business district.

Gikomba's growth into the most important market in Nairobi was helped by both the population explosion in Nairobi in the 1980s and 1990s and the lack of development of formal markets to meet the growing demand. The "temporary" nature of the secondhand clothes trade meant that the government dared not take it seriously, for fear of inadvertently "establishing" it—the authorities had not formally allowed any foreign competition in the textile industry thus far.

In the 1980s the average middle-class Kenyan had only a few clothes in his or her wardrobe (sometimes only three or four outfits in all). It was common to take one's clothes to the tailor for multiple repairs; having patched clothes was not considered a sign of dire poverty. Clothing was very expensive—the local textile industries were inefficiently run and passed their costs on to the consumers. The same was true of shoes—the cobbler trade was significant. Kenyans would take their shoes to the cobbler to be resoled several times; new shoes were very expensive and competed with other basic needs like housing and food.

Secondhand clothes eventually took over the market. Today, many shoppers say they go to Gikomba because it is affordable and they can get good-quality clothes from all around the world. Even street families who just a couple of decades ago had to go without clothing now wear brands like Gap, Nike, and Puma. Gikomba has emerged as a key wholesale market where traders from all over the country go to purchase bales of secondhand clothes. Other traders scour the market looking for trendy, newer clothes to resell at a premium in stalls in the central business district and in kiosks in the estates. "We target middle-class customers who find it a bother to go to Gikomba," says one of the traders in Langata.

KIOSKS—KINGS OF RETAIL

The most important source of entrepreneurship in Kenya's retail industry is the kiosk. Kiosks developed in the preindependence era, as many Africans sought to join the retail business. Due to the government's restrictive land-use laws, Nairobi suffered from a critical shortage of retail space.

Rather than bear the costs involved in launching a business through formal channels, many Kenyans instead chose to start up businesses in the informal economy. After independence, the development of kiosks was actually encouraged by the populist support of President Jomo Kenyatta and, later, President Moi. Both hoped that protecting kiosks would encourage African enterprise in general.

In time, kiosks emerged as important players in retail. They were cheap to erect, easy to maintain, and close to the consumer. They sold goods at affordable prices and quantities, and many kiosks extended credit to their customers. In fact, for a while they were the only retail stores outside of the prescribed municipal markets. As the population of Nairobi grew, the demand for goods and services that the kiosks provided increased. Cobblers, tailors, makeshift butchers, grocers, barbers, and others seeking to provide a service in urban Kenya opened a kiosk, with or without a license, and the government turned a blind eye to these establishments. Kiosks grew to become the kings of retail; today, they control more than 75 percent of the retail trade in Kenya.

Why the Success?

As Figure 3.1 indicates, the competitive edge enjoyed by kiosks is due to their location, price, small units of sale, and special services (such as extending credit to loyal customers). The importance of kiosks to manufacturers varies, but most agree that kiosks are an important partner and outlet for their products. For example, Unilever, which is a leading household name in domestic consumer goods, says that kiosks are responsible for 75 percent of their sales in Kenya.

FIGURE 3.1. Reasons Nairobi Residents Gave for Shopping in Kiosks

SOURCE: Neven et al., 2005.

Kiosks are located in areas that are easy for consumers to reach. They are generally concentrated along major roadways and in market squares with a high density of consumers. In a survey conducted by the Tegemeo Institute, Ayieko et al. (2003) found that supermarkets charge up to 60 percent more for fresh fruits and vegetables. As a result of this large markup, many of Kenya's poorest consumers prefer to go to kiosks for their produce. When it comes to other consumer products, supermarkets are often cheaper.

In addition to offering low prices and easy access, kiosks sell their products in small units. Other reports have established that fewer than 15 percent of Kenyans own refrigerators. As a result, they prefer to buy fresh produce in small quantities that can be consumed immediately. Most Kenyans also have a low cash flow. To make ends meet, they often purchase only one item at a time. Selling in smaller units means frequent visits to the kiosk by the consumer, making him or her familiar to the shopkeeper. A friendship often develops, creating a sense of consumer loyalty. One consumer said, "I am used to my local shopkeeper. I have been buying from him for over five years now."

Kiosks also extend short-term credit to consumers. Many consumers hold accounts with kiosks where they settle their bills on a monthly basis. This is especially true of salaried employees. One consumer explained, "My mum is one of them. She spends KSh3,000 a month on milk, bread, sugar, salt, and other consumables, which she picks up from the kiosk." Sometimes shopkeepers go so far as to lend money to their customers at minimal interest rates. Kiosks also provide quasi-postal services by delivering messages to different household members and serve as storage facilities, keeping keys, cash, and other petty items for their customers. These functions arise from the sense of closeness between the kiosk owner and the customer.

Membership in business support groups and microcredit institutions helps small businesses perform better. These support groups provide networking, increased access to credit, and the pooling of management skills and ideas. This model has been very successful for one microcredit supplier, Faulu Kenya, which works with small business owners and advances credit on a social guarantee basis.

Faulu Kenya organizes members in groups of ten, with each group trained in basic bookkeeping, marketing, and business management. Members are required to save some of their income with Faulu for a period of one year, after which they become eligible for small business loans. Other members within each ten-person group guarantee security for the loans.

Challenges

Although kiosks remain a vital part of Kenya's retail economy, kiosk owners face myriad hurdles that hamper the possibility of their growing into big retailers. A study conducted by enterprise development researcher Peter Kimuyu (2002) identified many factors that hinder the progressive growth of small businesses. He found that major obstacles included the informal nature of business, a lack of property rights and leases, the age of the enterprise, the education level of the entrepreneur, and poor access to banking, insurance, and other business support services. Hindrances attributed directly to the government included corruption, steep licensing requirements, taxes, poor infrastructure, and others. Kiosks in Kenya are mainly informal and suffer from the same hindrances.

Without the proper registration and licensing, it is impossible for a business to enjoy services like banking, insurance, and credit from suppliers. Most banks say that they find it difficult to provide services to the informal sector. The lack of credit provided to the informal sector is due largely to the fact that many small entrepreneurs do not keep proper records, cannot account for their sources of income, and have not demonstrated an ability to repay loans. Their business history is difficult to trace, making them a loan risk. More than 71 percent of traders in Nairobi have no credit. Those who do have credit obtain it from membership-based savings cooperatives and informal credit groups that charge up to 29 percent interest and require payment in monthly installments.

In addition to the lack of titles, most kiosks lack firm property rights that give their businesses collateral and help banks feel more confident when lending them money. Kiosks are most frequently erected on road shoulders, footpaths, playgrounds, and so on. These areas are mainly public land, and the presence of kiosks amounts to illegal squatting. Entrepreneurs who own kiosks have no claim to the land their business is located on. This condition makes the businesses temporary as far as the operating premises are concerned, regardless of how long the kiosks have been in existence.

Since there is little incentive to care for the kiosks over the long term, they are generally made of nonpermanent materials such as timber, nylon, and tin. Some kiosks consist simply of a makeshift roofing shelter and do not even have walls; others operate in the open air.

Recently, the government of Kenya has taken to demolishing kiosks and evicting traders without notice. The government claims that these kiosks pose a security threat and are an eyesore. This attitude is in line with the new government's policy that seeks to beautify Nairobi and reduce crime and insecurity. But given the instability and corruption in Nairobi, one would think that empty, open, "beautiful" areas would be far more dangerous than areas with kiosks and merchants. Most of the complaints by kiosk owners have fallen on deaf ears in the government, however, and the demolitions continue.

The key government agency dealing with the retail industry is the Local Authority. This body is charged with ensuring the proper running of basic infrastructure and services in a city or municipality. Local Authorities in Kenya, however, have a poor track record in providing services to residents. Many cities and towns are plagued by poor service delivery, a collapsing infrastructure, authorities that are nearly bankrupt and are riddled with corruption, and abuse of office. These authorities have failed to provide the environment necessary for retail enterprises to thrive. In fact, traders often report that the Local Authorities just want bribes from them for services that are not provided or as an incentive to provide services that are within their rights. In a recent index measuring perceived corruption published by Transparency International, the Local Authorities were listed as the most corrupt of the government agencies.

In general, the future of kiosks is insecure and unpredictable. Disruptions distort continuity and productivity, limiting the owner's ability to invest, as he or she is not sure what to expect. These conditions also limit the credit period the owner may receive, if he or she gets any credit at all.

This section has examined the business environment that kiosks face. By looking closely at the challenges facing kiosks, we can better understand the general retail environment for supermarkets trying to enter the formal economy. The rapid rise and spread of kiosks and informal retail operations in Kenya tells us a lot about current business conditions in Kenya. First, it helps us appreciate the power of markets and entrepreneurship. Despite high levels of regulation and corruption, people are still willing to take risks to improve their overall well-being. Second, the existence of kiosks demonstrates the relative lack of secure property rights in Kenya. When retailers are under a constant threat of predation or demolition of their firm, the relative costs of investing in long-term infrastructure are quite high. As a result, retail establishments never evolve beyond the mobile kiosk level. Finally, the fact that Kenya's king of retail remains the kiosk tells us that the overall retail system remains extremely inefficient. That Nakumatt and a few other large supermarkets have figured out a way to navigate all of these inefficiencies is an inspiring and insightful lesson in entrepreneurship on the one hand and a depressing story of excessive government on the other.

THE ROLE OF SUPERMARKETS IN KENYA

The first supermarkets in Kenya emerged in the 1960s, but their rapid growth is a recent phenomenon—they did not take off until the mid-1990s. Most supermarkets in Kenya are part of a chain, and they constitute 80 percent of all the stores in Kenya. Small, independent supermarkets make up a small share of the sector. Supermarkets have taken market share away from traditional food retailers such as kiosks, greengrocers, over-the-counter shops, market stalls, and street hawkers.

The supermarket sector in Kenya had estimated sales of US$520 million in 2002. It is growing at the rate of 18 percent annually. Neven et al. (2005) calculated that supermarkets have grown from a niche of 2 percent in Nairobi in the mid-1990s to 20 percent of the urban food market today.

There are four leading domestic supermarket chains; in descending order by size, they are Uchumi, Nakumatt, Tusker Mattresses, and the Ukwala Group. The two largest chains, Uchumi and Nakumatt, control 50 percent of the market. There are several other smaller chain supermarkets and single-store supermarkets. The majority of them are found in Nairobi. Uchumi is the only publicly traded supermarket in Kenya.

Although the majority of Kenya's supermarkets are found in Nairobi, approximately one-quarter of supermarkets are found outside that city.[10] The relative saturation of Nairobi and the rise of opportunities elsewhere have driven investment to other major towns. Mombasa, an intermediate city with a population of 700,000, has three chain supermarkets and three hypermarkets (thirty supermarket equivalents), plus an unknown number of independent supermarkets. Medium-sized cities and large towns also boast supermarkets. Nakuru, Eldoret, and Kisumu, intermediate cities/towns with populations of 200,000 to 300,000 people, have ten chain supermarkets and an unknown number of independent supermarkets. Nakuru and Eldoret are large-scale commercial farming areas, and Kisumu in western Kenya is a small-scale commercial farming area. According to Neven et al.

(2005), an estimated 900 to 1,400 smaller self-service shops have entered the retail sector. These shops include mini-supermarkets in smaller towns as well as convenience stores in residential areas and at gas stations.

The rapid rise of supermarkets in Kenya occurred against a backdrop of declining economic growth, high inflation rates, and high interest rates. Notably, most of the investment capital came from local sources; only one supermarket, Metro Cash and Carry, was foreign owned, and it closed its operations in the country in 2005 due to poor market penetration.

One of the key factors responsible for the spread of supermarkets in the 1990s was their appeal to middle-income consumers. In our own survey we found that shoppers preferred supermarkets because they had more products, were cheaper, were conveniently located, and offered a beautiful shopping environment. By contrast, consumers were more likely to buy fresh fruits and vegetables from kiosk vendors near their places of residence than at a supermarket.

In another survey conducted by Neven et al. (2005), the two most important reasons consumers gave for shopping in supermarkets were lower prices and the large assortment of goods. They found that 80 percent of households in Nairobi buy food from supermarkets at least once a month. Among this group of consumers, households with incomes of less than KSh15,000 make up 56 percent and account for 36 percent of supermarket sales. The upper-middle-income and high-income classes make up only 15 percent of shoppers, but they account for 44 percent of supermarket sales, reflecting their higher income.

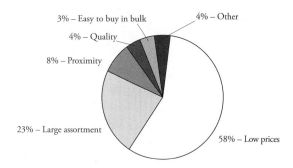

FIGURE 3.2 Reasons Nairobi Residents Gave for Shopping in Supermarkets

SOURCE: Neven et al., 2005.

Only 15 percent of households in Nairobi buy fruits and vegetables from supermarkets, with fewer than 1 percent of those with incomes of less than KSh5,000 buying their produce from supermarkets. Only 30 percent of the upper-middle-income segment and 67 percent of the high-income segment buy their fresh fruits and vegetables from supermarkets.

Nakumatt shop managers told us that most of their shoppers buy household goods such as foodstuffs, toiletries, soaps, and detergents. Shoppers in turn indicated that over half of their shopping basket consists of foodstuffs. Toiletries and other items were between 10 percent and 20 percent.

Uchumi

Uchumi Supermarkets, Ltd. has the largest retail network in Kenya. Started as a government-owned store in 1975, the company has grown over the years and currently operates seventeen retail supermarkets and hypermarkets in Nairobi, Nakuru, Karatina, Eldoret, and Meru. These consist of thirteen supermarkets and four hypermarkets. In addition to the seventeen stores, Uchumi operates six franchise stores—five in Nairobi and one in Kisumu. In 1992, the government divested from Uchumi by selling most of its shares to the public in an initial public offering. However, the government still maintains a controlling interest in the company.

In 2001, Uchumi embarked on a growth program to expand its network to fifty stores. It also planned to open stores in Uganda and Tanzania. This expansion strategy was successful for a while, with the opening of ten new stores, including two hypermarkets in Nairobi and one in Kampala, Uganda. The company also set up a new distribution center in Nairobi and installed a state-of-the-art information technology system that integrated its whole branch network. But Uchumi suffered a major setback in 2003 when it was unable to profit from its expansion due to high interest rates on short-term financing used in the expansion. After slow sales growth, management put a halt to the expansion program.

Almost every Kenyan has visited an Uchumi supermarket at some point in their lives. For a corporation that was established in 1975, its impact on the national consciousness and the multiplier effect it has had on the Kenyan economy is tremendous. Uchumi caters to the needs of Kenyans across a wide social stratum, from low-income to high-income groups. It has twenty-seven branches in seven urban areas in the country and one branch in Kampala, Uganda (now its flagship store). These branches target several different consumer classes, depending on their size and location. Hypermarkets located along major highways in Nairobi target upper-middle-income and high-income consumers, neighborhood stores target middle-income consumers, and city center stores located near major terminals attract middle- to low-income consumers.

Uchumi is credited with introducing the specialty shops concept to Kenya by taking on partners that provide services within the bigger store. As the term denotes, the partners have a built-in capacity to provide specialized services and products. The specialty partners cover a wide range of services and products, including laundry, in-store banking, courier services, gifts, pharmacy, textiles, footwear, and photo processing. In 1997 Uchumi also became the first large chain supermarket in the country to sell fresh fruits and vegetables.

Tuskermatt

Tusker Mattresses was set up in the 1980s in Nakuru. Five brothers run the modern Tuskermatt chain, a franchise started with small shops run by the late Joram Kamau, who died in December 2002.

In the middle of 2000, the brothers merged the Magic Super Stores with the Tusker stores to form what is now called Tusker Mattresses Ltd. The name had become a registered trademark back in the 1990s. "Tusker," as it is popularly known, is admittedly the quieter of the top operators, in a group that includes Uchumi and Nakumatt. It has a total of about 300,000 square feet of shopping space. Almost all of the stores are located next to bus stops, targeting the lower-income segment of the market. Besides the shops,

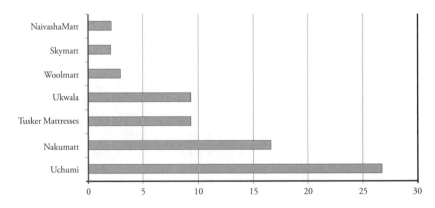

FIGURE 3.3. **Market Share of Supermarket Chains, by Number of Stores**

Tusker has aggressively invested in storage facilities and operations offices. Today, it is estimated that the company's sales are second only to those of the Nakumatt chain. Their success is attributed primarily to strategic locations and good customer care.

THE SUPERMARKET TODAY AND THE EMERGENCE OF NAKUMATT

As the previous section suggests, there has been a rapid expansion in Kenya's supermarket industry over the last ten years. The supermarket has reshaped the retail business directly and altered production practices in agriculture and other related industries. Supermarkets are rapidly penetrating urban food retail and are spreading well beyond their initial tiny market niche among the urban middle class into the lower-income groups. The main driver of this expansion, and the focus of the remainder of our study, is Nakumatt.

Nakumatt started as a small family-owned shop in the town of Nakuru in the 1980s. The retailer's annual revenue has grown from US$39,000 early on to more than US$130 million today. Nakumatt employs nearly three thousand people directly, and some estimates suggest that more than fifty thousand jobs are indirectly linked to Nakumatt. In 2005, Nakumatt won the prestigious East Africa's Most Respected Company in the Service Sector award. This award was initiated by Price Waterhouse to identify and celebrate the most respected companies in three East African countries, as chosen by their peers. The award strengthened Nakumatt's position as a leading company in the service sector. The company plans to go public soon to spread its ownership beyond the Shah family and raise more capital.

Nakumatt serves 1.5 percent of the Kenyan population and has a "smart shopper" loyalty scheme with more than 180,000 cardholders. Each month, the company handles about 1.5 million transactions that average KSh1,000 (approximately $14.40) per transaction. The overall result of these transactions is annual sales of KSh1.5 billion (approximately US$21.6 million).[11] The fresh foods and vegetables department alone enjoys a turnover of KSh35 million per month, and it has grown by more than 400 percent in the last two years. The company's gross margin is 3 percent of its turnover.[12] Like most large retailers, Nakumatt has high sales costs and makes up for its low margins by turning over its inventory quite rapidly.

Nakumatt has seventeen stores in five major cities and towns in Kenya. They are strategically located in urban centers where customers can reach them with ease. The largest supermarket in East and Central Africa, Nakumatt Mega, is on Uhuru Highway, Nairobi's premier highway and commercial backbone. The highway runs from Nairobi to Mombasa, Kenya's second biggest town (situated on the Indian Ocean coast) and Kisumu, the third largest town (situated on the western border on the shore of Lake Victoria). It also lies at the intersection of the industrial area and the beginnings of the suburbs west of Nairobi, close to the Nyayo Stadium roundabout. Nakumatt Mega symbolizes Kenya's coming of age in the mall culture and is part of a countrywide chain of supermarkets with nine stores in Nairobi, two in Mombasa, two in Kisumu, one in Eldoret, and one in Kisii. Mega has the floor space of ten soccer fields and stocks everything from lingerie to utensils, digital cameras, and groceries.

One would not have expected this success from Nakumatt's very humble origins.

A Soft-Spoken Visionary

Nakuru is the fourth largest town in Kenya. It emerged and developed as a railway stopover on the western route. When the government constructed the Great North Road, which traverses the entire country, it made it pass through Nakuru. Due largely to the location of the Great North Road, the town is a bustling hub for traders, transporters, travelers, and residents. Nakuru is also the capital of Kenya's largest province, Rift Valley, considered the country's breadbasket. It is therefore supported by an agricultural economy and is home to industrial giants such as Eveready East Africa LTD.

In 1978, Nakumatt, then known as Nakuru Mattresses, was a small retailer whose business consisted of selling mattresses in Nakuru, which was still a small town. The storeowner, a man named Medland Shah, worked closely with his son, Athul Shah. Athul began working for his father at the Nakuru store at the age of seven. By his teens he had a good understanding of the trade from his interactions with customers. Today, Nakumatt's operations manager, Thiagarajan Ramamurthy, describes Mr. Shah, who is now 46 and the managing director of Nakumatt, as a "soft-spoken visionary" whose entrepreneurial initiative helped Nakumatt grow to its current heights.

In 1986, Nakuru Mattresses Supermarket opened its doors. It was one of the first real supermarkets in Kenya, and it quickly became popular. Susan

Orengo, a longtime employee,[13] remembers when customers used to line up as they waited for the store to open. The 7,000-square-foot Nakuru Mattresses Supermarket would often be forced to serve customers in lots, as the store space was too small to contain the demand. Their major competitors at that time were Ebrahims and Gilanis supermarkets.

Ms. Orengo believes that Nakumatt's success in the early days was due to the discounted prices it charged. Supermarkets were a new phenomenon, and their owners sought to give great bargains in order to compete with kiosks. Consumers, in turn, developed a habit of shopping in set cycles and in huge quantities so as to get the best bargains.

In the wake of its success in Nakuru, Nakuru Mattresses Supermarket opened a branch in Thika (a small town 50 kilometers east of Nairobi), and then another in Nairobi, near the OTC bus station, in 1987.

In Nakumatt's formative stages, the company sought to change the face of shopping in Kenya. The company's first supermarkets in Nakuru, Thika, and Nairobi radically modified the concept of retail shopping. Until then consumers had been used to shopping at kiosks in the residential estates in the urban areas. Nakumatt introduced bargains and discounts, attracting a high volume of customers. Soon other investors followed suit by opening more supermarkets, creating more competition, and forcing the Shah family to innovate.

The Nakumatt branches in Thika and Nairobi were highly successful. Nakumatt then decided to sell the Thika branch and open up another, small branch in Nairobi, this time on Uhuru Highway, opposite the Nyayo National Stadium. The opening of this branch in 1992 would herald the beginning of the use of the name Nakumatt, a shorter, funkier version of Nakuru Mattresses. Three years later, the company opened Nakumatt Downtown, once again at a prime spot, this time in the central business district.

From Nakumatt Downtown to Nakumatt Karen

Since the opening of Nakumatt Downtown in 1995, Nakumatt has grown by leaps and bounds. Overcoming competition from other supermarkets, it has opened ten new branches all over the country. The growth of the company kicked off with the opening of Nakumatt Embakasi, Nakumatt Checkpoint, Nakumatt Ukay, Nakumatt Kisumu, Nakumatt Nyali, Nakumatt Likoni, Nakumatt Thika Road, and Nakumatt Village. These branches, the creation of Nakumatt Mega, and the sale of Nakumatt OTC gave the company a momentum that sustained growth through Kenya's economic depression in the late 1990s and early 2000s.

Kenya's economy has slowly recovered from the 2000 contraction. As the recovery has progressed, Nakumatt has enjoyed more rapid growth. The owners of Nakumatt have opened up state-of-the-art branches and transformed the concept of shopping in Kenya even further. The company has gone on to open five branches in Nairobi and three outside of Nairobi. Nakumatt Ngong Road introduced consumers to a new shopping experience by setting a shopping mall in the heart of four luxury estates in a prime location in Nairobi. The success of this store gave Nakumatt the confidence to open up five other stores, using the same award-winning mall concept.

Although it is hard to argue with Nakumatt's overall performance, it has faced challenges regarding finance, customer service, and stock control. In the 1990s the country went through an economic recession, a time that was far from optimal for entrepreneurs in Kenya, yet Nakumatt grew and succeeded. In the next section, we briefly discuss some of the business obstacles that firms such as Nakumatt face.

Nakumatt: A Uniquely Kenyan Business Model

Nakumatt is run by a dynamic management team that is committed to obtaining results. At various stages in the company's development, it has faced great difficulties. Interest rates currently stand at 9 percent, but in recent years they have been as high as 30 percent. One of these periods of high interest rates, the 1990s, were the most difficult years for Nakumatt as a company. Without financing, it was very difficult for the retailer to stock its stores, yet the strategy it pursued necessitated a fully stocked store with a wide variety of goods at low prices. Although Uchumi, the industry leader, was improving its stocks and expanding aggressively, Nakumatt was forced to come up with a different strategy.

According to Nakumatt's operations manager, Thiagarajan Ramamurthy,

> When the chain itself does not have money, the company has to depend on somebody else. Nakumatt used to invite people who had money to import goods and then supply Nakumatt. Nakumatt would sell the products and then pay for them. Nakumatt identified the products and would send people to visit China, Malaysia, Europe, UK, Dubai, India, and all these places. Most of these products had not been seen on the Kenyan market.

Having been in the retail business since he was very young, Nakumatt's managing director, Athul Shah, had built strong alliances and networks and was able to use them to enter into partnerships with importers once the company started to expand. Most of the importers were his friends. They would bring goods for consignment and Shah would sell the products and then pay them. This approach turned out to be a success, and very soon he was traveling with the importers to look for new goods for his customers. In this way the importers advanced Nakumatt credit.

EXPLAINING NAKUMATT'S SUCCESS

This section highlights some of the factors responsible for Nakumatt's success.

Human Resources

Nakumatt invests a great deal of time and money in its human resources. According to Ramamurthy, its manager of operations,

> . . . if you look at the 5 M's in business—material, money, market, missionary, and manpower, I always say, only manpower can handle the other four. . . . If you have the right management, money will come. If you have the right management, people will supply you. If you have the right management and right concept, people will come to you. If you have the right people, whether it is a branch or any missionary, it can all be handled well. So the major thing is the people. And you should know how to hire the right people . . . You should get the right people and motivate them and retain them, which are the main things. When I talk about people, I mean our own associates or employees, and our suppliers on the one hand and the customers on the other. At the end of the day the service industry centers around the people, so that is very important.

Nakumatt has one of the most interesting human resources policies in Kenya. While most companies are head-hunting and recruiting from the competition, Nakumatt has been busy developing its own staff, from the time they join the company. Nakumatt managers are all previous employees. No manager is hired from outside. Promotions are based on merit and duration of service.

When selecting new staff, Nakumatt looks for two main things. First, the candidate must have at least an O-level qualification. This helps with the understanding of basic Nakumatt operations. Second, he or she is required to have a good background, a clean school-leaving certificate, and a good conduct certificate from the police.

Nakumatt staff are also given opportunities to recommend people for a job. This policy helps ensure that only people with strong recommendations enter the company. It also builds social accountability: new employees do not want to disappoint the friend or relative who recommended them, nor do established employees want to recommend someone of dubious integrity to their employer. Many of the staff we interviewed placed a high value on this policy.

As soon as a person is recruited as a new employee, he or she must undergo a three-month training program. Nakumatt has invested in a state-of-the-art training facility at the head office. During training, the new employee is given a crash course in what we might call "the Nakumatt way." The company has a seventy-seat training facility and invests US$150,000 every year in employee training and development. Employees are also taken to visit manufacturers' and suppliers' premises in order to learn more about the products they are selling, where they are made, and how they are made. Nakumatt insists that it believes in employees listening to their supervisors, customer care, and personal and career development over the years.

All the Nakumatt employees we interviewed had been working with the company for more than six years. The managers had all been working with Nakumatt for more than ten years. Nakumatt is the kind of place where one joins as a driver and after eight years of dedicated service will have risen through the ranks to become a branch manager. There is opportunity for growth for most people as long as they are diligent in their work. One branch manager we talked to told us his story:

> I started as a shop assistant back in Nakuru when Nakumatt was still called Nakuru Mattresses Supermarket. . . . I was promoted to be a cashier in a Nairobi branch, Nakuru Mattresses Supermarket, Ukwala branch . . . in 1990 I was promoted to be a branch manager. (Moses, Nakumatt Mega branch manager)

From an early stage, the bigger vision of Nakumatt is communicated to employees until they own it. The idea is to make them feel as though they are a part of a much larger process. Nakumatt management is interested in maintaining a good name in society, something that they believe makes employees feel proud to be associated with Nakumatt. They pay their staff. The staff is also provided with morning and evening tea and snacks as refreshments. There are also branch competitions that staff can participate in.

The fact that all managers were once loaders or line attendants or shop assistants means that they understand their subordinates and will, on the whole, treat them fairly. And because the junior employees can see that their managers rose from their positions, they know that it is only a matter of time and hard work before they too are promoted.

Good Corporate Governance

In a country in which so many institutions and businesses plan only for the short term, Nakumatt has focused on a long-term vision. According to Ramamurthy,

> The second thing is the concept of good corporate governance. You should understand efficiency in operations. You should understand your numbers and focus. Some businesses think it is about budgets, and what you did last year and what you want to do next year. That is not our way of looking at it. We always look at our potential. When I am telling you that 98.5 percent don't buy at Nakumatt, I am telling you that our potential is that much. That is what our market is. Our concept or motto is related to the lifestyle of Kenyans. If you look at the quality, value, variety, service, and lifestyle, lifestyle is something that we want to bring to Kenya. We have already brought it up. We have changed the culture of shopping in Kenya; we can probably say that we have partially achieved that one in this part of the world. We have achieved in the urban areas, we are going into the rural areas today.

Outlook Toward the Country

Nakumatt believes that even in a poor country like Kenya there are consumers to sustain an expanding venture. It is a question of finding them. According to Ramamurthy, the operations manager, the people of Kenya are not poor; they are merely constrained by various circumstances that can be overcome. "Unless you project and position yourself in the market, you will not be able to attract the people to come and do anything here."

Positioning

As has been mentioned, Nakumatt started as an ordinary retail store, before it transformed itself into a supermarket. In its beginnings, it targeted all consumer groups but mainly attracted low- to middle-income consumers. At the start of the 1990s, Nakumatt started focusing more on higher-income consumers. Today, 65 percent of supermarket shoppers are higher-income consumers who spend between KSh1,000 and 4,000, and sometimes even as much as KSh100,000 per visit. The lower-income consumers that Nakumatt attracts tend to spend less than KSh1,000 per visit. Although Nakumatt's focus has changed to higher-end consumers, its overall customer base contains all classes of consumers.

Customer Care

In 2005, Nakumatt won the prestigious East Africa's Most Respected Company in the Service Sector award. In 2004 it had been the second runner up for the award. Managing director Athul Shah remains as keen on customers as ever. His number-one drive is to deliver a unique shopping experience. This, he articulates to his employees, his suppliers, his partners, and his bankers, is done through the Nakumatt promise of Quality, Value, Service, Variety, and Lifestyle. When it comes to customer care, Nakumatt management leads the employees by example: Athul Shah and Thiagarajan Ramamurthy are sometimes found pushing customers' shopping carts on Saturdays or Sundays. They say this is to reinforce to employees what needs to be done and how customers ought to be treated.

From the time they are hired, Nakumatt employees are told about the importance of customer care. Every employee understands the importance of treating his or her customers well. One employee puts it like this: "I am not employed by Nakumatt . . . I am employed by the customer." He added that during their training they would sometimes be paid directly from the cash till, and this drilled the importance of the customer. With no cash in the till, they would have had to wait for their salaries.

Nakumatt's aggressive expansion strategy has the customer in the center. The opening up of stores away from the city center and away from Nairobi helps fulfill Nakumatt's plans to be closer to the people. According to Ramamurthy,

> We have to move to the areas where people cannot come from. If
> I am positioned only in the urban areas, how will people living 200

or 300 miles away be able to come and enjoy the benefits of what Nakumatt is giving to others? So we have to go and open the branches in those places.

As Nakumatt expands, its prices remain uniform. Whether one buys in Nairobi, Kisumu, Kericho, or Mombasa, Nakumatt prices are the same. The company's brand image precedes it. Whenever a new store opens, dozens and sometimes hundreds of people wait in line to be among the first to go in.

The company's managers visit the United States every year to assess the changes taking place in the retail industry. They pay attention to the top American retailers and observe their operations in various cities around the country. The Nakumatt Smart Card is one idea borrowed from American retailers. This reward and loyalty scheme is one of the most advanced and successful in the world. It has created a sense of value for Nakumatt customers. Since 2003, more than 50 percent of Nakumatt sales have been to Smart Card holders. The retailer has about 180,000 Smart Card holders, 85 percent of whom use their cards actively. Smart Card holders can collect points and access discounts on goods and services from Nakumatt and more than thirty participating outlets. Other customer-focused schemes include the Nakumatt wedding list service, a wedding gift registry.

Nakumatt also has a gift card that allows the beneficiary to spend the value of the card in small amounts on different occasions.

Partnering with Other Retailers

The Uchumi supermarkets developed the concept of partnering with other retailers in the late 1990s. However, Nakumatt perfected this idea during its aggressive expansion over the last four years by following U.S. retail trends. The "shops in shop" have given rise to Nakumatt's slogans of "All Under One Roof" and "You Need It, We've Got It!" The concept allows different specialty retailers to sell their products in the same floor space as Nakumatt. Depending on the size of the particular Nakumatt store, one can find everything from a bank to a car dealer, a drapery specialist, an interior decorator, a shoe shop, a bookstore, a restaurant, an organic food store, a pharmacist, a bread shop, an electronics shop, and a meat shop.

We spoke to several "shops-in-shop" partners. All of them said that they have benefited from Nakumatt's huge customer base, the company's expansion, the brand success, and their customer care. Light Mania, a company that specializes in lights for domestic and office facilities, used to supply Nakumatt with lights before it set up a shop in Nakumatt. After visiting the Light Mania shop in Westlands, Athul Shah is said to have challenged the company to set up a specialty section inside Nakumatt. The challenge was taken up and resulted in an in-store specialty shop. Today, Light Mania has specialty shops in Nakumatt Mega, City (Kisumu), Nyali, Village, Ngong Road, Embakasi, and Thika Road. The Light Mania shop in Nakumatt Mega leads in franchise sales.

Some of Nakumatt's partners are not inside Nakumatt stores, but are in the same shopping malls. This concept was pioneered at Nakumatt Ngong Road and is now used in all new Nakumatt branches. Nakumatt identifies a suitable location for a new branch, asks a developer to build a shopping mall, and comes in as the anchor. Other retailers often follow. This system has brought a new shopping experience to the areas into which Nakumatt has decided to expand. In each case, not only does the company open a supermarket that has a wide variety of products, but it is also accompanied by many other retailers who sell different products and services. The result gives meaning to Nakumatt's "All Under One Roof" slogan. As Ramamurthy puts it,

> If you have land, we ask you to develop it for us, Nakumatt signs a lease with you, and the bank finances the development . . . Nakumatt comes as an anchor tenant . . . So many other small shops are coming into these spaces we create. We will take a beauty shop, a barbershop and salon, a laundry, a butchery, a phone shop . . . if the shop does well, we extend the relationship to other branches of the supermarket. We got a pharmacist, Dr. Muturi, gave him one shop to start, and after that wherever we want to go, whatever size we give, he comes.

IMPEDIMENTS TO DOING BUSINESS IN KENYA

Successful entrepreneurs, such as Nakumatt, have had to go through a minefield of constraints—legal, financial, and social. Countless would-be entrepreneurs become discouraged by these constraints and simply give up on their business plans. According to a recent study linked to the World Bank, Kenya ranked "poor" when it came to the ease with which businesses can obtain licenses and credit and "extremely poor" in the following areas: starting a business, hiring and firing, registering property, protecting investors, paying taxes, trading across borders, enforcing contracts, and closing a business. The possible rankings ranged from "extremely poor" to "excellent" (Doing Business Project, 2007).

The study found that:

- It takes 25 steps and 360 days to enforce contracts in Kenya, with the cost of enforcing contracts being 41.3 percent of the debt companies owe.
- Entrepreneurs in Kenya make up to 17 payments, spend 372 hours, and pay 68.2 percent of their gross profit in taxes. It takes 8 steps and 73 days to register property. The cost to register property in Kenya is 4.1 percent of overall property value.
- It takes 11 steps and 170 days to complete the process of licensing and permits, and these costs are 40 percent of income per capita.
- Entrepreneurs in Kenya can expect to go through 13 steps to launch a business. Doing so takes more than 54 days on average, at a cost equal to 48.2 percent of gross national income (GNI) per capita. There is no minimum deposit requirement to obtain a business registration number.

Nakumatt's success becomes all the more interesting when these general business conditions are taken into account.

In a study conducted by the Government of Kenya on impediments to trade in the country, administrative barriers, infrastructural barriers, policy barriers, and legislative barriers were identified as the main obstacles. Business leaders interviewed by Steadman and Associates in the East Africa's Most Respected Company survey (Price Waterhouse Coopers, 2005) also indicated that poor infrastructure and security are the key problems facing businesses in Kenya. In the area of human resources, businesses struggle to attract and retain good staff.

The Legal and Regulatory Environment

Kenyan laws concerning the retail sector are less concerned with creating incentives than with exercising command and control over the economy. The legal code is extremely specific about what a business can and cannot do. Unlike other sectors such as agriculture, tourism, or banking, however, there is no overriding authority that has any say regarding the informal sector, which by nature eludes the formal rules.

The laws that affect the retail sector were actually drawn up to fulfill a different function. The retail sector is run without any underlying philosophy and consists of thousands of business enterprises, each of which is required to have myriad registration certificates and licenses in order to operate. These translate into tools of control and revenue generation and barriers that purport to protect the consumers.

A retailer is required to register the business, obtain a national and municipal license, VAT and PIN numbers, a Health Inspection Certificate, National Hospital Insurance Fund and National Social Security Fund registrations, and environmental approval, among many other government-related permits. Registration is needed periodically in order to sell certain products such as liquor, fertilizers, meats, medicines, and so on. If the retailer is importing its products, another set of regulations applies, requiring additional documentation. Opening secondary branches entails a duplication of certain licenses and registration; the process to obtain them must always be followed as if one were applying for a new license.

Kiosks are by their very nature informal and often operate outside the realm of all these licenses, because some entrepreneurs are brave enough to ignore the confusing rules and because following the rules is too expensive. The government has been slow to restrict kiosks, fearing the political ramifications that might result from a crackdown. The Moi regime was characterized by soothing declarations in which informal sector practitioners were spared the full wrath of the law in return for loyalty and popularity; to some extent, the Moi legacy has been carried over to the new administration when it comes to the informal sector.

Although the government is slow to crack down on kiosks, it is also hesitant to legitimize them because they are often erected illegally in areas that are designated as road reserves. The authorities have consistently refused to recognize informal settlements in Nairobi, denying them critical infrastructure. In recent years, the Kenyan government has indicated that it will reform business licensing and registration requirements to make it easier to do business in Kenya. In February 2005, a working committee on regulatory reforms for business activity in Kenya was set up. Its objective was to substantially reduce the number of licensing requirements in Kenya and make the process more transparent. The working committee completed its first phase in September 2005. It reviewed eighty-six licenses that have an impact on business, eliminating thirty-five of these and simplifying four others.

The working committee is now required to apply the guillotine strategy[14] to the remaining licenses that affect business activity in Kenya. It will review an estimated 514 licenses, establishing a permanent electronic registry at the attorney general's office in Kenya. It also plans to create a mechanism for performing a quality review of licenses, in accordance with the specific terms of reference contained in the revised guidelines.

The Challenge of Store Space

Because of the high cost of borrowing, it was unrealistic for Nakumatt to own the premises where it located the stores. Although the market leader, Uchumi, has been busy buying up the properties its stores are housed in, Nakumatt does not have the money to do the same, and so the company instead leases space from property owners. In order to convince property developers to build malls and stores in areas it wants, Nakumatt must sign a lease before the property is developed. This gives the developer the confidence to go ahead and construct a building for the supermarket chain to use. Nakumatt generally signs eleven-year leases with property owners, renewable for another ten years.

As we have already stated, property rights in Kenya are unpredictable and often subject to predation. Although the leases can, in one sense, be viewed as a benefit in that they grant Nakumatt more flexibility in an unstable legal environment, the terms that must be worked out with landowners are often subject to change and constant renegotiation. These unexpected business expenses create an added burden for Nakumatt.

NAKUMATT TODAY

As of 2006, Nakumatt had sales of KSh220 million per year and was aiming for the KSh300 million target by the end of the year. The retailer plans to open more stores and sell some of its shares to the public in an initial public offering by June 2009. Nakumatt's ambitions also include opening retail stores in Uganda, Tanzania, Rwanda, Burundi, and even Sudan. Since the company looks at itself as one of the pacesetters in Kenya's economy, it is determined to take the leadership in opening up the region. It is committed to opening more stores in the rural areas, where they say there is a lot of untapped potential. The Kisii store is the flagship of this new venture.

In the past two years, Nakumatt has initiated nonprofit programs aimed at improving the lives of the communities in which they operate. For example, in 2006 it worked with Adopt-a-Light, a local company in charge of setting up street lamps throughout the city, to light up informal settlement areas in Nairobi.

Nakumatt's success in Kenya has led to the rise of a new class of farms growing fruit and vegetables in Kenya. There is a distinction between farmers supplying fresh fruit and vegetables to supermarkets and those supplying the traditional wet or open-air markets. Supermarket suppliers tend to have medium-sized farms, rely on hired labor (80 percent of the workforce), and be more technologically advanced. They are also more likely to use modern irrigation systems and fertilizers. There is a lot of pressure on supermarket suppliers to produce high-quality produce throughout the year.

On average, the prices of fresh fruit and vegetables in supermarkets are higher than in traditional outlets (kiosks and open markets). However, the volume of sales of fresh fruit and vegetables in supermarkets is gradually rising and will continue to rise, a tendency that can be attributed to the fact that younger shoppers are beginning to shop for fresh fruit and vegetables in supermarkets and that prices have recently started to become more competitive.

At Nakumatt, the fresh fruits and vegetables business has quadrupled in the past two years (it started selling fresh produce in 2001). The retailer now buys about $500,000 worth of fresh fruits and vegetables per month. All Nakumatt branches now have a fully stocked, modern fresh fruit and vegetables section.

Nakumatt has also set up a subsidiary company to handle farm products. Having developed relationships with the farmers, the Fresh & Juicy Ltd. Company buys directly from them and supplies Nakumatt. They set the quality standards for the fresh produce, the amount to be supplied, and the payment system. The suppliers are paid on a weekly basis and can easily expand their businesses from the sales.

Nakumatt has blazed a trail in the retail market. It sells more than 40,000 items in more than 277 categories. Nakumatt claims that all of Kenya's leading producers, importers, and suppliers of retail products sell their products through its stores. The company uses a centralized procurement system and sources everything locally. It is not involved in importing, producing, or packaging any of the goods sold in its stores. It focuses its energy and finances on customer care, brand building, and chain expansion. Nakumatt outsources product lines to firms that operate on a consignment basis, which means that Nakumatt gives them the space to display their goods and the firm manages that space. When Nakumatt has sold the goods, the firm is paid, with an agreed-upon discount that goes to Nakumatt.

Nakumatt chooses suppliers based on two criteria: quality and reliability. It supports leading brand names. The retailer normally identifies the products it wants to sell, especially new products, and then asks the suppliers to bring them in. Occasionally, suppliers approach Nakumatt with new products, and it will accept them. The managing director travels more than four times a year to China, Malaysia, Europe, and North America. He takes importers with him to trade shows, where he identifies new products for the stores. The importers then bring the products in. A supplier's products must be targeting the same consumer segments that Nakumatt serves.

Nakumatt's management works closely with leading brands and manufacturers to increase sales volumes. They periodically design and implement sales promotion strategies. The success of these strategies is evident. For example, after taking deliberate steps to work with Nakumatt, sales of Coca-Cola through Nakumatt grew by more than 100 percent over two years.

Unilever, which considers Nakumatt a key account, said that working with the retailer is easy because it is professional in its approach and quick to implement new ideas. According to Unilever, Nakumatt is more sophisticated than other retailers and distributors. It has contracts, better trading terms, a more formalized business, and better-looking shelves. According to one Unilever manager, "Being our biggest customer, any time we have an innovation, Nakumatt are the first to get the benefits, considering how we take them through the marketing links."

Today, visiting a Nakumatt is like visiting a mall in the United States or Europe, with glistening tiles, wide aisles, innovative shopping carts for children,[15] advertising and branding in the store, and a large variety of goods on display. Something always impresses me whenever I visit a Nakumatt. Right after I park my car in a secure environment, I will encounter either a bouncing castle filled with children of all colors or a 70-inch plasma screen that welcomes visitors with lively pictures and interesting advertising. There is always something new to look at: new furniture, a new brand of perfume, some new lotions and bath soaps. Nakumatt also has departments where you can buy gifts or indulge yourself in exotic products.

Kenyans who have traveled abroad no longer gawk in amazement at the stores—they have similar stores at home. And when they are exposed to a new product in their travels, they can also find it at Nakumatt. Visitors to the country and foreign residents can always find their preferred brands of products in their stores.

Working at Nakumatt, working with Nakumatt, and shopping at Nakumatt have become the ultimate urban experience for many Kenyans. Nakumatt has indeed changed the face of Kenya's retail. With its superstore-in-mall concept, it has transformed sleepy towns and backward shopping centers into first-class shopping malls with all sorts of amenities: movie theaters, restaurants, clothing stores, jewelers, pharmacies, art galleries, media stores, shoe shops, electronics shops, food courts, meat shops, book shops and so on. And consumers have flocked to these places; a shopping frenzy has emerged, to the joy of manufacturers, importers, and other retailers.

For Nakumatt employees, Nakumatt is *mama na baba*.[16] Imagine a place where, regardless of your entry position, you have a chance to become a line supervisor, a shop supervisor, an assistant manager, and ultimately a branch manager. Nakumatt's policy of engaging new employees at lower levels and then promoting them upward as they move along their careers is a great step forward in a country where most casual workers and semiskilled laborers almost never have a chance to engage in any sort of career development beyond the job they start with. The best they can hope for in good institutions are small increments in the package they take home and perhaps promotion to a supervisory position, but the chances of being a manager are zero unless one studies and gets a degree. Nakumatt takes the initiative to develop and promote its employees. This approach, and other Nakumatt strategies, helped Nakumatt earn the prestigious award of East Africa's Most Respected Company in the Service Sector in 2005.

Nakumatt suppliers enjoy increasing sales revenues, good professional relationships, and easy market entry points for new products and brands, as well as a growing customer base because of Nakumatt's expansion. The Kenyan retailer provides space for innovative and useful products to be seen and purchased by consumers. Whenever they succeed, new appetites are created in consumers, resulting in a ripple effect through the supply chain.

Nakumatt has also been a key player in real estate development. As the anchor tenant in new shopping malls, it has created the necessary activity and interest needed for the success of the malls. Its long-term lease agreements create confidence in the developers, who are now able to obtain financing for building malls. Other tenants also gain confidence because they know that as long as Nakumatt is around, there will be customers coming in and out of the mall.

PROBLEMS OF CORRUPTION

Before we conclude our discussion of the business environment in Kenya, we must provide the reader with one important caveat: Nakumatt's success has not been free from scandal. A number of corruption and money laundering charges have been brought against the company. In the spring of 2006, the Central Bank of Kenya (CBK) announced its intention to close down Charterhouse Bank. Charterhouse is a privately owned bank that faces accusations from Kenyan lawmakers that it helped Nakumatt and six other firms dodge US$250 million in taxes. Charterhouse Bank has denied the accusations.

Earlier, Kenya's opposition party, the Kenya African National Union (KANU), had presented to Parliament an unpublished 2004 report alleging fraud by Nakumatt with the purpose of evading taxes. The report alleged that Charterhouse Bank operated multiple accounts for Creative Innovations, Sailesh Prajipati, Tusker Mattresses, Kingsway Tyres, and John Harun Mwau group, among others. It charged that Creative Innovations supplied Nakumatt with imported goods without maintaining proper documentation. It further stated that Sailesh Prajipati received large cash deposits and checks from Nakumatt but did not have any account-opening forms or records of accounts available. Uchumi supermarkets paid ten times more in value added tax (VAT) than Nakumatt, despite the fact that Nakumatt is a larger operation than Uchumi, which eventually went bankrupt.

In one of Kenya's biggest corporate scandals, opposition politicians accused government officers of playing a role in protecting the Nakumatt chain. They produced a letter sent by former central bank governor Andrew Mullei to the treasury in March of 2006 alleging that Nakumatt had evaded taxes. Early in 2006, Mullei was suspended to face abuse of office and corruption charges. Many questions were raised when it was revealed that Mullei had been suspended a few days after recommending to the minister of finance that he withdraw Charterhouse's license.

It will be a long time before we know all the facts, but the allegations against Nakumatt raise an interesting question about the relationship between entrepreneurship and the rule of law. In those countries where there is no rule of law, or where the rule of law is limited in scope, successful entrepreneurs will eventually face an institutional system full of incentives to use influence to gain advantage. The mercantilist system thrives on the collusion between government bodies and private parties in the absence of institutional safeguards for the protection of property rights across all of society. Although it is too early to ascertain how many of the allegations against Nakumatt are true, the preliminary information would seem to indicate that this admirable venture built thanks to the entrepreneurial skills and creativity of its founders and managers, and the very hard work of its employees, grew so successful that it eventually became unable to partake in the common practices of the formal economy.

That Nakumatt's success has not been completely free from scandal illustrates the complex legal and regulatory environment facing any firm trying to do business in Kenya. Our study does not excuse anything the Nakumatt owners and managers have done. But we also believe that we should not allow the perfect to become the enemy of the good. Although Nakumatt could very well have engaged in corrupt business practices, there are still important entrepreneurial lessons to be learned from the company's overall success.

CONCLUSION: YOU NEED IT, WE'VE GOT IT

Over time, the retail landscape will no doubt change. Although we have spoken positively of both kiosks and Nakumatt, the two are clearly in competition with each other. Both are serving important functions in the Kenyan economy, but the existence of kiosks is almost entirely due to political inefficiencies. If Kenya's government can find ways to lower the costs of doing business, one of the most promising signs of progress will be a decline in the number of kiosks. The decline in kiosks should not be a result of demolition, but rather competition from formal establishments playing by the rules of the game. Until major changes are made in the regulatory burden facing businesses, however, a mixed retail sector that is filled with supermarkets and kiosks will remain.

Although it is certainly possible for other stores like Nakumatt to emerge from shaky beginnings to become business leaders in Kenya, there is little margin for error, given the high costs of doing business in Kenya. Moreover, it is nearly impossible to emerge as a major retailer in a way that is free from all charges of corruption—the incentives just aren't there for entrepreneurs to play the game in a completely clean manner.

When it started, Nakumatt was a small retail shop selling blankets, mattresses, and similar goods in Nakuru. Today, Nakumatt is a retail giant and in three years' time it will be listed on the Nairobi Stock Exchange. In following the story of Nakumatt, the key conclusion that we can reach is that it is perfectly possible to grow a big enterprise in Africa. Nakumatt's challenges were the standard challenges that any business faces anywhere in the world: finance, employee policy, customer retention, relations with suppliers, competition, the nature of the economy, and so on.

Although it's possible to grow a large business in an unstable environment, the government could make this growth a lot easier by getting out of the way. Instead, government forces entrepreneurs to work harder than they should have to to come up with innovative and ingenious ways to both market their products and also abide by all kinds of unnecessary business laws. The case of Nakumatt provides us with a fascinating story of how entrepreneurs can succeed in one of the worst business environments, but it also makes us pause and wonder why things had to be so difficult in the first place.

NOTES

1. Our discussion of the retail environment of Nakumatt is based on traditional data sources and original field research that was conducted by June Arunga throughout 2006.

2. Unless otherwise stated, the facts in this discussion are based on World Development Indicators Online (World Bank, 2006).

3. In December, 2007, President Mwai Kibaki refused to relinquish power after an election that, according to many observers, was thoroughly rigged in his favor. Kibaki's decision to cling to power stoked up tribal, regional and even religious resentments, replacing institutions with violence as a means of allocating power, wealth and prestige. More than 1,000 people were killed, many more were mutilated or raped, and a quarter of a million were made homeless. International efforts to mediate between Kibaki and opposition leader Raila Odinga finally produced a power-sharing arrangement in March, 2008.

4. We use per capita income with constant 2000 US dollars as our measure. This rate comes from the World Development Indicators Online (World Bank, 2006).

5. For more on rent-seeking, see Krueger and Tullock.

6. A businessman devised a scheme in which he purportedly exported gold and diamonds worth hundreds of millions of dollars, although Kenya is not a producer of either mineral. He then presented fictitious export compensation claims for payment by the Central Bank. Many high-level officials were involved in this scheme, which cost Kenya hundreds of millions of dollars.

7. According to the World Bank, Kenya has a GDP of US$34.7, roughly that of a medium-sized state in the United States. Microsoft earns at least three times this amount annually.

8. All of these data come from World Development Indicators Online (World Bank, 2006).

9. Small mom-and-pop stores.

10. The high concentration of supermarkets in Nairobi is similar to the distribution of supermarkets that Reardon and Berdegue (2002) found in several Latin American countries.

11. This conversion was based on the exchange rate of 1 KSh=0.0143USD on January 2, 2007.

12. By comparison, Walmart's is 3.5 percent and Bakers Pies in South Africa makes between 2.5 percent and 3.5 percent.

13. Ms. Orengo has worked for Nakumatt for nineteen years. She joined the business when it was still a small retail store in Nakuru.

14. The guillotine process is defined as an independent, neutral, and objective process whereby licenses are reviewed according to the following criteria: is it legal, necessary, and business friendly; can it be simplified by conversion into a notification or amalgamation, reducing the target group, reducing the reporting frequency, applying the silence is consent rule, or establishing time limits for responses? The recommendations of the review will be implemented through the budget.

15. Special shopping carts for parents have steering wheels and carlike seats under them for children to ride in

16. A very Kenyan cliché to mean "all that matters," used especially by one of the leading political parties that at one time was convinced that it was all that mattered in the country.

REFERENCES

African Centre for Economic Growth. 1992. National Micro and Small Enterprise Baseline Survey. Nairobi.

Akumu, Washington. 2004a. Nakumatt's Branch Expansion Picks Up Pace. *Daily Nation, Business Week*, September 28.

Akumu, Washington. 2004b. Shopping Mall Targets Christmas Opening. *Daily Nation, Business Week*, September 21.

Ayieko, M. W., D. L. Tschirley, and M. W. Mathenge. 2003. *Fresh Fruit and Vegetable Consumption Patterns and Supply Chain Systems in Urban Kenya: Implications for Policy and Investment Priorities.* Nairobi: Tegemeo Institute of Agricultural Policy and Development, Egerton University.

Central Intelligence Agency (CIA). The World Factbook. Available at https://www.cia.gov/cia/publications/factbook/print/ke.html.

Doing Business Project. 2007. *Doing Business: Kenya.* World Bank and International Finance Corporation. Available at www.doingbusiness.com.

EastAfrican. 2000. Fiery Lesson for Investors. Editorial, September 11.

Easterly, William. 2001. *The Elusive Quest for Growth.* Cambridge, MA: MIT Press.

———. 2006. *The White Man's Burden.* New York: Penguin Press.

Emerging Market Economics and Almaco Management Consultants Ltd. 2005. *Trade Facilitation Project in Kenya: Study of Administrative Barriers and Other Impediments to Trade in Kenya.* London: Emerging Market Economics Ltd.

Foreign Policy. 2005. The Failed States Index. July/August. Available at http://www.foreignpolicy.com/story/cms.php?story_id=3098.

Kimuyu, P. 2002. *Micro-Level Institutions and Revenue Generation: Insights from Kenya's Small Business Sector.* Nairobi: Institute of Policy Analysis and Research.

Krueger, Anne. 1974. The Political Economy of the Rent-Seeking Society. *American Economic Review* 64: 291-303.

McCormick, Dorothy. 1998. *Enterprise Clusters in Africa: On the Way to Industrialisation?* Brighton, UK: Institute of Development Studies, discussion paper 366.

McCulloch, N., L. Winters, and X. Cirera. 2001. *Trade Liberalization and Poverty: A Handbook.* London: Centre for Economic Policy Research.

Muguku, C. W. 2002. *Trade Liberalisation and Entrepreneurship: Responses to Constraints and Opportunities by Micro and Small Garment Producers in Nairobi.* University of Nairobi.

Munene, Mugumo. 2005. Fire Guts Gikomba Stalls Yet Again. *Daily Nation*, January 17.

Neven, D., et al. 2005. *The Rapid Rise of Supermarkets in Kenya: Impact on the Fresh Fruit and Vegetable Supply System.* Michigan State University and Kenya Agricultural Research Institute.

Nyoro, J. K., J. Ariga, and I. Komo. *Kenyan Case Study on Fresh Fruits, Vegetables, and Dairy Products.* Nairobi: Tegemeo Institute of Agricultural Policy and Development, Egerton University.

Price Waterhouse Coopers. 2005. *East Africa's Most Respected Companies Survey 2005.*

Randiki, M. J. 2000. *Capacity Utilisation in Micro and Small Enterprises (MSES): A Case Study of Small Garment Enterprises in the Nairobi City Council Markets.* University of Nairobi.

Sulule, P. M. 2003. *Constraints of Micro Business and the Livelihoods of Petty Traders in Nairobi and Kampala.* University of Birmingham.

Transparency International website: http://www.tikenya.org/

Tullock, Gordon. 1967. The Welfare Costs of Tariffs, Monopolies, and Theft. *Western Economic Journal* (now *Economic Inquiry*), 5: 224-32.

Wahome, Muna. 2005. Bottl1er to Rebrand Retail Outlets. *Daily Nation, Business Week,* November 10.

Weatherspoon, D. D., and Thomas Reardon. 2003. *The Rise of Supermarkets in Africa: Implications for Agrifood Systems and the Rural Poor.* Malden, MA: Blackwell Publishing.

World Bank. 2006. World Development Indicators Online. Available at http://publications.worldbank.org/WDI/.

4

The Nigerian Clothing
Design Industry

THOMPSON AYODELE

SUMMARY

The *adire,* or clothing design industry, employs thousands of people in Abeokuta in southwestern Nigeria, most of them women with little or no education who have used their entrepreneurial drive to make a living and create wealth where there was previously only misery. These entrepreneurs have received no government aid. In fact, through action or omission, the government has placed and continues to place many obstacles in their way. Yet they have been able to combat poverty much more effectively than foreign aid and official poverty-reduction programs. By creating thousands of small businesses and seizing opportunities under spontaneous institutional arrangements that offer a good measure of security and therefore a predictable environment, they have generated employment and profits. Even the less well-off among the *adire* entrepreneurs earn more money than other Nigerians make through the minimum wage in government jobs or formal-sector companies. The earnings of the top 40 percent of *adire* entrepreneurs compare favorably with the income earned by many managers in both the public and the private sectors. Thanks to the rise in their standard of living, many of these Nigerians have assumed responsibility for their own health care and other basic services.*

BACKGROUND

Situated on the west coast of Africa, with a population of more than 130 million people, Nigeria is a nation of many and diverse ethnicities. Currently,

---

*See page 207 for a list of abbreviations used in this chapter.

it has thirty-six states, including the Federal Capital Territory, Abuja. These states are divided into six geopolitical zones, namely Southwest, Southeast, South-South, Northeast, Northwest, and North-Central. The Southwest, which is the focal point of this case study, comprises six states: Lagos, Ogun, Oyo, Osun, Ondo, and Ekiti. These states are mainly peopled by Yorubas; their language is also Yoruba.

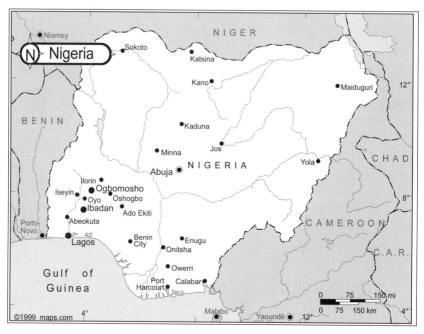

Figure 4.1. Map of Nigeria

SOURCE: ©maps.com

Indigo Dyeing as a West African Tradition

Indigo dyeing and design is an old, established tradition in West Africa. For example, the Bamana, a Mande-speaking people in northeastern Bamako, in Mali, have long been known for making mud cloth. Similar practices are present elsewhere in the region—for example, among the Fanke in Ghana and the Egbas in southwestern Nigeria (Jones, 2006; Sherertz, 2006). These activities were traditionally an expression of each culture and served as symbols of identity. As such, they were passed from one generation to the next.

The Yoruba word *adire* has its source in "*adi*" and "*re*," which can be translated as "tie" and "dye," respectively. *Adire* is a resist and/or indigo-dyed cloth. The emergence of *adire* dates back more than a century. During the early period, locally woven handspun cotton was used for various designs (Clarke, 2002). It is interesting to note that originally *adire* making was not seen as an economic enterprise or an alternative to farming, the predominant occupation of the time. It was a cultural trait rather than a profit-seeking venture.

The *Adire* Revolution

In the early twentieth century, there was a departure from the earlier practice of *adire* making. Contacts with European textile merchants ensured access to large quantities of factory-produced shirting material. Apart from being available, this material was also affordable. As the drudgery of having to weave local cotton gave way to abundant shirting material, opportunities for growth appeared. A new dyeing technique that used cassava starch as a resist agent was also discovered and quickly adopted.

These developments brought a revolution to the practice of clothing design. *Adire* making gradually came to be seen as more than a symbol of cultural heritage and eventually evolved into an industry. Women effectively came to dominate the enterprise.

Although other towns in southwestern Nigeria are also involved in *adire* making, Abeokuta sets the pace. In the 1920s and '30s, *adire* was a local craft in that town. It attracted buyers from all over West Africa and even some other African regions. In 1926, Royce (1940, 4) reported 2,200 *adire* cloth makers and dyers in the Abeokuta township alone and estimated that they dyed about $200,000 worth of cloth every year, representing about 30 percent of the total trade in cloth. Today, Abeokuta is well known as the leading productive and commercial center of the *adire* industry. Nearly half of the population has a connection with the trade.

In the 1940s, the thriving *adire* industry was rocked by a crisis of quality, due primarily to the influx of new, less skilled entrants and the use of lower-quality materials. This development led to the near-collapse of the industry. Some believe the industry has never entirely recovered from that downturn (see, for example, Clarke, 2002).

Even if it has become an industry, *adire* cloth remains an integral part of Yoruba culture. The nature and type of the cloth a person wears say much about his or her mood and the status and prestige that people accord to him or her. Consequently, different motifs of *adire* are tailored for different purposes and occasions. Each of them communicates certain messages decipherable by average people.

Who Are the *Adire* Makers?

The state of Ogun is made up of three major tribes: the Egbas, the Ijebus, and the Yewas. The Egbas specialize in the making of *adire* and batik. With the advent of Islam and Christianity in the area, a number of them converted to one of these new religions, but even today many of them hold on to their traditional beliefs and practices.

The Egbas are made up of four tribal groups, and the territory they inhabit is under the control of the Egba Native Administration. There are two districts of non-Egbas: Ota and Imala. The state of civilization and economic development of Egbaland deserves a brief description. The Egbas have been known as keen traders for many centuries. In 1936, it was estimated that the Egbas obtained nearly US$1 million annually in revenue from trade in cocoa and palm oil, while revenue from the *adire* industry represented some US$250,000—about $45 per capita among the adult population. No statistics are available for the aggregate trade value for these periods, but these estimates indicate a high level of wealth creation.

Of the four Egba groups, the Egba-Alake is the one known for *adire* making. Within the Egba-Alake district, the Itoko and Asero people are the "gurus" of the industry. They are mostly rural dwellers who rely on batik and *adire* for their daily livelihoods. Nearly all of them have involved their children in the every stage of the business, from production to selling. Many of their children assist them in the process of putting stripes or lines on the fabric before it is tightly folded and sewed. They are also of immense help in organizing the necessary ingredients and tools used in the making of *adire,* and in selling and distributing *adire* to the buyers.

THE MAKING OF *ADIRE*

Indigo, or *elu,* is a major ingredient in the making of *adire*. It is grown primarily for its commercial value and is widely cultivated in many parts of the Egba division. The farmlands of the Kemta, Itoku, and Ijemo townships that lie to the north and northwest of Abeokuta best support the growing of *elu,* which involves planting the stem and then tending it until it is mature enough for harvest.

Cassava is grown primarily as a staple as well as to provide shade for the young *elu* plants. The planting usually takes place at the beginning of the rainy season. Cassava starch is used as the dye resist agent.

The Preparation of the Dye

The leaves—especially the young ones—of the *elu* tree are plucked when it is at least two years old. Once a sufficient quantity has been gathered, they are pounded in a wooden mortar. The leaves almost immediately turn dark as the color is expressed. Pounding continues until the leaves break up into a fibrous, pulpy, dark blue-green mass. The pulp is rolled into balls and placed on a flat lodge called a *pepe,* where it is dried, either in the sun or by heating with fire.

The balls are sold in the market. Contrary to what one might expect, the preparation of the *elu* is done entirely by men. Before the balls of *elu* can be used for dyeing, they must be mixed with a special preparation known as *aluba,* which fulfills the functions of caustic soda.

Making the *aluba* requires careful attention. Two native pots are placed one on top of another. The upper pot is filled with water, to which ashes of special woods have been added. The selected woods are *epin, oni,* and palm fiber. Ashes of cocoa pods can also be used to good effect. The ashes are stirred into the water and the mixture is allowed to stand while it slowly percolates through the upper pot and falls into the pot beneath, where it is collected.

The preparation of the *aluba* takes three to four days. For this reason, the more convenient caustic soda was often used instead in the past, until it was forbidden by the Alake, the paramount ruler of Egba, and the Council in 1929 because of the effects it had on the finished products.

The *elu* balls are broken and stirred into the solution by means of a stick. Water is then added until the requisite concentration and color are obtained. The mixture is allowed to soak for five to seven days. After that, the dye, or *aro,* is ready for use.

Adire Cloth

Adire is divided into two broad categories: *adire eleko* and *adire oniko (eleso).* In each case, white shirting and brocades are used.

Adire Eleko

Adire eleko employs cassava starch as the resist agent. The design on the fabric can either be painted freehand or stenciled. Different motifs exist, each with a unique name. Currently, motifs such as *ibadan dun* (*ibadan* means "sweet"), *jubilee,* and *olokun* ("sea goddess") are in vogue.

For a stencil design, the motif required is cut from thin strips of metal. The thin metal stencils are placed on the fabric and the pattern is filled in with cassava starch mixed with water into a stiff paste, called *agidi.* The stencils are then removed and the paste is allowed to dry. The fabric is carefully dipped into the dye and then dipped again. After each immersion, the fabric is dried. This is to let the *agidi* dry so that it does not wash away prematurely. The process continues until the desired color has been achieved. The fabric is then dried in the sun. When it is found that the pattern covered by the *agidi* has resisted the dye, the *agidi* is flaked off.

One can only imagine the great care and skill required to ensure that the paste does not wash away or flake off when drying or before the dyeing is complete. Otherwise, the exercise becomes futile.

Adire Oniko (Eleso)

Adire oniko is named after raffia, a natural fiber known as *iko.* In this process, *adire* is made by folding, tying, and/or stitching fabric with raffia before dyeing. This is also known as the "bamboo process." The raffia serves as the resist agent. Crochet cotton is now sometimes used in its place.

After the raffia has been tied into the desired motif, the fabric is dipped into indigo. It is then immersed in the dye for a very brief period. Care is taken to see that the dye does not soak through the raffia and extend beyond the desired region.

When the dyeing is complete, the fabric is dried and the raffia is removed. Nowadays, the design on the fabric is routinely created by a machine called a "machine *adire.* "

The Economics of the *Adire* Business

Taking into account the commercial worth of each of the shops and the number of people involved in the *adire* business, altogether the industry represents some US$20 million. The *adire* market is generally competitive, although certain elements of oligopoly are clearly visible. The activities of a few entrepreneurs can significantly affect the whole industry.

General agreements exist at the industry level as to the specifications, requirements, and standards for *adire* making. However, differences in the quality of the shirting material used, varying degrees of indigo concentration, and the relative attractiveness of the different motifs generate product differentiation in the mind of buyers.

In the *adire* business, transactions are conducted through physical meetings in a shop owned either by the occupant or by another person, on a cash-and-carry basis. The business is highly localized and affords rapid skills and practice diffusion among operators. There is virtually no documentation of deals or recording and keeping of transactions. The business, in short, is done primitively.

Within Nigeria, there are usually no middlemen in the chain of distribution; *adire* makers and consumers meet via physical contact to conduct transactions. Moreover, government-created transaction costs and a certain ignorance of the dynamics of international transactions on the part of these entrepreneurs hinder direct exports abroad. *Adire* cloths find their way abroad principally through Nigerian expatriates. Partly for reasons of cultural heritage and partly for profit, Nigerians abroad purchase *adire* cloths, serving as sales outlets in faraway lands.

Bargains are often reached after much haggling over price between the different buyers and sellers. Relatively rich people pay far more for the same piece of cloth than their poorer counterparts because of their tendency to haggle less.

Adire cloths are always in great demand on the eve of festivities and in periods of cultural renaissance. In recent times they have become popular among the elites. This could imply a persistent demand in the future. Although one cannot with precision determine the elasticity of demand for *adire* cloth, its supply is certainly price inelastic. This can be explained by the fact that there are many constraints on production, so that the supply responds slowly to price changes. For instance, the use of modern technology supporting large-scale production is limited. The inadequate supply of credit is another hurdle.

Adire entrepreneurs don't devote monetary resources to advertising or public awareness campaigns to promote *adire* among non-Yorubas. The product is unwittingly "advertised" when people catch a glimpse of a sample of cloth at a museum or cultural festival, or whenever a prominent Egba (such as President Olusegun Obasanjo) wears clothing made of *adire* cloth.

Manufacturers of conventional fabrics, on the other hand, spend huge amounts of money advertising their products in various media outlets to promote their brands.

POVERTY IN NIGERIA[1]

From the point of view of income, expenditures, and nutrition, poverty principally refers to those whose resources are insufficient to meet the basic physical needs of food, clothing, and shelter for continual survival. Economists and development experts differ in their definitions of poverty, but there appears to be a consensus that poverty entails a low income level, poor health, malnutrition, and a low level of education or even illiteracy (Todaro and Smith, 2003). It has been described as the most serious problem on earth because hunger, malnutrition, degradation, disease (and avoidable deaths) have their roots in poverty (Magleby, 2006). Poverty is characterized by dismal living conditions from the point of view both of health and the general environment, widespread ignorance, and frequent social unrest.

A somewhat less obvious manifestation of poverty is social exclusion. Poverty-stricken people are deprived of the chance to take full part in mainstream society (Birchall, 2003).

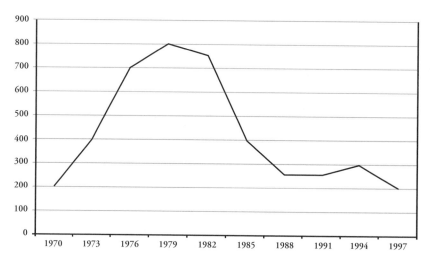

FIGURE 4.1. Per Capita Income in Nigeria, 1970–1997 (in current U.S. Dollars)

Note: 2000 and 2001 are GDP per capita, whereas 2003 and 2004 are GNI per capita. See www.finfact.com/biz10/globalworldincomepercapita/htm.

The level of poverty in any country is related to the average level of income and the degree of income distribution. For a given degree of income distribution, the lower the average level of income, the higher the incidence of poverty, and vice versa. For a given average level of income, the more unequal the degree of income distribution, the higher the prevalence of poverty, and vice versa (Todaro and Smith, 2003).

Nigeria's per capita income has remained perpetually low.[2] In 2004, Nigeria's per capita income was ranked 145th—the bottom rung of the income ladder. Figure 4.2 shows the rise and fall of per capita income in Nigeria over a period of three decades.

Income inequality has also not improved appreciatively. Although the average Gini coefficient for Africa as a whole was estimated to be 0.451 in 1996, Nigeria's figure was 0.507 at the beginning of the 1990s. Another source states that in 2000 the top 2 percent of Nigerians, with respect to income, collectively earned the same amount as the bottom 55 percent—a sharp contrast to 17 percent in 1970 (Mbeki, 2005).

Given this background, endemic poverty is almost a given, and so it is little wonder that relevant indicators confirm the existence of poverty in Nigeria. More than 60 percent of Nigerians live below the poverty line. Life expectancy at birth is 47.08 years, and the infant mortality rate is 97.14 deaths for every 1,000 live births (CIA, 2006).

The incidence of poverty differs among a cross-section of people. Certain groups of people are more vulnerable than others. Largely because of their lower earning capacity occasioned by weak physiques and lack of agility, children and the elderly are, on the whole, more prone to poverty than other members of society. Similarly, ethnic minorities and people on the margins of society generally have a higher chance of being poor, for they might be socially excluded (Todaro and Smith, 2003). Indeed, resource allocation within a household is often biased against certain members of the household, such as women and children.

Household endowments—the physical and human assets—have been identified as critical in determining whether or not a given household is poor (Olaniyan, 2000). A household with a relatively higher level of physical and human assets is not as vulnerable as one with little or none. Logically, when income falls below a certain threshold, a household with physical assets may dispose of part or all of its assets to supplement the dwindling income. On the other hand, a member of a household who possesses human assets such as good educational qualifications has a far higher chance of finding and keeping well-paid employment.

Discerning observation also reveals that some parts of the world, including Nigeria, are more poverty prone than others. For instance, poverty worldwide appears to be more concentrated in the tropics than in temperate regions, perhaps on account of the more fertile soil and benign climate of the latter. In the same vein, Gallup and Sachs (1998) have shown that, all else being equal, the closer a place is to the equator the less it grows and the more prone it is to poverty, owing to the harsher climate. Nigeria's case is no different. Poverty seems to be more prevalent in the savannah than in the rain forest (although the latest surveys indicate a more mixed picture). Figure 4.3 summarizes the situation.

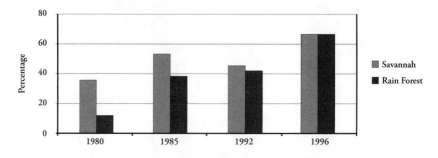

FIGURE 4.3. Incidence of Poverty Between Rainforest and Savannah (1980–1996)

SOURCE: Federal Office of Statistics.

Worldwide, poverty has always been more associated with rural areas because farming and subsistence activities are more vulnerable (Todaro and Smith, 2003).

Nigeria's poverty level has had a dramatic history.[3] From a relatively modest level of 27 percent in 1980, it increased to more than 65 percent in 1996, with most Nigerians living on less than US$1 per day (Ogwumike, 2001). In 1997, 90.8 million and 70.2 million Nigerians earned less than US$2 and $1 a day, respectively (World Bank, 2002). Surveys by the Federal Office of Statistics (FOS) consistently show a higher level of poverty among farmers than nonfarmers. In 1996, it was 73 percent versus 58 percent for nonfarming activities. In addition, these surveys reveal a positive correlation between poverty and household size. Figure 4.4 depicts how widespread poverty is among urban and rural households in Nigeria.

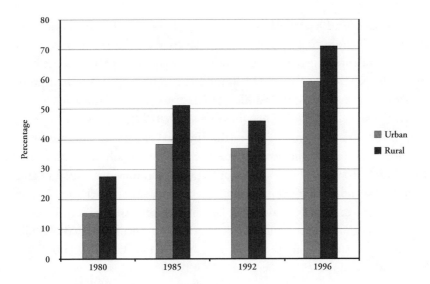

FIGURE 4.4. Urban vs. Rural Poverty in Nigeria (1980–1996)

SOURCE: Federal Office of Statistics.

Poverty Reduction Measures to Date[4]

A conscious attempt to tackle poverty through public policy has taken place in the post-Structural Adjustment Program (SAP)[5] era that started in the mid-1980s. These policies were originally adopted in order to cushion the unintended effects of the adjustment program, which sought to redress fiscal and monetary imbalances. Since then, nearly all of the programs targeting poverty have entailed some form of government interventionism. These policies tend to see the poor as "victims" (Prahalad, 2004) who need help, rather than as human beings who are part of the solution to the challenge of development. Those policies are briefly reviewed below.[6]

The National Directorate of Employment (NDE). This program came into existence in 1986 to combat growing unemployment. Upon completion of training for specific trades, participants were given microcredit.

The Better Life Program (BLP). The BLP was rolled out to focus on rural women. Inputs and microcredit were also dished out at discounted rates.

The Peoples Bank of Nigeria (PBN). The PBN was set up to cultivate saving habits and extend microcredit. A Community Bank (CB) also carried out less sophisticated services.

The Family Economic Advancement Programme (FEAP). This initiative, a pet project of the wife of the late General Sanni Abacha, was conceived in order to support the establishment of cottage industries. It turned out to be an avenue for squandering public funds rather than alleviating poverty, as the wives of elite Nigerians became the immediate beneficiaries of the program. By 2998, more than US$100 million had been spent on the Family Support Programme (FSP) and FEAP (*TELL* magazine, 2006).

National Poverty Alleviation Programme (NAPEP). NAPEP went into effect in 2001 in response to the disturbing level of poverty and in view of the high expectations the people placed on the civilian administration that took office in 1999. It is more comprehensive than previous measures and purports to address the manifestations of poverty, such as lack of access to water, low income, poor health, and lack of access to essential medicines.

To make good on its promises, the federal government allocated N10billion in 2000, later raising the amount to N17billion (US$76,923,076.9m and $130,769,230.77m, respectively).[7] For the first time, some government departments were saddled with poverty alleviation responsibilities.

The battle against poverty is far from won. Most of the aforementioned policies were blighted by one or more factors, which can be categorized as follows:

- Politicians and dictators alike expanded these programs to add to their undeserved credit. They were not created with the genuine intention of curbing poverty. Sometimes, they gave these policies and programs political toga. And once the ploy became obvious, the general perception was that the programs were "political booties" or "national cakes" that must be shared by anyone fortunate enough to be able to grab some. Hence, the purposes for which they were created were wholly defeated.
- Virtually all those poverty alleviation measures were noncontributory. In case of failure, they placed the burden on the government and not on the individual. Common-sense economics tells us that people respond to incentives, but when those incentives are lacking, they behave unpredictably and their desire to innovate is jeopardized. People also become prodigal in spending someone else's—especially the government's—money.
- Most poverty alleviation is characterized by leakage to nontarget groups. Closely related to this is the fact that officials and/or the coordinators of these programs frequently used the funds to line their pockets and tended their own interests rather than those of the poor.
- The different programs were not sustained; a change of government usually brought about the death of the existing programs and the birth of

other poverty-amelioration policies. Policies and programs would change frequently even under the same government.

Foreign Aid and Oil Dependence

During all these years, many politicians and opinion leaders supported foreign aid. They argued that investment financed by an injection of cash from overseas would reduce the vicious circle of poverty. Due to the nonavailability of the necessary data, the exact amount of foreign aid Nigeria received in the past three decades cannot be adequately ascertained. However, at the end of 2004 Nigeria's total external debt was US$33 billion (*Business Day*, 2006).

Generally, foreign aid throughout Africa followed the same trend. In the early 1970s, when the percentage of aid as a proportion of GDP was low, GDP growth per capita was high. In the late 1970s, the proportion of aid grew exponentially but GDP growth collapsed and was even negative for several years (Erixon, 2005). The living standards of more than 60 percent of Nigerians plummeted during this period. Far from reducing the vicious circle of poverty, foreign aid actually fueled it. Most of the projects on which the Nigerian government embarked with foreign aid money did not bring direct benefits to the poor. For instance, Ajaokuta Steel gulped US$4 billion but never reached its planned capacity. By the time the military government relinquished power in May 1999, various reports asserted that the project had generated payoffs of about US$2 billion to various government officials (Erixon, 2005).

It is not surprising that the chairman of the Economic and Financial Crime Commission (EFCC), Nigeria's foremost antigraft agency, Mallam Nuhu Ribadu, has asserted that, since independence, Nigerian leaders have stolen US$500 billion in development assistance funds given to Nigeria by Western countries (*Daily Independent*, 2006).

Nigeria in recent decades received huge transfers of financial resources from abroad. Notably, the funds were meant to provide social amenities, the development of infrastructure, and the construction of some key industries for meeting other national obligations, such as putting together a census and, more importantly, achieving sustainable growth.

However, corruption has severely hampered these efforts. According to Kofi Annan, former secretary-general of the United Nations, "Corruption hurts the poor disproportionately by diverting funds intended for development, undermining the government's ability to provide basic services, feeding inequality and injustice, and discouraging foreign investment and aid" (Annan, 2003). Despite the efforts of the EFCC, it has been reported that it is still business as usual in government departments and parastatals (*Nigerian Tribune,* 2007).

When President Olusegun Obasanjo came into power in 1999, he found that the nation's biggest problem was corruption. For example, a former police chief was said to have amassed US$975 million while in office. According to Ribadu on the occasion of the launch of the EFCC's "FIX Nigeria Initiative" in Abuja, "the money carted away to foreign banks could have recreated the beauty and glory of Western Europe six times all over in Nigeria" (Nigerian Tribune, 2007).

Similarly, the country is facing problems of ethnic politics, with various ethnic groups clamoring for resource allocation and a power shift. The ethnic card is a veritable arsenal for politicians who use it for their selfish interests. This has given rise to various ethnic militias such as Oodua Peoples Congress (OPC) in western Nigeria, Arewa Peoples Congress (APC) in northern Nigeria, and Bakassi Boys of the southeast. These developments have drawn the attention of the various ethnic groups away from national development. This is connected to the huge concentration of power at the center while the states are weak (Irobi, 2005).

Although ethnic militia groups appear to have been tamed by the authorities, a dangerous scenario is currently at play in the Niger Delta region under the name of Movement for the Emancipation of the Niger Delta (MEND). This group has claimed responsibility for a spate of kidnappings of oil workers. These actions have disrupted the crude supply, with huge financial consequences for the country's oil revenue. More than six hundred thousand barrels daily, valued at $4.75 billion, have been lost to the Niger Delta crisis, and three hundred thousand barrels of oil worth $8.5 billion were reportedly stolen in the region (*The Punch,* 2007a).

Some one hundred hostages have been seized in a year of increased violence in the Niger Delta region. Hostages are generally released unharmed after a ransom is paid, although casualties have occurred during gun battles between the attackers and security forces. Besides the reported brutal murder of thirteen traditional chiefs, about nine Chinese workers were recently abducted (*The Punch,* 2007b). In view of these kidnappings, the U.S., Philippine, British, and Chinese governments have consistently warned their citizens to stay clear of the region.

Despite the vast energy stores lying beneath southern Nigeria's soil, the region's people remain desperately poor. Nigerians continue to suffer from decades of misguided politics despite huge oil revenues. Many blame their plight on corruption and mismanagement by the federal government. Although the deregulation of the telecom sector has helped in creating additional jobs and helped business, overall the reform program of the present government still meets resistance from entrenched interests, making it difficult to pass crucial legislation. Government officials sometimes dilly-dally over the implementation of the reform program. In addition, capacity constraints and poor data management continue to impede the pace of reform implementation (IMF, 2005).

Government overdependence on oil is also a factor working against the current reform agenda. Expenditures on reform are based on the proceeds from oil and gas. Economic reforms would have been better off if the government had allowed the non-oil sector to develop and the general infrastructure, particularly the power supply, had been improved.

As a result of all this, the manufacturing sector in Nigeria is suffering a serious decline and may collapse soon. For example, the textile industry suffered a 64 percent reduction in the number of existing firms between 1994 and 2005 (*The Punch,* 2006).

THE ENTREPRENEURIAL APPROACH TO POVERTY REDUCTION

Although the approach to underdevelopment has shifted from redistribution and resource transfers to poverty alleviation measures in the past decade, the results continue to be unsatisfactory. Redistribution failed, especially considering the massive flow of foreign aid to developing countries meant to alleviate poverty in the 1980s and 1990s. But recent poverty alleviation measures have also failed to foster development. They have provided only temporary relief and served as ephemeral palliatives. In the long run, palliatives do more harm than good to the poor. The alternative is entrepreneurship, especially by the poor. As our findings related to the *adire* industry in southwestern Nigeria demonstrate, entrepreneurship is a much more potent tool against poverty.

Entrepreneurship brings growth and employment; once profits are made, wealth is created. When reinvested, this wealth multiplies. Even though access to good health care, education, and nutrition are important, they cannot by themselves lift the poor out of poverty. Entrepreneurship does this by empowering the poor economically so they can meet their own needs.

Some market-based approaches have been gaining ground very recently. The United Nations Development Program (2004) has recognized that the private sector can be very useful for poverty alleviation because, insofar as it contributes to economic growth, it creates income and employment, and it empowers the poor by providing them with essential services and increasing their choices. Many institutions are beginning to understand that entrepreneurship ultimately improves the quality of people's lives in a way that redistribution and poverty alleviating mechanisms do not.

For the private sector to perform this role creditably, however, the foundations and pillars upon which entrepreneurship thrives and flourishes must be present. These foundations and pillars—as identified by international bodies that have warmed to the idea of entrepreneurship, including the UNDP—are as follows:

Foundations

- Global macro environment
- Domestic macro environment
- Physical infrastructure
- Rule of law

Pillars

- Level playing field
- Access to financing
- Access to skills and knowledge

Once these factors are in good shape, entrepreneurship can improve the lot of the poor sustainably. By contrast, where property rights and the rule of law are not entrenched, entrepreneurship suffers (Magleby, 2006). This aspect has been missing from recent international efforts to empower small and medium-sized enterprises in Nigeria.

Recognizing the important role of the private sector in the drive toward poverty reduction, the government of Nigeria launched the National Economic Empowerment Development Strategy (NEEDS) in 2004. NEEDS envisions a strong, dynamic private sector that will propel Nigeria's economy. It is poised to increase financial resources to the private sector by promoting the goals of the Small and Medium Industries Equity Investment Scheme (SMIEIS)[8] through the removal of bottlenecks and red tape in the public sector and the incorporation of the informal sector into the mainstream economy (National Planning Commission, 2004, 54).

The intentions are good. There is no question that if the informal entrepreneurs were incorporated into the formal sector they would benefit from the relatively benign and favorable operating climate surrounding the latter. Nevertheless, the document does not spell out how this incorporation will be brought about, and little effort has been made to create secure, predictable, and stable conditions for small and medium-sized businesses to prosper. Absent the right institutions, the process of incorporation into the formal economy cannot be completed. According to a survey of thirteen African countries by the Economic Commission for Africa, small and medium-sized enterprises in Nigeria face many hurdles, including a stifling regulatory framework and an inadequate infrastructure. Indeed, research focusing on two different periods rated Nigeria's regulatory framework and infrastructure as "disabling."

Many scholars have concluded that certain types of institutional environments facilitate entrepreneurship and therefore wealth creation. Beyene (2002) has chronicled the efficacy of small and medium-sized enterprises in generating employment and fostering economic growth in both high- and low-income economies. He points to small and medium-sized enterprises as the prime movers behind economic success in some Asian economies, thanks to strong legal institutions.

Birchall (2003), for his part, explores the potential of cooperative societies in alleviating poverty. According to him, these groups are often overlooked or neglected by development experts. When members pull resources together for a common goal, and they all actively participate in the venture, they eventually prosper. However, he cautions that dependence on external resources can undermine the management of the group. Policies aimed at helping small and medium-sized companies in Nigeria have tended to emphasize dependence on external resources.

In a case study of women in Cameroon, Dinga-Nyoh (2005) argues that the determination to conquer poverty motivated the women to engage in microenterprise. After surviving many years and overcoming all sorts of obstacles, their enterprise became their occupation and they were able to eke out a living and become successful. She notes that the institutions behind the success were transparency, the rule of law, and property rights.

What Does the Entrepreneur Do?

Though said to have originated in the French word *entreprendre*, which means "to undertake," (Kibas, 2004) the term "entrepreneur" is now widely used to mean one who brings together various factors of production to create wealth or add value to existing wealth. In the process, the entrepreneur adds utility to meet the needs of both existing and potential consumers. Armed with their skills and craft, entrepreneurs scan the environment for viable productive activities.

The entrepreneur makes decisions on resource allocation at each stage of the process, choosing among alternatives. In his drive to meet the ever-growing needs of consumers, he constantly innovates and responds to their concerns. From time to time, in order to remain competitive and survive in the marketplace, the entrepreneur devises and switches to production techniques that entail lower costs without compromising quality. He aims to meet the challenges of the environment in which he operates.

The entrepreneur assumes the risk of uncertainties in the economic, social, and political climates. These risks often substantially affect his business activities. For all these, and for supplying his entrepreneurial services, he earns profits, just as labor, land, and capital generate wages, rent, and interest, respectively (Williams, 2005). The prospect of earning profits in the future propels him to be savvier in the pursuit of wealth creation. In the face of uncertainties and challenges, the entrepreneur presses ahead.

MICRO, SMALL, AND MEDIUM-SCALE ENTERPRISES: THEIR DISTINGUISHING ATTRIBUTES

It is often difficult, in practice, to clearly distinguish among micro, small, and medium-scale enterprises. For the convenience of various stakeholders, different institutions have adopted different benchmarks. Table 4.1 shows employment and asset-based classifications in Nigeria, according to various institutions.

Given these definitions, it is easy to conclude that micro and medium-scale enterprises dominate the Nigerian economy. These entrepreneurs tend to operate informally out of necessity—they are trapped in subscale enterprises (UNDP, 2004, 8). Essentially driven to informality by the huge costs of being formal, they have no legal existence, but they compete with legally recognized enterprises and multinationals. A typical entrepreneur in this category possesses an insignificant market share.

TABLE 4.1. Different Institutions' Definitions of Micro, Small, and Medium-scale Enterprises in Nigeria, Based on Employment and Assets*

Institution	Micro	Small	Medium
IFC	<10	10–50	50–100
CBN		<50	<100
NASSI		<40	
Accenture		<50	<500
Asset-Based Definitions (Excluding Real Estate)			
IFC	< $ 2.5m		
CBN	<N1m	<N150m	
NASSI	<N40m		
FMI	<N50m	<N200m	

*Employment-Based Definitions

Source: Nigeriabusinessinfo.com, 2006

The majority of Nigerian entrepreneurs have not registered their businesses. Doing so involves many bureaucratic procedures, all of them difficult to follow. To bypass these costly and time-consuming bureaucratic hurdles, entrepreneurs resort to bribery.

Obtaining a license in Nigeria takes much longer and costs more than in developed countries. Usually, sixteen steps are needed to obtain a license, and the procedures usually take more than a year (Doing Business Project, 2006). By implication, entrepreneurs either have to wait more than a year before commencing business or join the legions of informal businesses that are found all over the country. As could be expected, entrepreneurs prefer to operate their businesses informally.

Access to credit on the part of entrepreneurs (including *adire* entrepreneurs) is very restricted. The majority of young entrepreneurs lack collateral because most of the assets that could be used to secure loans are unregistered. They would have to borrow from family members or delve into their meager personal savings in order to offer some kind of guarantee. Very little information regarding credit facilities is available from private bureaus and the public registry.

Registering a property is not a smooth process either. To register a property, one needs to go through sixteen procedures that take about eighty days and cost about 21.2 percent of the value of the property being registered.

Entrepreneurs also face exorbitant taxes, tariffs, and other levies. More than one hundred different taxes are imposed on businesses, although statutorily "only" thirty-nine different forms of taxes are approved for all tiers of government. The government, at various levels, imposes various levies on entrepreneurs that lead to multiple taxation. The number of taxes paid by entrepreneurs increased from 99 in 2005 to 105 in 2006 (Nigerian Economic Summit Group, 2006).

A decrepit infrastructure, dysfunctional public utilities, the rising cost of import rates and machinery, high interest rates, and inconsistent economic policies have all increased the cost of doing business. Entrepreneurs spend a great deal of money, for instance, on privately provided and alternative sources of infrastructure. The country's epileptic power system, the lack of pipe-borne water, and other poor infrastructural facilities are major impediments to entrepreneurship.

The cost of alternative power generation in Nigeria is about three times what it is in other countries. Unable to cope with these costs, the tire giant Michelin has indicated that it will cease business operations in Nigeria effective in May 2007.

The Nigerian trade system is affected by endemic corruption at every level of public life. Entrepreneurs worry about a lack of transparency in business transactions, a director's liability, and scant personal protection (Doing Business Project, 2006). In the same vein, Nigerian entrepreneurs are faced with a court system that is very slow and inefficient and involves systematic and unnecessary adjournments. The system fails to enforce contracts between debtors and creditors and between suppliers and customers. Enforcing a commercial contract involves twenty-three procedures, and it takes more than a year for a lawsuit to be settled.

The Informal Sector in Nigeria

As in other developing economies, the informal economy makes up a significant portion of the economic activity in Nigeria. It pervades both rural and urban areas. The total value of Nigeria's informal sector is estimated to be ten times that of the Nigerian Stock Exchange. These activities include roadside trading, street hawking, water packaging, informal money lending, repair work, and others. The informal sector serves as an employment substitute for those with low education and skills[9] and a source of income for women, whose roles have traditionally been limited to the household. It provides an escape route for evading the overly burdensome registrations and regulatory procedures present in the formal sector.

TABLE 4.2. Characteristics of the Informal Sector in Nigeria

	Urban	Rural
Motive	To scratch a living To accumulate a surplus	To scratch a living
Status	Landless or squatter May own land, often with weak titles	May own land but with limited or no legal title
Products and Services	Lack uniformity Lack standards Mostly consumer goods Services are less technical and often personalized	Same
Education	Below secondary or secondary education Limited financial literacy	Mostly below primary school Lack financial literacy
Labor	Employs casual labor in addition to family labor	Uses family labor
Finance	Family savings Grants from relatives Loans from money lenders or cooperatives Rotational Saving and Credit Society and Association (RSCA) Plow back the surpluses	Same

The share of Nigeria's urban informal sector employment was calculated to be as high as 50 percent in 1981 (Sethuraman, 1981). Sethuraman's 1997 estimates put the informal urban labor force in Africa at 61 percent, with "little variation across countries." In spite of the modest economic progress made in Nigeria in the 1980s and '90s, recent estimates still indicate that between 45 percent and 60 percent of the labor force is employed in the urban informal sector (Nwaka, 2005). The World Bank's estimates put the size of Nigeria's informal economy at 57.9 percent in 2003 (Doing Business Project, 2006). Yet little has been done by the authorities in terms of policy formulation to integrate the activities of this resilient sector into the mainstream economy.

Moreover, as was noted earlier, the burden of employment creation increasingly falls on this sector as the formal sector continues to struggle to accommodate additional educated and skilled workers.

The Liabilities of the Informal Sector

Although informal entrepreneurs constitute a potential reserve of wealth creation and poverty reduction, under present conditions they are condemned to low productivity. Their activities are legitimate but also illegal because the cost of complying with the law is too high. The following are some of the liabilities that result from the illegal nature of their legitimate activities.

Undercapitalization. Nearly all informal-sector operators contend with a very small capital base. Although it is the lifeblood of any business, capital is acutely insufficient in relation to the desired size of the venture. This deficit undermines profitability because it reduces the volume of transactions. The gradual withdrawal of resources from the business, either in cash or in kind, for consumption leads to the erosion of capital and threatens the very existence of this sector.

Primitive techniques. Although it is generally recognized that the adoption of modern and improved technology leads to higher productivity for labor and capital, the informal sector is still mired in simple and outdated technology. The cost of acquisition is simply beyond the reach of the informal entrepreneurs. The rudimentary technology leads to lower productivity and, ultimately, higher costs.

Huge compliance costs. The entrepreneurs of the informal sector face a plethora of government regulations and guidelines, from difficult registration procedures and exorbitant fees to product standardization requirements and on-site inspections by officials. The cost of abiding by these regulations is burdensome for small entrepreneurs.

The bias against the informal sector. There is a strong antipathy toward the informal sector on the part of both the government and the formal sector. Formal private enterprises often see informal activities as a threat. They frequently team up with regulators to clamp down on informal enterprises. Government policies also discriminate against the informal economy, as has been specifically demonstrated in Nigeria[10] as well as other countries (Sethuraman, 1997).

THE *ADIRE* BUSINESS AND THE INFORMAL SECTOR

The *adire* business, a subset of the informal sector, has all the attributes of informality discussed so far. The dyed *adire* fabric is not certified by the Standard Organization of Nigeria (SON). Therefore, the strict rules and regulations dictated by this official body are not imposed on the trade. Most of the traders start and carry on their businesses on meager initial capital, usually as little as US$100. With no access to financing from the formal sector, most of them rely on the Rotational Saving and Credit Association (RSCA), an *esusu,* or membership-based lending association, run by cotraders who plow their profits back into the association. *Adire* entrepreneurs may not have formal collateral to secure loans from financial institutions, but they are well known within their communities and therefore are worthy of credit.

Not surprisingly in the context of informality, nearly all the *adire* entrepreneurs rent the lock-up stores they use to conduct their business. Unlike what happens with other informal activities in Nigeria, however, the owners of the stores enjoy clear and enforceable property rights over these properties, which were originally occupied by squatters. In many cases those squatters obtained occupancy certificates from the state authorities and passed the properties on to their children through customary law. The community developed rules over time to ensure that each person's property was protected and that any violation was met with immediate action. The properties originally had a residential use, but since the area is now a commercial center, they are currently used as stores.

About This Case Study

Numerous academic and policy papers, seminars, and conferences have asserted the potential of entrepreneurship in the battle against poverty in Nigeria and elsewhere. But nearly all of these assertions have been made in the abstract rather than in reference to specific, real-life cases. This study, based on extensive field work among *adire* entrepreneurs, looks specifically at this thriving industry, asking a number of questions. How does entrepreneurship reduce poverty? What level of income do the entrepreneurs earn from their petty businesses, and how can we conclude that they live above the poverty line? How sustainable is this income? Do the entrepreneurs cover their basic needs through these businesses, or do other activities supplement their income? In short, this case study looks at the neglected aspects of entrepreneurship among the poor.

ADIRE WEALTH CREATORS

In order to obtain comprehensive information about the *adire* industry, a systematic enumeration of *adire* entrepreneurs was undertaken. This was carried out by twenty field officers who spent one month in the field under the supervision of more senior officers. The focus was mainly on the Itoku and Asero parts of Abeokuta, two locations well known for *adire* making.

The exercise showed that there are more than 4,854 *adire* entrepreneurs in the downstream (selling and distribution) sector of the business. Since some degree of *adire* entrepreneurial activity takes place in a few areas outside of the two locations we studied, the number of *adire* entrepreneurs we have stated represents a conservative estimate.

To capture the essential data regarding the *adire* industry, we designed a well-structured but simple questionnaire. The forms containing the questionnaire were administered by field officers who were tutored and trained to conduct interviews and take data. All the forms were returned.

Structurally, the questionnaire was divided into two sections. The first section focuses on demographics, while the second looks at financial and economic variables involving the *adire* business.

Given the great number of *adire* entrepreneurs, who in some cases are sparsely distributed, we selected 1,100 entrepreneurs according to a cluster sampling technique. This sampling technique is widely used in field surveys and is particularly appropriate in the case of *adire* entrepreneurs, given their spatial distribution. Where necessary, the entrepreneurs were engaged in conversation to follow up on information that the questionnaire was silent about or that was deemed relevant by the field officers.

The following sections present an analysis of demographic variables based on the responses to the questionnaire.

The Respondents' Sex

Among the *adire* entrepreneurs who were surveyed, 28.9 percent of the respondents were male and 70 percent—an overwhelming majority—were female. This indicates that the common opinion that the *adire* business is the exclusive preserve of women is not entirely correct. Upon further probing, it was discovered that males are in fact more predominant in the upstream activities (production), while females dominate the downstream (sales and distribution) aspect of the *adire* business.

The Respondents' Age

Figure 4.5 shows the age breakdown among the survey respondents. Not surprisingly, 90.6 percent of the respondents are still in their prime. Their skills and abilities would have declined had they not been involved in the *adire* industry. It is interesting to note that people older than 65 who could have retired and/or been pensioners in the public system were also still earn-

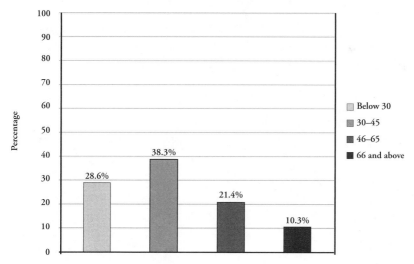

FIGURE 4.5. Ages of *Adire* Sellers

Note: 1.5 percent of the responses were missing or invalid.

ing their livelihoods in *adire* enterprises. They account for 10 percent of the total number of respondents.

The Respondents' Educational Level

Figure 4.6 shows the highest level of education completed by the survey respondents.

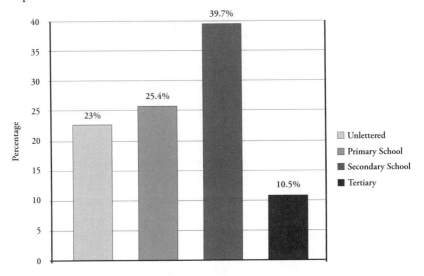

FIGURE 4.6. Educational Level of *Adire* Participants

It is worth noting that many illiterate people who have been shut out by the educational requirements of the formal economy are subsisting in the *adire* industry. As many as 23 percent—almost a quarter—of the *adire* entrepreneurs belong to this category. Had they not entered the clothing design industry of Abeokuta, they could at best have become farmers or artisans with much lower earning capacity.

It is also true that some individuals holding certificates from tertiary institutions, who would usually be chasing the few white-collar jobs available, are operating alongside people with much lower educational qualifications in the *adire* business. Indeed, one in ten *adire* entrepreneurs have passed through tertiary institutions. Many resort to *adire* making when they no longer have any hope of getting white-collar jobs. This confirms the earlier assertion that the burden of employment creation in Nigeria is increasing falling on the informal sector, as the formal sector seems to have reached the point of saturation. Other demographic variables in our study include household size, the number of dependents, and marital status. These are not reported, for the sake of brevity.

Respondents' Previous Occupations and Level of Involvement

The respondents were also asked what their occupations were before venturing into *adire*. Figure 4.7 summarizes those responses. It is clear that a majority of the respondents were traders before, but in another line of business. As many as 16 percent of the respondents were formerly artisans and technicians. It is plausible to speculate that they were lured into the *adire* business by the thought that the "grass was greener" and that they would find better opportunities there.

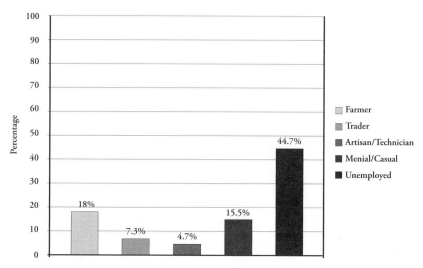

FIGURE 4.7. Previous Occupations of *Adire* Sellers

Note: 6.6 percent of the responses were missing or invalid.

The respondents were then asked about the level of their involvement in the *adire* business. As could be expected, 85.9 percent and 12.5 percent of them are involved full-time and part-time, respectively. This means that the *adire* business occupies the productive time of the overwhelming majority of the respondents.

How Long Have the *Adire* Entrepreneurs Been in the Business?

Figure 4.8 summarizes how long the survey respondents have been involved in the *adire* business.

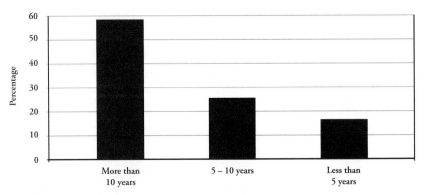

FIGURE 4.8. Length of Time *Adire* Sellers Have Been in Business

Note: 1.7 percent of the responses were missing or invalid.

As the figure shows, well over 80 percent of the respondents have been in the business for at least five years. More than 50 percent have spent more than ten years in the business. The conclusions we can draw are that these people are not fly-by-night entrepreneurs and that their businesses fare well enough for them to have stayed with it for a long time. If they were not able to make an acceptable living, they would have ventured into other activities, since the exit cost is almost zero.

Respondents' Number of Employees

The respondents were asked about the number of people they employ in the *adire* business, and 45 percent reported no hiring. This seems to confirm the popular opinion that informality relies heavily on family labor. But, significantly, more than 50 percent of the *adire* entrepreneurs hired at least one unit of labor. Of those, four out of ten hired more than four units of labor. Consequently, employment beyond the family does indeed take place in the *adire* business.

Respondents' Daily Sales

The survey respondents were then asked about their daily sales. The question was asked in order to ascertain the profit generated by the *adire* entrepreneurs, over and above their costs of production. An examination of their accounting records would have been a more reliable way to obtain this information, but these were either not available or not even kept. Therefore, proxy sales figures were used instead.[11]

Assuming a conservative 20 percent profit margin (in reality, the average profit margin for informal entrepreneurs is more than this), 19 percent of *adire* entrepreneurs earn up to US$1.53 worth of surplus per day. Moreover, 22.2 percent, 20.3 percent, 14.7 percent, and 20.8 percent of *adire* entrepreneurs earn average daily surpluses of $4.61, $10.77, $16.16, and $18.46, respectively.

To put these earnings in context, the daily surplus of the bottom 19 percent of *adire* entrepreneurs is well above the daily salary of state government and federal government civil servants who are paid the minimum wage, which is just $1.41. Similarly, the daily surplus of the second lowest quintile of *adire* entrepreneurs is the equivalent of more than twice the daily salary of federal government workers who are paid the minimum wage and at par with the daily earnings of most graduates working in moderately prosperous private firms. More significantly, the average daily earnings of the top 40 percent of *adire* entrepreneurs compare favorably with what some managers in both the private and the public sectors earn daily.

This analysis points to the fact that the skills of *adire* entrepreneurs are more valued and rewarding in that industry than in government employment and in some formal private businesses. The fact that about 78 percent of these skillful entrepreneurs earn an average daily surplus of between $4.61 and $18.46 means they cannot be considered poor Nigerians.

It is interesting to note that revenue accrued from the sales of *adire* would have been far greater had *adire* entrepreneurs been able to sell their products directly at international market prices. Although the local price market of *adire* ranges between US$12 and $20, the corresponding international figure is between $75 and $650.[12] *Adire* products differ in both quality and size; hence the wide interval between the low and high end of the ranges.

Respondents' Other Sources of Income

Another survey question was whether respondents receive income from sources other than the *adire* business. Although 30 percent responded yes, 69.3 percent said no. This question aimed to ascertain whether income from *adire* activities was being propped up by remittances from more prosperous relatives who reside either in Nigeria or abroad.

We asked those who responded yes to tell us about their other sources of income. Figure 4.9 depicts the various responses to this question.

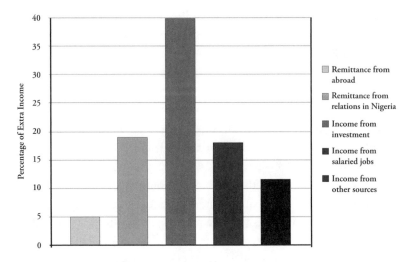

FIGURE 4.9. Other Sources of Income for *Adire* Entrepreneurs

Note: 2.19 percent of the responses were missing or invalid.

Income from investment represents by far the single biggest source of income for the respondents, accounting for as much as 40 percent of the responses. This indicates that previous surpluses invested by these entrepreneurs are now yielding returns. Indeed, follow-up conversations revealed that quite a large number of *adire* entrepreneurs have made a fortune, especially in real estate.

Remittances from relatives in Nigeria are sizable but not significant enough to prop up these entrepreneurs. Income from salaried jobs is also noticeable, accounting for 18 percent of extra income, but this relates to part-time entrepreneurs only.

Respondents' Distribution Channels and Exports

As shown in Figure 4.10, when asked about the distribution channels for their *adire* cloth, more than half of the respondents reported selling directly either to consumers or to middlemen. Sales to each were reported to be roughly equal.

When the respondents were asked about the destination of *adire* exports, their responses indicated that *adire* is much in demand in Africa, followed by Europe, North America, and, finally, Asia. The result for Asia is not surprising. Over the years, Asia has shown a comparative advantage in textile production internationally.

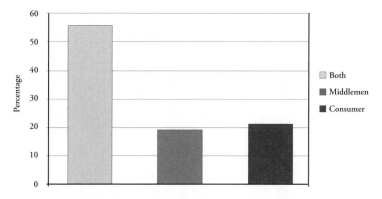

FIGURE **4.10. Distribution Channels Used by *Adire* Entrepreneurs**

Note: 1.7 percent of the responses were missing or invalid.

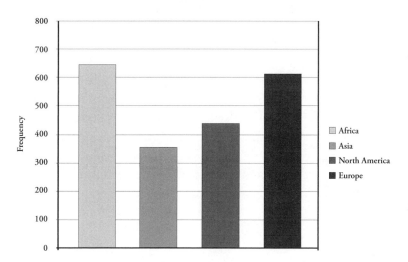

FIGURE **4.11. Destinations of Exported *Adire* Cloth**

Note: 3 percent of the responses were missing or invalid.

It is instructive that none of the *adire* entrepreneurs surveyed are directly involved in the export of the product. Were they to become involved, their earnings would quadruple.

Respondents' Sources of Credit

It is well known that an adequate and timely availability of dependable and low-cost financing is crucial to the survival of any business undertaking. There is near unanimity among experts regarding the fact that, in less developed countries, small and medium-scale businesses do not have the same ability as large-scale enterprises to access credit from formal financial institutions. With this in mind, we queried respondents on their sources of credit. The results were revealing, as shown in Figure 4.12.

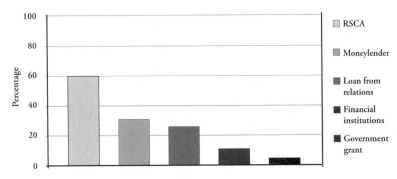

FIGURE 4.12. Sources of Credit for *Adire* Entrepreneurs

As many as 60 percent of *adire* entrepreneurs rely on the Rotational Saving and Credit Association (RSCA). This source of financing, though flexible and accessible, has a high rate of default. For example, internal wrangling may lead some members to withdraw. Moreover, RSCA loans often come in small quantities, so they need to be supplemented with other sources.

Next is the moneylender, whose loans come with harsh conditions. The moneylender may charge as much as 100 percent interest, demand collateral, and change the terms of the loan at will. Note that the RSCA and moneylenders give credit/loans to those who are known within the community, unlike formal financial institutions, whose clients are not necessarily members of that community.

Despite much hype about SMIEIS, the financial institutions' share of loans to the *adire* businesses is by all accounts very low. At the time of the writing of this report, more than US$346 million was available under SMIEIS for small and medium-scale businesses (*Daily Newspapers,* 2006). It is unclear why these industrious *adire* entrepreneurs have not benefited from SMIEIS. It may be related to the stringent requirements of the banks. The proportion of government grants is minuscule or negligible.

Obstacles to Obtaining Raw Materials

Respondents were subsequently asked about the obstacles they encounter in obtaining raw materials. Figure 4.13 depicts the result.

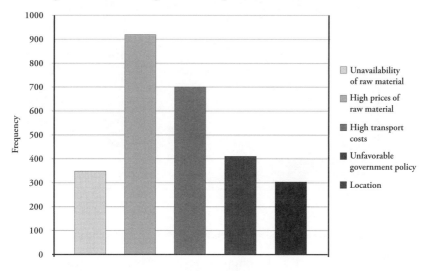

FIGURE 4.13. Obstacles in Obtaining Raw Materials

The high prices of raw materials topped the list, followed closely by high transport costs. When we probed the factors behind this situation, we found that government policy was responsible. The federal government's outright ban on the relatively cheaper textiles from Asia, ostensibly to protect local producers, has contributed immensely to the high price of the shirting material used for making *adire*. Thus, *adire* entrepreneurs have had to settle for the more costly local textiles even when importation would make more sense. A lower cost of textiles would lower production costs, boost sales, improve profit margins, and, ultimately, enhance the welfare of these entrepreneurs.

Respondent's Level of Government Assistance

The survey respondents were also asked if they have ever received government assistance. This question seemed necessary in view of the various ongoing poverty reduction/alleviation measures undertaken both by the states (including Ogun) and by the federal government. Figure 4.14 shows the response to this question.

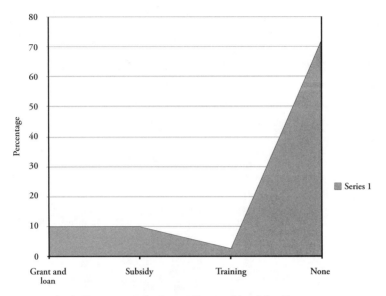

FIGURE 4.14. Government Assistance Received by *Adire* Entrepreneurs

More than 70 percent of the respondents have never received any form of government assistance. They have survived on their own and been able to fend for themselves. This result makes a mockery of several government poverty alleviation programs and constitutes a clear indication that the interventionist approach is not necessarily the only measure available to reduce poverty. Government handouts aimed at easing the conditions of poverty-stricken people foster dependency, whereas the *adire* industry has encouraged responsibility.

It should be noted that the state of Ogun and the federal government have separately expended millions and billions, respectively, on poverty alleviation measures. The National Poverty Alleviation Program (NAPEP) alone received well over US$23 million from the government in 2004 for its various programs.

Respondents' Business Registration

Figure 4.15 shows the response to the survey question asking respondents whether they had registered their businesses with the appropriate authority.

Fifty-three percent of the respondents reported that their businesses are registered with the appropriate authority, and 44 percent said theirs are not. Our research indicated that the respondents who indicated that their businesses were registered had actually misconstrued the question to be asking whether they were registered with the association of adire sellers, which is not a government organization. The Traditional and Modern Kampala/ Adire Manufacturers' Association is open to anyone involved in making or selling adire within the town. It has a few unwritten rules regarding the avoidance of crime and operates under customary law. It also opposes government policies that may inhibit the spread of the adire industry, such as

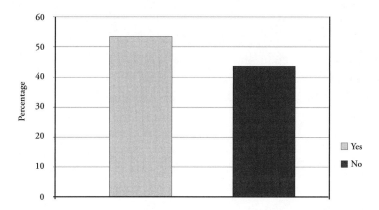

FIGURE 4.15. Responses to the Question "Is Your Business Registered?"

any increase in the local government squatters' fees. Usually a representative is sent to negotiate terms with various government departments. Nonregistration on the part of new entrants may invite reprisals from the association, which sometimes include a fine.

This practice corroborates the view of Peruvian economist Hernando De Soto about informality when he writes, "Their only alternative is to live and work outside the official law, using their own informally binding arrangements to protect and mobilize their assets" (De Soto, 2000, 23).

The association has executive members who are voted into various positions for a specific period of time. They meet regularly, sometimes weekly or bimonthly. Usually the executive members, headed by a market leader, attend the meetings. Nonexecutive members can also attend, but this is rare except in cases where the association requires the member to attend to iron out a dispute. Because the association does not have any means of informing members of whatever decisions are reached, each of the executive members transmits the decisions to members orally.

The association has rules that are unwritten and no formal constitution guiding its operations. By custom, these rules are nevertheless obeyed. They involve good moral conduct and the avoidance of conflicts and criminal tendencies that might hurt the reputation of the association and its members.

Members enforce the rules through fines and by asking for public apologies to the association. Some of the disciplinary measures involve suspending the offender from operating his or her business for a certain period of time or banning the person from operating within that vicinity.

If the offender refuses to heed a decision, the association sends representatives to the offender's family and friends to explain the need to obey the association's decision. If there is no compliance and the offender stays open for business, the association can call in the police to intervene. This is usually the last resort after other peaceful avenues have been exhausted.

Respondents' Response to a Boom in Sales

To know how financially literate the respondents are, we asked them what measures they adopt in order to take advantage of a boom in sales. Figure 4.16 presents their responses.

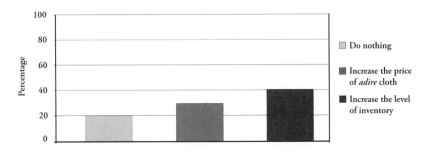

FIGURE 4.16. How *Adire* Entrepreneurs Respond to a Boom in Sales

To reap the benefits of a boom, more than 40 percent of respondents say they increase the level of their inventory holdings. Similarly, more than 30 percent report that they increase the prices of their products. Around 20 percent of respondents do nothing. Overall, it can be that said that, from a financial standpoint, they are modestly literate.

Respondents' Health Care

Since poverty is closely linked to poor health, respondents were asked if they go to a hospital when they are sick. The percentage responding yes was 81.7 percent, while 15.5 percent said no. How are those who said no cared for when they come down with an illness? A sizable number of respondents live in the ancient part of the city and may not have much contact with modern health care. Therefore, they still use traditional methods of treatment.

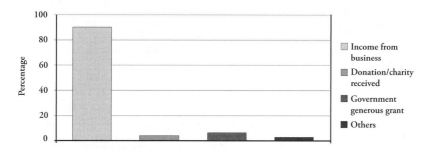

FIGURE 4.17. How *Adire* Entrepreneurs Pay for Health Care

We then asked the *adire* entrepreneurs how they cover their health care bills. As shown in Figure 4.17, 90 percent of them use income derived from their business. A negligible proportion of respondents rely on donations and charity or government grants (the so-called "free" government health care program). The fact that the burden of health care—one of life's most basic necessities—falls squarely on the businesses themselves indicates an inseparable link between the *adire* enterprise and the owner's responsibility for her or his own survival.

Respondents' Standard of Living

Respondents were also asked if they feed and take care of their families with the profits obtained from their businesses. Eighty-five percent responded yes, while 11 percent evaded the question. This reveals not only the aversion of many Nigerians involved in the adire industry to sensitive questions but also the tendency to remain as secretive as possible vis-à-vis outsiders. This attitude supports our opinion, stated earlier, that their sales figures are grossly underestimated.

We then asked if their living conditions have improved since they started their businesses. The responses measure the degree of satisfaction on the part of these entrepreneurs. Figure 4.18 shows the results.

FIGURE 4.18. Have the Living Conditions of *Adire* Entrepreneurs Improved?

Note: 2.5 percent of the responses were missing.

About 95 percent of *adire* entrepreneurs reported an improvement in their living conditions since they ventured into the *adire* business. This finding is consistent with the responses to some of the preceding questions. In fact, most of the respondents have been in the business for more than ten years and could not have remained in it had their living conditions deteriorated over time. Even in a repressive climate, entrepreneurs could not be forced to continue to run a business if, at the end of the day, they were worse off.

The percentage of those who evaded the question—2.5 percent—is as large as the combined number of those who responded no and cannot say. The result reaffirms that respondents are reticent, especially when confronted with questions that deal with their modest prosperity.

Demographics of Respondents' Daily Sales

We inquired into how the *adire* entrepreneurs' daily sales—and by extension the surplus accrued—varies according to the level of education, sex, and age. Tables 4.3, 4.4, and 4.5 show the results.

As Table 4.3 shows, the relationship between the level of education and *adire* sales is statistically insignificant. The variations in sales across the various levels of education are not systematic and happen by chance.

Females make more sales than males, as can be seen in Table 4.4, and they are more prosperous and dominant in the *adire* business than their male counterparts. The findings confirm the females' edge in the *adire* industry.

TABLE 4.3. Daily Sales of *Adire* by Level of Education

Education	$7.69 or less	$7.70 to $38.46	$38.47 to $69.23	$69.24 to $92.31	Above $92.31	Total
Unlettered	48	69	55	31	47	250
Primary	52	62	71	40	48	273
Secondary	84	89	71	79	102	425
Tertiary	20	24	25	12	30	11
Total	204	244	222	162	227	1,059

*x^2 =20.89, df=12, not significant, p>0.050

TABLE 4.4. Daily Sales of *Adire* by Sex

Sex	$7.69 or less	$7.70 to $38.46	$38.47 to $69.23	$69.24 to $92.31	Above $92.31	Total
Male	72	83	73	37	41	306
Female	133	161	150	125	188	757
Total	205	244	223	162	229	1,063

*x^2 =24.98 df=4, significant, p<0.01

TABLE 4.5. Daily Sales of *Adire* by Age

Age	$7.69 or less	$7.7–38.46	$38.47–69.23	$69.24–92.31	Above $92.31	Total
Below 30	89	84	55	33	43	304
30–45	63	106	91	59	90	409
46–65	34	41	47	44	68	234
Above 65	19	13	29	21	28	110
Total	205	244	222	158	229	1057

*x^2=62.1, df=12, significant, p<0.05

Table 4.5 shows the daily sales of *adire* by age. As the table shows, age differences among *adire* entrepreneurs are responsible for some variations in sales. Certain age brackets sell more than others.

Testimonials of Four Adire Entrepreneurs

Overall, the ingenuity of the *adire* entrepreneurs and their struggle to ward off poverty appear to have been rewarded with modest but unequivocal success. To round out the statistics, we end by giving four of the many personal testimonials we collected.

1. "My name is Mrs. T. A. Animashaun. I am 50 years old. I started my *adire* business 30 years ago, when I was 20. Before that time, I sold Guinea brocade cloth. *Adire* is good and profitable. I started with just $167 and the business is now worth $12,000. I have not been doing any other business. I will never stop doing this. I have sponsored seven children and now I feed ten children daily,[13] besides my having acquired assets worth more than $35,500."

2. "I am Mrs. Fatimo Akinbo. I am 30 years old. Before 2002, I was not involved in any business. On 23rd October, 2002, I started my *adire/ kampala* business. It is really moving well, and now there is capital to reinvest into it. It is good and profitable. I started with a token of $417. I now have a business that is worth more than $5,917. I do not engage in any other business beside the *adire/kampala* business. I do not have plans to stop it or in the future. I have sponsored two children and now feed two every day. I have acquired assets that are worth more than $10,083. I wish to continue with this business. Actually, this is the only business I learnt."

3. "I am Mrs. Amoo S. I am 42 years[14] old. I started my *adire* business 30 years ago. Many have ventured into another business, but I cannot stop making *adire*. The business is fine, enjoyable and profitable. I started with $417 but now the business is worth $8,167. I have sponsored four children with it and now feed nine children. I have assets worth $40,667. Look! It is lucrative."

4. "My name is Mr. Monsuru Akingbade (a.k.a. A. I. Monsor). I am 35 years old. I started 20 years ago. Prior to that time, I was not doing any other business. The business is okay for me. It is somewhat profitable. Having started with $42, my business is now worth $7,083. If there is better-yielding business I can also venture into that. I have sponsored three children and now feed six daily. I have acquired all possible things since I started the business. I will like to continue it to make ends meet."

CONCLUSION

Over the decades, *adire* making has moved from being an activity perceived as a mere expression of cultural identity and heritage to becoming a huge business enterprise in which thousands of Nigerians currently earn a living. They have made and continue to make headway in their efforts to escape poverty in spite of the many roadblocks placed in their path, mostly by the government. And their success represents a notable contrast with the different poverty alleviation programs implemented by successive governments. The success of these entrepreneurs would be dramatically increased if many of the current obstacles they face, including being prohibited from selling directly overseas, were removed.

The *adire* story shows that entrepreneurship leads to wealth creation and wealth begets wealth. Our findings refute the view that the poor are necessarily victims to be helped. The poor can become rich if the environment is made conducive to entrepreneurship.

With more a favorable operating environment, Nigerian entrepreneurs could create wealth in other areas. *Adire* entrepreneurs have demonstrated this: they feed, clothe, and shelter their families solely with income from their clothing design businesses. Just as tellingly, as many as 40 percent of *adire* entrepreneurs have at least five dependents whose needs are also met by the business.

Like other studies on development, our research tells us that entrepreneurship—that is, the capacity to discover opportunities and act upon them even in the most adverse circumstances—is a powerful tool against poverty. The results of the research mock the extended opinion—especially in Nigeria and other developing nations—that government agencies alone, through their poverty alleviation measures, can effectively address the poverty challenge. As this study clearly shows, the majority of the *adire* entrepreneurs have not been the beneficiaries of government assistance at any time. Yet they go on with their business and create wealth that many would have thought out of their reach.

Indeed, the government stands in the way of these industrious entrepreneurs. The ban on textile imports, for example, has kept the cost of *adire* production relatively high. This ban forces entrepreneurs to resort to substitutes that are more expensive, drives down their profit margins, and eventually undermines the fortunes of the business. When we asked *adire* entrepreneurs to describe the ways in which the government has been a problem for them, they mentioned its inability to provide infrastructure, the unfriendly attitude of state officials, and the prevailing business climate, which puts legal, bureaucratic, and regulatory obstacles in the path of their development.

Adire businesses empower and provide employment for women, who are less likely to get a decent job and are more vulnerable to poverty than men. Since women spend much of their income on the nutritional needs of the household, this implies an improvement in the intake of calories, and thus better health for household members. *Adire* businesses have been empowering women in Abeokuta, and can continue to do so in even more effective ways in the future, only if the business environment is enabling. Much of the money currently being spent by various tiers of government on empowering women would be more valuable if devoted to the provision of basic infrastructure.

Our study makes clear that the bedrock of any poverty alleviation measure should focus on facilitating the entrepreneurial activities of the poor themselves. The focus should be on this, rather than on transferring resources that serve primarily to further the politicians' agendas.

NOTES

1. The word "poverty" here and in the rest of this report refers to absolute poverty, using the income definition of poverty—that is, living on less than US$1 per day.
2. In 2003, GNI per capita was just about 1.2 percent of OECD high-income countries.
3. Unless otherwise stated, data used in this section was extracted from FOS household surveys conducted during the periods. However; we do not know the exact definition of poverty adopted by FOS.
4. The list here is by no means exhaustive. It can aptly be described as "representative" of the policies instituted so far.
5. SAP was adopted in 1986 at the behest of the IMF in response to many economic imbalances that had undermined the Nigerian economy. Among other things, SAP prescribed the removal of subsidies on all commodities, the privatization of state-operated enterprises, allowing the naira to float, and strict adherence to fiscal discipline.
6. This section is largely based on Ogwumike, 2001.
7. $1=N130 or N=$0.0077.
8. This scheme mandated that every commercial bank set aside and invest 10 percent of its profit before tax (PBT) in SMEs. Banks demand, among other conditions for granting the facility, a bankable project and project feasibility study.

9. Nigerians with high education are also increasingly turning to the informal sector. The formal sector and various governments are unable to absorb the thousands of graduates the educational system churns out annually.

10. For example, unregistered enterprises are excluded from bidding on government contracts. A certificate of registration is a prerequisite, but other preconditions may be beyond the reach of informal enterprises. The same holds for the corporation's brief.

11. In spite of repeated assurances by field and senior officers that any information given would not be divulged or used for tax purposes, we found that the sales figures reported were grossly underestimated. We realized this when we multiplied the average number of yards of adire cloth reported sold per day by the average price per yard for *adire* cloth. However, *adire* cloth varies in both price and quality, and extrapolating the actual earnings in this way could lead to distortion or amount to mere guesswork. Therefore, we made do with the given figures, which should be taken with a grain of salt.

12. See www.adire.clara.net/salegallery.htm or www.adire.clara.net/adiregallery.htm for different types of adire and their prices at the international level.

13. It should be noted that this includes adire apprentices and children of close relations who are being brought up by adire entrepreneurs.

14. Many people learn the adire business through their parents or close relations. When they reach a certain age, they are given permission to establish their own business outfits. The initial capital for setting up is usually donated by their parents or relations.

REFERENCES

Annan, Kofi. 2003. Statement in support of the United Nations Convention Against Corruption. October.

Beyene, A. 2002. *Enhancing the Competitiveness and Productivity of Small and Medium-Scale Enterprises (SMEs) in Africa: An Analysis of Differential Role of National Government Through Improved Support Service*. Available at http://www.eldis.org/static.html. Retrieved April 21, 2006.

Birchall, J. 2003. *Rediscovering the Cooperative Advantage: Poverty Reduction Through Self Help*. Available at http://www.ilo.org/dyn/empent.html.

Business Day. 2006. September 25. Available at www.businessdayonline.com. Retrieved April 21, 2006.

Central Intelligence Agency (CIA). 2006. The World Factbook. Available at http://www.cia.gov/cia/publications/factbook/geos/ni.html. Retrieved June 20, 2006.

Clarke, D. 2002. *Adire: Resist-Dyed Cloths of the Yoruba*. Available at www.adireafricantextiles.com/adireintro.htm.

Daily Independent. 2006. October 19. Available at www.independentngonline.com.

The Daily Newspapers. 2006. May 3, 50.

De Soto, H. 2000. *The Mystery of Capital: Why Capitalism Triumphs in the West and Fails Everywhere Else*. London: Black Swan.

Dinga-Nyoh, S. 2005. Women as Entrepreneurs in a Formal and Informal Economy. Available at http://www.fordham.edu/economics/vinod/docs/ding-pap-doc. Retrieved April 27, 2006.

Doing Business Project. 2006. World Bank and International Finance Corporation. Available at http://www.doingbusiness.org/ExploreEconomies/Default.aspx?economyid=143.

Erixon, F. 2005. *Aid and Development: Will It Work This Time?* London: International Policy Network.

Federal Office of Statistics. 1999. Poverty Profile for Nigeria, 1980–1996. Lagos.

Gallup, J. L., and J. Sachs. 1998. Geography and Economic Development. *Journal of Political Economy.* December.

International Monetary Fund (IMF). 2005. Nigeria, Article IV: Consultation Concluding Statement.

Irobi, E. G. 2005. *Ethnic Conflict Management in Africa: A Comparative Case Study of Nigeria and South Africa.* Parker, CO: Outskirts Press.

Jones, K. M. 2006. *History, Origin, and Significance of Mud Cloth.* Available at http://www.library.cornell.edu/africana/about/mudcloth.html. Retrieved June 20, 2006.

Kibas, P. 2004. Entrepreneurship: Key to Africa's Development. In *Reclaiming Africa*, ed. James Shikwati. Kenya: Inter Region Economic Network.

Magleby, K. 2006. *MicroFranchises as a Solution to Global Poverty.* Available at http://www.omidyar.net/group/poverty/file/7.35.11055472357.

Mbeki, M. 2005. *How African Political Elites Undermine Entrepreneurship and Economic Development.* London: International Policy Network.

National Planning Commission. 2004. *National Economic Empowerment Development Strategy (NEEDS).* Abuja, Nigeria: Communication Development Incorporated.

Nigeriabusinessinfo.com. 2006. Available at http://www.nigeriabusinessinfo.com/nigeria-smes. Retrieved April 18, 2006.

Nigeria Economic Submit Group. 2006. Policy Brief no. 2. September.

Nigerian Tribune. 2007. Rope Around Governor's Neck. October 10.

Nwaka, G. I. 2005. The Urban Informal Sector in Nigeria: Towards Economic Development, Environmental Health, and Social Harmony. *Global Urban Development Magazine* 1:1 (May). Available at http://www.globalurban.org/Issue1PIMag05 / NWAKA%20article.html. Retrieved May 5, 2006.

Ogwumike, F. O. 2001. An Appraisal of Poverty Reduction Strategies in Nigeria. Lagos. *Central Bank of Nigeria Economic and Financial Review* 39: 45–71.

Olaniyan, O. 2000. *The Role of Household Endowment in Determining Poverty in Nigeria.* Ibadan, Nigeria: University of Ibadan. Available at: http://www.csae-ox-ac.uk/conferences/2000-OA/pdfpapers/olaniyan-95.PDF. Retrieved April 28, 2006.

Prahalad, C. K. 2004. *The Fortune at the Bottom of Pyramid: Eradicating Poverty Through Profit.* New Jersey: Wharton School Publishing.

The Punch. 2006. December 20, 16.

The Punch. 2007a. Niger Delta's Worsening Violence. January 22, 16.

The Punch. 2007b. Nine Chinese Oil Workers Abducted. January 26, 12.

Sethuraman, S. V. 1981. *The Urban Informal Sector in Developing Countries.* Geneva: International Labour Organisation.

Sethuraman, S. V. 1997. *Urban Poverty and the Informal Sector: A Critical Assessment of Current Strategy.* New York: United Nations Development Programme.

Sherertz, S. 2006. The Art of the Quilt. Available at http://www.yale.edu/ynhti/curriculum/units/1995/4/95.04.04.x.html#d. Retrieved June 20, 2006.

TELL magazine. 2006. August 3.

Todaro, M. P., and S. C. Smith. 2003. *Economic Development.* India: Pearson Educational Publishing.

United Nations Development Programme (UNDP). 2004. *Unleashing Entrepreneurship: Making Business Work for the Poor.* New York: UNDP.

Williams, W. E. 2005. The Entrepreneur as Hero. *The Insider.* Washington DC: Heritage Foundation.

World Bank. 2002. *World Development Report 2002.* New York: Oxford, 234–235.

ABBREVIATIONS USED

BLP	Better Life Program
CB	Community Bank
CBN	Central Bank of Nigeria
ECA	Economic Commission for Africa
FEAP	Family Economic Advancement Program
FMI	Federal Ministry of Industry
FOS	Federal Office of Statistics (now National Bureau of Statistics)
GDP	Gross domestic product
GNI	Gross national income
IFC	International Finance Cooperation
IMF	International Monetary Fund
NAPEP	National Poverty Alleviation Program
NASSI	National Association of Small Scale Industry
NDE	National Directorate of Employment
NEEDS	National Economic Empowerment Development Strategy
OECD	Organization of Economic Cooperation and Development
PBN	People's Bank of Nigeria
PBT	Profit before tax
PPP	Purchasing power parity
SMEs	Small and medium-scale enterprises
SMIEIS	Small and Medium Industries Equity Investment Scheme
UNDP	United Nations Development Program

5 Barter Clubs in Argentina

The Market's Response to the Failure of the State

MARTÍN SIMONETTA, GUSTAVO LAZZARI, AND
GABRIEL GASAVE

SUMMARY

Argentina's barter clubs emerged spontaneously. It could be said that their origin was the result of a romantic search for solutions to the problems of unemployment and poverty when Argentina's economy collapsed at the end of 2001 and millions of people found themselves in dire financial straits.

Perhaps it was the dream of getting along without money; or perhaps it was a desperate search for solutions amid unemployment. What happened was that people got together to swap. Eventually, they found a way to create a private currency to sustain their exchanges. Once the financial health of the nation had been restored, however, the clubs declined.

It could be said that barter clubs created a parallel economy with its own currency, based on exchanges of every kind, free from official taxation and the asphyxiating regulations that beset the normal operation of the labor market in Argentina.

This chapter analyzes the phenomenon of barter clubs as an example of the informal economy rising to the surface, allowing the creation of wealth and the survival of citizens despite the failure of the state.

> Argentina is a peculiar country. It puts us to the test at every moment and does not have the stability we might wish. Last December [2001], for example, when the depositors went to retrieve the capital they had accumulated, they found that the cashiers who handle electronic currency would not return the money to them.
>
> *Rubén Rivera, cofounder of the first barter club**

---

*Quoted in Hintze, 2003, 145.

THE ARGENTINE CRISIS AND THE RETURN TO BARTER

In 2001 and 2002, Argentina experienced the worst economic crisis in its recent history. After long periods of deep recession and the dismemberment of the country's formal political institutions, the existing economic model fell apart. Bank accounts were confiscated, public-debt payments to private creditors were halted, the convertibility that, for ten years, had linked the value of the peso to the dollar was ended, and a megadevaluation of the peso occurred, during which it lost 70 percent of its value.

Within less than two months, Argentina had been governed by five presidents. The parade of leaders began with the forced resignation of Fernando de la Rúa on December 20, 2001, after he ordered the confiscation of savings accounts at the recommendation of his minister of the economy, Domingo Cavallo.

The ensuing wave of poverty affected more than half the population of Argentina, giving rise to such harrowing scenes as the hordes of people who, looking for food, dug into garbage cans in the various neighborhoods of Buenos Aires. The unemployment and underemployment indices rose to unprecedented heights, and joblessness affected 20 percent of the economically active population (see Figure 5.1).

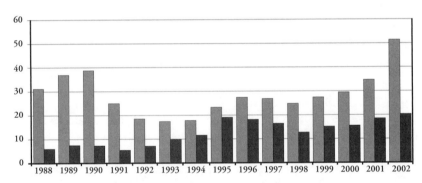

FIGURE 5.1. Poverty and Unemployment in Argentina, 1988–2002

SOURCE: National Institute of Statistics and Census–INDEC.

Because of the dire economic situation, and because of the confiscation of bank deposits, large segments of society, among them the impoverished middle class, found it impossible to carry out their daily transactions. One night, around Christmas 2001, many Argentines went to bed quite wealthy and were reduced to poverty the next morning as a result of the freezing of bank deposits.

Over time, the failure and retreat of the government became increasingly evident, as it abandoned its self-assigned duties. Crime rose to record levels; the judiciary system approved the confiscation of bank deposits (known as the *corralito,* or corralling), a flagrant violation of property rights; and all contracts made under the so-called Convertibility Act, which for years had established a fixed relationship between the peso and the dollar, were voided.

The painful economic and social crisis that resulted from the financial crisis of 2001 and 2002 gave an unexpected boost to different expressions of individual initiative, triggering a spontaneous search for basic subsistence in the short run and laying the grounds for a gradual recovery in the long run.

The Meaning of the Barter Club: A Private Response to the Disappearance of the Local Currency

This section looks at the real meaning of the barter clubs. That meaning emerges not from the statements of the protagonists but from reading between the lines of those statements.

It must first be said that, although the clubs became a massive phenomenon after the 2001–2002 crisis, they had, in fact, originated in 1995 and became popular during the 1999 downturn, which was triggered by international factors. In that year alone, it is estimated that two hundred thousand Argentines joined barter clubs. The 2001–2002 crisis, when between 2.5 million and 6 million people joined the barter clubs, elevated this social phenomenon to new heights.

Rosa Cattana was the coordinator of the Río Cuarto Barter Club in the province of Córdoba. In an interview with the Faculty of Economic Sciences of the University of Río Cuarto, she said that the barter club "is a group of people who gather to exchange products and services without using money. They use tickets or vouchers called credits (as in 'credibility'). Whoever receives this credit does so because he believes in the system" (Cattana, 2003).

Rosa Cattana's statement is more than just a simple explanation. Although it says that no money is used in a barter club, it also points out that people "use tickets or vouchers called credits (as in 'credibility'). "The name of the voucher is not capricious. To call it a credit and to associate it with the word "credibility" means it is "new money." It even has a similar name. The fiduciary currency, or fiat money, is called a "credit" of credibility. Both institutions rely on the trust that the users of such "rectangles of paper" place in the system in order to carry out their transactions.

Unwittingly, Rosa Cattana clarified the issue further when she said that "whoever receives this credit does so because he believes in the system." Like the population's acceptance of monetary currency issued formally by the central banks, acceptance means confidence in the system. In monetary terms, that confidence translates into what is called the "demand for money," that is, people's desire to have liquid money in their pockets or current accounts.

When people lose confidence, they cease to demand money, and that leads to a loss of the money's purchasing power. The monetary sign—the unit of currency—falls and dies under a crushing monetary hyperinflation.

In this sense, Argentina is a textbook case. Between 1967 and 1992, four units of currency were destroyed: the national peso (*moneda nacional*), the peso per Law 18.188, the Argentine peso, and the austral. All were replaced amid economic chaos, with the official excuse that "removing zeros" from the currency would expedite transactions.

In those four changes of unit, thirteen zeros disappeared. In other words, the product that today (2006) someone buys for 1 peso could be valued at 10,000,000,000,000 pesos *moneda nacional*, or national currency. Clearly, it is easier to work with a smaller number of zeros, but the truth is that the peso, the national currency, died, as did the other monetary signs.

Each of those currencies died because the people lost confidence in them. The paper used to print the current pesos is neither better nor of greater value than the paper on which *moneda nacional* pesos, or Law 18.188 pesos, were printed. Those monetary signs died because of what Rosa Cattana described with naive cruelty: people just ceased to believe in them. Their demand for money was reduced and the consecutive official currencies passed away. During the crisis that unfolded in Argentina, money ceased to accomplish its function as a means of exchange and a store of value.

All of this changed with the convertibility regime established by the new Argentinean government in the 1990s, although in the end that regime also collapsed, giving rise to the barter clubs. Understanding how the convertibility regime worked and why it reached a crisis point is critical to understanding the massive expansion of the barter clubs in the new millennium.

Convertibility implied a change from pesos to dollars and vice versa at a fixed rate of 1:1 in a free and voluntary fashion. The Central Bank was, in practice, a teller's window for conversion. When someone turned in pesos, the bank would turn out dollars, and vice versa. Then, in 2000, because of political instability and bad economic management that triggered big deficits, the economic agents (depositors, investors, and the general public) began to perceive that a default in the public debt was inevitable. The pessimists around them predicted a confiscation of bank deposits and even safety deposit boxes.

Beginning on December 3, 2001, the government-decreed *corralito* made it impossible to withdraw funds, and the debt default occurred on December 26. Although safety deposit boxes were not confiscated, there was widespread fear that such a step would be taken. Driven by that fear, many Argentineans opted to turn their pesos in to the Central Bank and exchange them for dollars. Dollar bills were exempt from confiscation.

In fact, reserves dropped by 25 percent in 2001 and bank deposits declined by 22 percent that year. With people withdrawing money from the banks to buy dollars, and even using money stored elsewhere to acquire the foreign currency, the local currency was evidently headed for extinction.

The "replacement" money—that is, the dollars—performed the function of storing value but were not used as a means of exchange. Instead, people chose to hoard the dollars and reduce their commercial and banking transactions. The years 2001 and 2002 saw a record number of bank accounts closed down and checks rejected for lack of funds. Business experienced a virtual breakdown in their chain of payments.

The money was disappearing not in the midst of an inflationary crisis, such as those that had destroyed four Argentinean currencies in the past, but under a brutal recession. A while later, the office of statistics of the Argentine government, known as the INDEC, announced that during 2002 the gross domestic product (GDP) declined a little more than 10 percent, the second worst drop in the twentieth century (see Figure 5.2).

Why did barter clubs operate only sporadically and in small numbers in the 1990s? Because the people still had confidence in money. Why did the number of members and clubs increase exponentially during the 2001–2002 crisis? The answer to this question conveys the real meaning of the barter clubs.

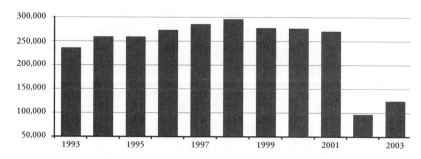

FIGURE 5.2. The Argentine GDP: From Recession to the Big Bust
(IN MILLIONS OF US DOLLARS)

SOURCE: Ministry of the Economy and Production.

The boom in the barter clubs resulted from the substitution of an informal currency that was relatively credible for a formal currency that was not trusted. In that respect, they soon ceased to be "barter" clubs, because an informal currency came to underpin the various exchanges between the participants. The barter clubs were not a permanent solution but a private attempt to solve a public problem.

The state, as the provider of currency, had failed once more. This fiscal deterioration mortally wounded people's confidence in the currency, leading to an attempt to replace currency through the barter clubs.

In this context, ordinary people without formal economic training or access to learned advisers began to carry out their transactions voluntarily with the help of pieces of paper called credits that, as Rosa Cattana stated so accurately, depended on their trust and faith in the system.

Almost 6 million people placed their trust in the system represented by the barter clubs. This essential fact explains the clubs' impressive growth. They exemplified the best of private initiative in an extreme situation and illustrated how the instinct for self-preservation releases the citizens' creative powers in times of crisis, when the government fails to maintain a basic framework of coexistence.

Unable to access the market for goods and services, and faced with the high cost of living within the formal economy, thousands of citizens—aware of their ability to produce goods and services valued by other persons—began first to exchange them through barter. In time, this gave way to a new form of indirect exchange: the use of a private currency, or rather of different private currencies that spontaneously appeared in the various barter clubs that emerged throughout the country.

TABLE 5.1. Magnitude of Barter, According to Various Sources (1995–2001)

	Source	Date of source	Nodes	Partici-pants	Remarks
1995	Primavera, Heloisa	May 2000	1 (May)	20 (May)	The first node was inaugurated in Bernal in May 1995.
1996	Ovalles, Eduardo, Center for Studies of the New Majority	5/08/2002	17	1,000	
1997	Ovalles, Eduardo, Center for Studies of the New Majority	5/08/2002	40	2.300	
1998	Ovalles, Eduardo, Center for Studies of the New Majority	5/08/2002	83	5.000	
1999	Ovalles, Eduardo, Center for Studies of the New Majority	5/08/2002	n/d	180,000	
	González Bombal, Inés: "Sociability in the declining middle classes: The barter experience," Universidad Nacional de General Sarmiento (UNGS)	Nov. 2001	400	320,000	Estimated data, based on newspaper *Clarín* 20 Aug, 2000.
	Barter magazine 2: 3, H. Primavera, publisher	Dec. 1999	500	200,000	Estimated data published in editorial of magazine.
2000	Ovalles, Eduardo, Center for Studies of the New Majority	5/08/2002	400	320,000	
2001	Ovalles, Eduardo, Center for Studies of the New Majority	5/08/2002	1.800	600,000	
2002	Stancanelli, Pablo, *Le Monde Diplomatique*	June 2002	5.000	2,500,000	Data from the Center for Studies of the New Majority.
	Ovalles, Eduardo, Center for Studies of the New Majority	8/05/2002	5.000	2,500,000	
	La Nación newspaper, 31	8/24/2002	8.000	6,000,000	Estimated figures. The number of participants refers to the people who benefit somehow from barter.

Source: Data based on ICO/UNGS research project, "Social Enterprise in the Labor Economy," September 2002.

The barter clubs reached their highest level of membership soon after the crisis broke out, with eight thousand markets for exchanging goods and services known as *nodos* (or clusters) and 6 million participants, according to the newspaper *La Nación*, or five thousand nodos created directly by 2.5

million people, according to the Center for Studies of the New Majority. Table 5.1 lists estimates of the barter clubs' membership at various times, according to different sources.

Reflections on Direct Exchange

Throughout history, humans have conducted daily exchanges using abundant and varied mechanisms of nonmonetary exchange.

In *The Mystery of Banking,* professor Murray Rothbard (1983) presents a marvelous summary of the system of direct exchange, or barter, and the problems that the system began to create with the passing of time and the advancement of societies. It explains why that system was eventually abandoned and how a return to a variant of it can be only a temporary and exceptional solution in the face of an economic crisis of enormous proportions, such as Argentina experienced during the dawn of the second millennium.

Rothbard reminds us that, prior to the appearance of the first coins, communities conducted their exchanges by means of direct exchange or barter. The various goods were produced by those people who specialized in them, and their surpluses were exchanged for products they did not produce. Every product or service had a price, in terms of other products or services, and all the participants, as happens in any free and voluntary transaction, felt that they benefited subjectively as a result of those transactions.

However, under the barter system, the exchanges were basically limited for three reasons, to wit:

- For a person to obtain something he desired, (a) he had to find someone who might offer the good or service he needed, and (b) that person, by coincidence, had to have a need to acquire at that exact moment what he had to offer. The need for this "double coincidence of desires" was a fundamental difficulty for the viability of barter. Add to this the fact that there also had to be an agreement about the relationship of the goods or services to be exchanged. (If, for instance, someone who owned four pottery vessels wished to buy a horse, he first had to find a horse vendor eager to acquire pottery vessels, and second, the horse vendor had to be willing to exchange the animal he owned in a relation of 1 to 4, not 1 to 6).
- The second inconvenience was that most goods are not susceptible to being divided or fractioned without losing value or being denaturalized.

If someone wished to exchange his house for a carriage, clothing, and some domestic fowl, how would he carry out those three operations? Would he divide his house into as many parts as the goods he needed to exchange? A house is indivisible; once fractioned, it loses its value. The indivisibility of goods was, therefore, an obstacle that hindered the barter system and was very difficult to overcome.

- The third and final problem Rothbard describes regarding barter is that of economic calculation. People, just like firms and businesses, must be capable of calculating losses and profits in each of their transactions. In a barter system, it was impossible to make this calculation. Within the framework of a modern industrial economy, we find that doing business by barter would not be viable over the medium and long term.

As Rothbard points out, the system could not exist beyond the incipient economy of a small town. But human beings are ingenious, and little by little they figured out how to create one of their most prodigious inventions: money.

The vendor of vessels who needs a horse asks himself, "What does the vendor of horses need? A merchandise called 'X'? Very well, then, I'll get 'X.'" He doesn't get "X" because he needs it as an end in itself but in order to exchange it for the horse he needs. There is now a demand for merchandise "X" because people know that it can be used as a means of exchange. That is how money made its appearance, when the participants in a market selected, freely and spontaneously, a type of merchandise that could be used as a means to access the goods and services desired. Historical examples of "X" were fish, furs, salt, tobacco, cattle, and so on. The choice always turns to merchandise that is already in widespread use, is in great demand, and is well accepted by the majority of the people.

How is it, then, that at some time in history, some societies—including Argentina's—resorted again, circumstantially, to barter? And how is it that from those exchanges new forms of currency arose?

BIRTH OF THE GLOBAL BARTER NETWORK

Paradoxically, the barter clubs originated in groups based on principles contrary to the free market, such as self-supply and the rejection of profit-making operations.

Argentina's barter networks were born on May 1, 1995, when Horacio Covas, Carlos de Sanzo, and Rubén Rivera, professionals who had jointly accomplished some productive enterprises, brought together neighbors in the town of Bernal, Buenos Aires province, to promote the production of food in family vegetable gardens that could later be exchanged or swapped according to the needs of each family (González Bombal, Leoni, and Luzzi, 2002).

While the problem of hunger was not a pressing social theme in Argentina at the time, the phenomenon of unemployment was beginning to assume great urgency, and so barter was presented as an alternative to the lack of job opportunities in the formal market.

For the three promoters, barter was the fusion of two streams of thought that began in 1994: an ecological trend, represented by the Program of Regional Self-Sufficiency, created by de Sanzo and Rivera, and an entrepreneurial trend, in the form of Covas's Professional Network. Later, in 1996, a third stream was added: the Network for the Exchange of Knowledge and Social Cybernetics, promoted by Heloísa Primavera and Carlos del Valle, which stressed permanent training as the principal condition for the network's growth.

Carlos de Sanzo recalls that, during its first six months, the Bernal Barter Club operated amid an atmosphere of small-town enthusiasm:

> We, the club members, took turns going to a place where we'd leave various products, such as cakes, meat pies, pizzas, garments, and crafts, and the credits were added to our respective exchange cards. Then we'd go out and reenter as consumers, and our purchases were discounted from the balance of the card (the data were kept on a balance sheet)" (de Sanzo, 1998).

The experience spread and in a short while arrived in Buenos Aires, with a remarkable increase in the number of participants. This was the birth of a network of barter clubs that originally was called the Global Barter Network in Solidarity and later the Global Network of Multireciprocal Barter (GBN). Each club constituted a *nodo* or cluster in the network.

In 1996, barter acquired great popularity nationwide and began to occupy more space in the media. That year, several *nodos* were inaugurated in the western region of urban Buenos Aires; these later formed the Western Zone Barter Club.

In 1997, the first Industrial Nodo of the Global Barter Network was inaugurated on the grounds of the former La Bernalesa textile factory in

Quilmes, province of Buenos Aires. About six hundred people took part, exchanging goods and services (electricians, shoemakers, barbers, teachers, accountants, psychopedagogues, masseuses, taxi drivers, tile layers, craftsmen, dressmakers, cooks, ice-cream manufacturers, and farmers, among other trades and professions). For their work, they obtained "barter tickets," a scrip whose value was specified in credits: 1 credit was the equivalent of 1 peso.

That year also saw the First Congress of Multireciprocal Barter, promoted by the Global Barter Network. In subsequent years, the network expanded throughout the country, basically in the provinces of Río Negro, Santa Fe, Córdoba, and Mendoza. By late 1998, more than four hundred clubs had formed in Argentina.

The Second National Congress of Multireciprocal Barter was held in 1998 and, in April of that year, a No-Money Congress was held. At that time, a regionalization of the Global Barter Network was agreed upon, which divided the network into zones called Capital, North, West, and South of Greater Buenos Aires.

It has not been easy to accurately establish the number of participants in the barter clubs. The available information was supplied by network authorities, who usually have only approximate data. This vagueness in the number of participants arose from the fact that many of the participants were members of more than one club or network and therefore may have been registered in more than one place. Also, participation in the activities of the *nodos* extended beyond the members, usually including their relatives.

If we stick to the official statistics, the first available data goes back to May 2002. At that time, the Standing Survey of Homes conducted by the National Institute for Statistics and Census (INDEC) included a special section on job quality. According to the published results, 87,800 people in the country worked offering goods or services for a barter club. The districts with the largest numbers of participants were Greater Buenos Aires (55,800), Mendoza (17,900), Mar del Plata (3,600), and the city of Buenos Aires (3,300) (INDEC, 2002).

Information provided by the press shows sustained growth in the barter clubs. In 1996, one year after the inauguration of the first *nodo*, there were about 1,000 members. In 1997, the number rose to 2,300, and in 1999 they reached 180,000. One year later, the growth was exponential: 320,000 persons participated in 400 *nodos* in 15 provinces and the federal capital. In 2001, the number of participants rose to 500,000 in more than 20 provinces (refer back to Table 5.1).

The three founders of the barter club movement noticed that the great crisis was having the effect of leaving many people out of the formal market. The founders saw that these excluded people were unable to reinsert themselves into the formal economy and lacked the initiative to think about self-advancement, accustomed as they were to a model in which their work activities were organized and managed by others. With these observations in mind, the barter clubs attempted to help people move out of an organized system and enter a system of self-advancement. They emphasized the education and training of the participants. The different courses they offered were intended to reeducate people, to instill in them the desire to produce and generate wealth.

That's how the Solidarity-Based Barter Network (SBN) emerged. To set itself apart from the Global Barter Network, the SBN redefined itself by stressing horizontality and democracy in the decision-making process; the cooperative organization of labor; the emission, distribution, and control of credits, with the approval and participation of the members (the sale of credits was forbidden); and the creation of assemblies of members in all spaces of the network for the purpose of making decisions. These differences were established not only in the city and province of Buenos Aires but also in various provinces in the country's interior.

Rodrigo Cervantes Ramírez says that competent individuals were displaced from the formal market in Argentina, in addition to those who, on the basis of age or knowledge, were not required. Even though these competent people were qualified, they couldn't be absorbed by the formal labor market. The situation was not merely transitory, because many people had looked for work for many years, and were still looking. A person knew that, if he lost his job, he might not find another. Those people who found themselves plunged into poverty formed the bulk of the barter club membership. The media called them "the newly poor," by virtue of the fact that in the past they belonged to the middle class. It may be that the barter clubs succeeded because of a strong entrepreneurial spirit on the part of their middle class members, trying to regain their lost status (Cervantes Ramírez, 2004).

Early in 2002, there were said to be 4,500 *nodos* in operation and four times more participants than the previous year. It should be pointed out that, before the corralito was instituted, about 20,000 people joined every month. After the financial system collapsed, 5,000 people joined every day

(Leoni and Luzzi, 2006). Table 5.2 gives a brief chronology of the growth of barter clubs in Argentina. Figures 5.3 and 5.4 show the growth in membership and the number of *nodos* during the same period.

TABLE 5.2. A Brief Chronology of the Barter Clubs in Argentina

1995	First barter clubs are formed
1996-2000	Sustained growth. Membership rises from 1,000 to 300,000 as recession and joblessness increase
2001-2002	Barter clubs in full bloom with membership of 2 million. The big crisis and the freezing of bank deposits make barter the only means of subsistence for an important segment of Argentina.

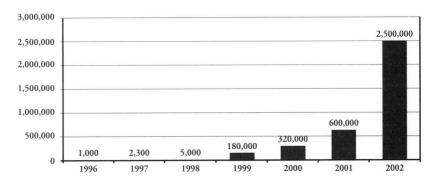

FIGURE 5.3. Evolution of the Membership of Barter Clubs in Argentina

SOURCE: New Majority.

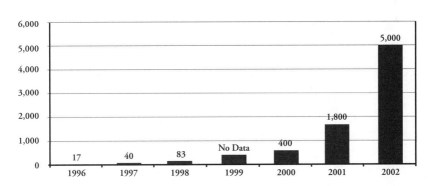

FIGURE 5.4. Evolution of Barter Club Nodes in Argentina

SOURCE: New Majority.

General Operation of Barter Clubs in Argentina

If we had to choose the central characteristics of the Argentine model of barter clubs, the following would be at the top of the list:

- They issued their own currency almost from the start.
- They established a permanent system, with regular weekly gatherings that allowed the members of the small groups to bond.
- From the moment that the first exchanges were made between clubs and the network was created, each club began a complementary association with the network or at least with several other clubs (or nodes) in the network, implying a multiple association.
- Each *nodo* enjoyed a clear autonomy in relation to other *nodos,* in an effort to preserve the fundamental principles of the network (described later) and the various forms of articulation and creation of a consensus to solve common problems.

As we stated earlier, during the economic crisis experienced by Argentina in 2001, the clubs worked to cushion the fall of certain social sectors and kept the conflict from becoming worse. The informal economy created by the barter clubs constituted a spontaneous and creative response by a segment of the population that was excluded from the economy as a result of the state's inefficiency.

Origin and Evolution of the System of Credits

Barter credits (sometimes called tickets, vouchers, or bonds) were created shortly after the first barter clubs were established, as a way to avoid the inconvenience of an accounting system within the clubs. Initially, the system was true to its name and the exchanges were always made between two participants, who established an equivalence between the products or services they offered.

Later came what was called "multireciprocal barter," an exchange involving more than two persons. By then, the gatherings resembled street fairs, filled with vendors and buyers. It was no longer necessary for the vendor of a product to receive a good or service in exchange from the buyer.

Each member of a club held a card that contained a record of his purchases and sales and his positive or negative balance at the end of each gathering. Later, all that information was entered into a computerized balance sheet that contained a roster of all members and all of the club's operations.

Obviously, a system like this was feasible only with a limited number of participants and, basically, with a small number of clubs. Once the clubs began to grow and expand into other sectors of the urban area and the capital city, accounting by means of balance sheets became unmanageable. That's when the organizers created the credits (vouchers), which simplified the calculation of transactions and the expansion of exchanges.

From that time on, the barter clubs formed a market in which members exchanged goods and services using their own currency: the credit. The market's creators also used the concept of a "prosumer," meaning someone who is both a producer and a consumer and who makes exchanges with others without resorting to intermediaries. A prosumer is thus a person who produces, has surpluses, and exchanges them, becoming a consumer. This concept was defined by Alvin Toffler in his 1980 book *The Third Wave*.

Members of barter clubs were referred to as prosumers. Prosumers brought in their products and carried out exchanges with others in the group by means of credits. The principal characteristic of the credit in this new economic scenario represented by the barter clubs was its acceptance as a means of exchange. Official money is a means of exchange accepted by all, but, unlike the credit, it's an imposed means. The state establishes by law the power of money to cancel all debts, both public and private, and does not depend on the acceptance of the person who receives it. The Argentine peso, the dollar, the euro, and all currencies in general have this obligatory power, which emanates from their character as an imposed medium.

In contrast, the barter club credits had no such power. Their acceptance depended on the parties involved. "If I don't want to accept it, I won't," said Rubén Rivera in an interview. Thus, this is the most important characteristic, the cornerstone—the credit permits diversity (Cervantes Ramírez, 2004, 3).

The barter club credits were not coercive in terms of their power to pay off obligations between parties. The acceptance of the credit was by mutual accord between the persons involved in the exchange. The acceptance of the informal currency was therefore a fruit of interaction, not of imposition.

Just as state-issued money has a value that has been established in advance, the value of the credit was set through interaction and established at the moment the goods are purchased or sold.

Cervantes Ramírez says that the three founders of the barter club system were obsessed with the convenience of decentralizing the instruments of compensation or exchange, trying to turn away from forms of payment that they considered "imperialist systems." According to them, the dollar and the euro are imperialist currencies—currencies of domination that reflect a territorial space.

Paradoxically and to a great degree, the intention of the people who devised this informal system was to implement some of the concepts on monetary issues advanced by economist Friedrich von Hayek in his book *The Denationalization of Money* (1977). In other words, let the economic agents decide what money is, and how much of it there will be, and don't allow that service—which is essential for the development of a society—to be imposed in a monopolistic way by means of legal coercion.

As expressed by Heloísa Primavera, coordinator of the Social Management Area of the Master's Program on Public Administration of the School of Economic Sciences, University of Buenos Aires, the use of the word "credits" had its origin in "the 'confidence' placed on the participants, who received a certain number of vouchers to begin the operations. From the outset, the same amount was delivered to each of the club members; that guaranteed at least an equity, i.e., the amount of currency for the operations" (Primavera, 2001).

Allocation of Credits

In today's barter clubs, the allocation of credits begins with a loan granted by the coordinators of each *nodo* to their members. This loan carries no interest.

When a new member joins the club and begins to participate in it frequently, he is given 50 credits. The purpose of this number of credits is to motivate the member's participation in the various swaps conducted. The coordinators of each *nodo* request these credits from the coordinators of the network, who are in charge of controlling the number of members in each club and are responsible for issuing the credits.

Historically, the issuance of credits was conducted in the central nucleus, where the first barter club was created: the garage in de Sanzo's home in Bernal, municipality of Quilmes, where, on May 1, 1995, twenty-three people formed the first barter club in Argentina. The club members left their products there and received a computer card that recorded the product delivered. They could then use the card to obtain something that was brought in by another participant. Those cards were called credits.

Unlike other instances in which "social currencies" have been created—such as the SELs (local exchange systems) in France—the Argentine credit is not the creation of each club but an instrument that's common to all of the clubs, with a centralized distribution. For that reason, their potential is much greater, because the more universal credits not only accelerate exchanges within the small group of people who form each *nodo* but also greatly increase the quantity and variety of goods and services to which each member can gain access.

Of course, this approach has disadvantages, too. At the same time that it broadens the horizon of possibilities for participants, it reduces the members' links with their original communities. In other words, participants are not obliged to remain faithful to the *nodos* in which they registered, each producing exclusively for his or her *nodo* and channeling the resources obtained there.

An unintended consequence of the universal credits was that, beginning in 2001, some clubs strengthened while others gradually weakened, even when the number of their members was on an upswing.

How did the credits work in practice? There was a sort of value system. A potential prosumer arrived at a barter club with his product, to which he assigned a price in terms of credits. He was given a card that bore the number of credits, after about 20 percent had been deducted for administrative costs. The same procedure was carried out for services requested, in which case the prosumer delivered an "order of service" for a specific amount expressed in credits.

With the incorporation of credits into this parallel economy, the currency went from being scarce to being abundant. The premise was that the credit had to be imbued only with its ability to serve as a means of exchange and lose its attribute as a store of value and a means to transfer value in time. In other words, the premise was that the credits should not accumulate.

During its first year of operation, the Bernal club opened every Saturday afternoon for members to exchange different kinds of products. At the start, these were basically food—fruit, vegetables, and prepared food—as well as garments, fabrics, and handcrafted articles. Shortly thereafter, the activities began to be more varied; for example, a dentist was invited to join the group so he could offer his services in exchange for bread baked by a neighbor. In other words, the possibilities for barter were not limited to the exchange of products but included the interchange of services, thus multiplying the number of transactions.

The club members carried an identification card that attested to their membership. The established rule was that someone who did not produce anything that could be exchanged was not allowed in. Members paid between 2 and 5 credits to enter the clubs, which usually operated in a storeroom. The credit was printed on filigreed paper and had twelve security measures that made it practically forgery-proof.

The barter club was set up in several levels. Food was always at the top, while services such as hairdressing, gardening, and auto repair were in second place.

Despite the popularity of multireciprocal barter, direct exchange never totally disappeared. In addition to using credits, many prosumers exchanged their products directly. For example, a bagful of bread would be traded for a bottle of detergent. This shows that barter was at the heart of all interchanges being made. It also means that even though the possibility existed to advance to a system that might be considered more "evolved," the basic swap had no reason to disappear.

Determination of Prices at the Barter Clubs

There is no price list in the internal market of the barter clubs. As the founders explain, the prices are the result of the interaction between supply and demand. In fact, they say, that's the essence of barter: the price is arrived at during the interaction, not before. The same product may have different prices during different transactions, in accordance with the subjective values the parties involved assigned to the goods or services being exchanged.

The participants take as a starting reference the price of the product in pesos and, accordingly, establish a price in credits that varies according to the product. The market for raw materials is not the only market that depends on the variables of the Argentine peso. The entire system is comparable to the formal system. The similarity of the credits to money makes understanding the system all the easier. Originally, to help the participants adapt to the system, a parity was established of 1 peso to 1 credit. That relationship was neither fixed nor established by the founders or written on any document. According to the founders, people intuitively compared the credit to the peso.

By using the prices in the formal market to define the prices of the products they want to exchange, members keep the barter system very close to the exchange scheme of the state's monetary system. However, that's precisely what the founders were trying to avoid, according to the theory on which the barter clubs were based.

What the barter clubs do, in effect, is to take as a reference, or guideline, the relationship between the various goods in the formal economy. That is, if the ratio in the formal market between a specific pair of jeans and a shirt is 2 to 1 (that is, if at market prices, the price of a pair of jeans is the price of two shirts), that ratio is used as a standard for a transaction involving similar goods, whether it is a direct exchange, a plain swap, or a transaction expressed in credits.

Profile of Barter Club Participants

During the crisis experienced by Argentina in the late twentieth century, most of the people who suddenly found themselves excluded from the formal market were competent and well trained. These people, though qualified, couldn't help being displaced and could not rejoin the formal labor market. It was these individuals who, finding themselves in poverty overnight, were the most likely to join the barter clubs. For that reason, the various *nodos* noticed a great entrepreneurial spirit among their members. These were competent individuals who found themselves out of the market and wanted to regain their place in society.

The barter clubs operated as a center for certain sectors of the middle class looking for a way to manage with a fixed income. That income could be the product of informal work, a pension, and so on. The important thing was that, if any of the members of a family had a small income in pesos, he or she could buy raw materials and begin some sort of productive activity. That way, the family could manufacture goods that they could later exchange.

Families that had several jobs, among them a formal job, acted within the barter clubs as links between the formal economy and the informal one. The barter club facilitated this linkage. The plurality enabled a division of labor and a diversification of the sources of income. Being able to earn income in more than one way prepares people for diversity. In the barter clubs, the borders between the formal and the informal economies were erased; both worked together as an alternative response to the economic crisis.

Today, many members see the barter clubs as another source of income, broadening the range of ways to obtain resources and gain access to goods and services. The barter club is also a market that values and gives relevance to certain resources that the formal market does not take into account. Things that cannot be placed within the formal market have found a profitable place in the barter clubs. This initiative does not go counter to the official system but complements it.

The members of the various barter clubs come from different social groups. One group worth highlighting is the Bolivian immigrants. They find the barter clubs very useful, because certain products that they cannot sell in the formal market, such as fruit that they grow themselves, are highly valued in the barter clubs. They sell their goods in the formal markets for Argentine pesos and also exchange them in the barter clubs for credits. As this example demonstrates, people go almost spontaneously from the formal economy to the informal one. Those products without much value in the formal market become a resource in the barter clubs, forming the basis for an alternative market. The barter clubs put people in contact with one another and create a network. Their objective is not to waste any resource but to recycle and give relevance to everything.

Organizational Structure of the Barter Clubs

From their beginnings, the barter clubs were characterized by a strong emphasis on self-management, a horizontal organization, and autonomy from the state and other organizations.

Opposed to the construction of a vertical organization with a hierarchic and stable structure, the founding nucleus leaned toward the creation of many autonomous groups—the clubs or *nodos*—and linking them by means of networks.

In an article titled "Scraping the Canvas: The Experience of a Barter Club in an Urban Area of Buenos Aires," researchers Fabiana Leoni and Mariana Luzzi (2006) write that, from the beginning, the clubs were guided by a set of "basic rules," standards that are not written down in codes or regulations but are transmitted informally by the coordinators to the members of the *nodos*.

Among those basic rules are the following:

- The obligation to carry out the transactions only in credits (transactions in pesos, or in credits and pesos, are forbidden).
- The obligation to produce for trade—that is, of participating either as a consumer or a producer.
- The commitment to circulate the credits obtained—that is, not to hoard them.

- The commitment to carry out all transactions within the fairs or gatherings organized by the nodes, not outside them.

Each barter club constitutes a self-contained unit that shares with the other clubs a space for linkage, expressed originally by the Global Network of Multireciprocal Barter and later by the different zones into which the network was divided. The communication among the various clubs and the solution to problems and challenges common to all gave origin to these spaces of convergence; monthly assemblies were convened that brought together the coordinators from each zone or region.

However, a vestige of centralization was present in the creation of the Global Barter Network. An advisory council was designated that would perform administrative functions for the network, such as creating new clubs and issuing and distributing the credits. Thus, any group that wished to found a new barter club had to apply to the advisory council, which provided the necessary information, trained the coordinators, and issued the necessary credits so the club could begin its activities.

According to the *Guidebook for Starting a Nodo,* written and distributed by the Global Barter Network, for a new node to be founded, a minimum of twenty participants is required, who must gather at two or three meetings and discuss the materials issued by the network before they can begin trading in an "inaugural fair."

Within each club, the organization relies on the principles of horizontal decision making and relative autonomy vis-à-vis other clubs. Each club has a coordinator, elected by the club members in assembly. The coordinator organizes each gathering or fair, registers new members, teaches them the principles of the activity, and ensures a linkage between the club and the network. Every member of the group is able to perform the function of coordinator and, at least in theory, the position rotates among all members. The figure of the coordinator is, without question, one of the defining elements of each club.

A process common to most clubs, which emerged as a consequence of an increase in the number of participants, is the formation of "collective coordinations," where the coordinator's functions are shared by several members.

The clubs have an unusual status, since they are not structured as true organizations and generally do not have a permanent venue. They exist only through the fairs and gatherings they organize. It could be said that the *nodos* are the fairs. In fact, the only way to find a barter club is to go to the gathering place at the appointed day and time. If you arrive before or after, you'll find hardly any indication of the club's existence. Other than the hours devoted to bartering, you'll find only schools, bars, parish houses, soccer clubs, and ordinary private homes.

The barter clubs, or "barters" as they are usually called, do not maintain close relations with the institutions or spaces that shelter them. Rather, their connection usually simply involves a lease arrangement paid for in credits or pesos, limited to the availability of the locale where the fair is held.

The life of a club begins at the moment the coordinators arrive at the gathering place and begin to organize the fair. They set up the tables that will serve as stalls for the vendors, erect the bulletin boards needed to promote the services offered by the members and to post news about the club, and set up the tables where the members will check in and the admission will be charged.

In like manner, the *nodo* dissolves the moment the fair ends, and it is not re-created until the next reunion. The coordinators are then in charge of straightening up and cleaning the meeting place to return it to its original condition. They are the club's direct references, and a club will often be identified as "so-and-so's *nodo*," although its official name does not mention the coordinator or any of his or her more evident characteristics.

Most of the *nodos* take the name of the barrio, the street, or the place where the gatherings are held. Such is the case with Almagro, Autopista, and La Bernalesa, the last of which took the name of an old factory in Bernal. In other cases, the name symbolically points to the new, positive, and even liberating character of the barter club, such as We All Can, The Sun Rises for Everyone, Creative Hands, and Hope.

BARTER IN ACTION

Let's see how a new barter club begins its activities, so we may have a clear idea of how a club operates and what its objectives typically are. Of course, the characteristics of a particular barter club will depend to a great degree on the creativity of the promotional group and the history of the site.

The general rule has always been to choose a place that, in addition to being functional, is attractive, pleasant, neat, and clean, so that, even if it isn't luxurious, it is a pleasure to return to.

Once the fair begins to operate, it is very important that it get together on a regular basis, such as every week, even if only a few members show up each time, so the fair becomes identified as a regular exchange space. Most clubs seek a commitment from members that no one will withdraw earlier than three weeks from the start of the experience, so that each person can have an opportunity to take a turn as prosumer.

At the first meeting, the attending participants are asked to bring a certain number of products to barter, even if they are only some basic foods taken from their own pantry. The place is set up as if for a party and a certain minimum value is agreed upon that the participants can put into play. Ideally, that value should not exceed a sum that everyone can bring—for example, the equivalent of a minimum of 20 liters of milk and a maximum of 50.

The meeting begins with a kind of exercise known as "the game of the five columns," because it uses five facts about the participants, which each person must call out when it is his or her turn.

The indicators are:

1. Name, address, and telephone number. This information allows the creation of relationships of trust inside the group, because it exposes the identity of all people alike. Also, it permits later contact for the execution of transactions and the formation of a general catalog.
2. Main activity the participant performs or performed in the formal market, in the areas of products and services, that he is willing to offer within the network. This information allows the others to learn what kind of products and services they will find, so they may order them for their consumption or inform others about their availability.
3. Knowledge the participant can occasionally impart to other members of the network, without necessarily charging for it or dispensing it on a regular basis. This activity helps participants discover how they can be useful to others.
4. Products and services the participant obtains or obtained previously without the use of money; in other words, which of his needs were met through barter. Although someone attending the club for the first time does not have experience in a barter club, it is very important that such a person identify past situations in which he turned to barter, thus demonstrating how that activity was always present in various moments in

his life. For example, children exchange toys, teenagers swap clothing, parents take turns transporting their children to school, and so on.

5. Products, services, or "odd stuff" the participant would like to find but hasn't found, or needs that are unsatisfied. This is an opportunity for the individuals to realize that they are potential providers for other members of the group, either because they produce what others need or because they can begin to do so in a short while, as proof of their ability to develop new skills.

For the occasion, coordinators will distribute "barter vouchers" (given special names by the organizers), issued in an amount the coordinators will have to account for. It is estimated that a reasonable amount is three times the maximum number of partners at the start of the process.

Coordinators need to decide how many vouchers will be distributed to each person. They also require each participant to sign a document stating that he will return the vouchers if he withdraws from the club. In the event he spends them all, he will have to produce something new and barter it within the club, so he can obtain more social currency.

Let us look at a specific example. Organizers invite thirty people and calculate that 50 units (equivalent to 50 pesos) is the amount needed to form a fund of social currency that will allow enough transactions to make a difference in the budgets of the participating families.

At the first fair, each participant gets 20 units of that social currency, which in this case we shall call "sunflowers." It has been decided, as we said, that the total amount each participant will receive is 50 sunflowers, which, if converted into formal currency, would buy 50 liters of milk at the rate of 1 liter of milk for 1 peso.

At the first fair, each person must bring the equivalent in products of 20 to 30 liters of milk, for the purpose of barter.

How to calculate how many bills need to be printed and what their values should be?

Continuing with this example, if we estimate the value of 1 liter of milk to be 1 peso, and if we issue our sunflowers as equivalent to the peso, then 1 sunflower may be bartered for any product for the equivalent of 1 liter of milk.

If we calculate that 50 pesos is enough to begin to make a difference in a family's monthly budget, and if the group vows to produce at least 50 pesos' worth of products to barter at the fair, we can deliver 20 sunflowers at the first fair and then increase that amount by 10 sunflowers every week, until we reach 50.

So if we have a group of about 30 people, they will use 30 times 50 sunflowers, that is, 1,500 sunflowers. However, because we estimate that a good maximum number for a first group (node or club) is 100 participants, we should produce a total of 5,000 sunflowers, that is, 100 times 50.

The face values of the bills, their designs, and their drawings are usually the result of collective creativity. It is useful to have a large number of coins (0.25, 0.50, and 1) and a small number of bills (2, 5, 10, and 20), so the transactions are easy and the participants are not confused by the new calculations.

So the 5,000 (five thousand) sunflowers in this first issue could be composed of:

> 100 bills of 10 sunflowers (1,000S)
> 400 bills of 5 sunflowers (2,000S)
> 500 bills of 2 sunflowers (1,000S)
> 500 coins of 1 sunflower (500S)
> 500 coins of 0.50 sunflower (250S)
> 1000 coins of 0.25 sunflower (250S)

In all, we have the 5,000 sunflowers, and each participant will receive 50 sunflowers distributed in the following manner: one 10S bill, four 5S bills, five 2S bills, five 1S bills, five 0.50S bills, and ten 0.25S bills.

Issuing and Distributing Credits

From the start, the control over the issuance and distribution of credits was a key topic in connection with the operation of the network. According to the bylaws of the organization, one of the advisory council's tasks was to issue the 50 initial credits that belonged to each of the newly incorporated members. The idea was not only to guarantee the currency necessary for the exchanges but also to ensure that the amount of available credits would keep pace with the number of active participants. At no time could any member of the club hold more than 50 credits. Those credits are entrusted by the coordinators of each club to the coordinators of the network, whose job it is to keep tabs on the number of members and to look after the issuance of credits. This delegation of the issuance of currency to a central group (from the beginning located in the original club in Bernal) is done through a social franchise.

Beginning in 1999, differences grew within the organization with respect to this system of monetary creation. The main concern involved the people who were responsible for the issuance, amount, method of utilization, and transparency in the handling of the credits. The discussions pitted the founding nucleus of the network, which had become the network's advisory council, against former members of the western and capital zones, and the tensions finally led to the creation of alternative networks to the Global Barter Network.

The "dissident" voices demanded that the advisory council publish balance sheets that reflected the level of credit issuance. This statement of accounts would have two purposes:

- To maintain the required balance between the number of credits issued and the number of members.
- To provide transparency in the management of the network and its funds, inasmuch as the issuance of credits implied a cost being financed by the participants themselves.

The repeated refusals by the advisory council to publish such balances ended up shattering the network's unity. On top of that, charges were made that the advisory council had issued an overabundance of credits.

For example, in April 2002, Heloísa Primavera published in the newspaper *Clarín* an article denouncing "irregularities" in the Global Barter Network and describing the differences between the GBN and the newly created Solidarity-Based Barter Network (Primavera, 2002).

Because the Solidarity-Based Barter Network (SBN) promoted horizontality and democracy in the decision-making process, as well as the cooperative organization of labor, control over the issuance and distribution of credits, and the assembly of members in all spaces of the network, it had a strong presence in the capital and the province of Buenos Aires and was expanding gradually in the country's interior.

To many, the establishment of the SBN explained the reduction in the supply of goods at the clubs, a situation that contributed to an unchecked increase in prices within every barter club.

In addition to the dispute about the responsibilities of the advisory council, another problem became evident. In a context of accelerated growth, such as barter clubs had experienced since 2001, control over the issuance of a "unique" currency had become almost impossible. Every day, hundreds of people arrived at the various clubs, asking to register and totally unaware of the regulations and principles that ruled the activity. The coordinators, who were not prepared to deal with the mobs but were aware that the main objective of the newly arrived applicants was to satisfy their most immediate needs, proceeded to register anyone and everyone.

Likewise, the franchise centers, although they had been decentralized and reorganized by zones, found themselves overwhelmed. No one was in a position to monitor whether a person had registered in more than one *nodo* and whether the mass of credits issued was multiplying artificially through the emission of 50 initial credits to each new member.

In a sense, the problem of issuing an excessive number of credits was caused not only by negligence or a lack of transparency on the part of those responsible for monetary control, but also by the dizzying growth in the number of participants, combined with the fact that a unique social coin existed for the entire network.

Partly due to this growth, some members of the SBN began in mid-2002 to harshly criticize the big clubs and to try to convince people to return to the small *nodos*, believed to be self-sustaining units. To that end, some clubs decided to ameliorate the limitations posed by the crisis. Along with other complementary measures, they tried to reduce the volume of currency available in each *nodo*. To achieve this, the members of some clubs were asked to reregister. This involved returning 50 of the credits in their possession, which, once revalidated by the coordinator by means of a rubber stamp, would become the only credits accepted in that *nodo*. The plan was to return to the initial situation, in which each member had the same quantity of monetary resources and was obliged to invest part of them in the production of new goods (or the supply of services). In addition, it was hoped that this measure would help lower the prices, which should be adjusted to a context of bare liquidity.

Another practice that apparently also affected the number of credits in circulation was forgery. In mid-2002, it was believed that 30 percent of the credits in circulation were counterfeit.

The main result of the inflationary phenomenon—caused either by overissue or forgery—was the crisis that barter clubs experienced beginning in mid-2002, resulting in a massive shutdown of clubs. The excessive number of credits caused a distortion in the relative prices within the system on one hand, and discouraged the production of goods for barter on the other. This became evident when people who were bartering prepared food realized they faced an imbalance between the value of the credits and the prices in the formal economy and, seeing that they were at a disadvantage, abandoned that activity.

Heloísa Primavera explained it thus:

> The inflation that appears in the barter club does not appear because of a deviation of prices in the formal market but because of unbridled emission in the discretionary distribution. It is internal . . . absolutely endogenous. At the moment that that group needs 1,000 credits to operate and has 50,000 . . . I don't know what to do with the vouchers, then she says to me: "That blouse is worth 2,000." "Well, okay . . . after all, I have 50,000. What am I going to do with the rest? (Primavera, 2002)

As a way to respond to this crisis, the clubs moved to limit access to the organization and tried to reactivate their operation by enforcing three main rules:

- The production of goods or the supply of services is an indispensable condition for participation in the nodes.
- The parity of 1 credit to 1 peso is maintained.
- Members are obliged to report the illegal sale of credits.
- In addition, the Global Barter Network issued, in October 2002, a credit with a new format, with more sophisticated security measures and a new characteristic—it had an expiration date.

Later on, the founders of the Global Barter Network developed new measures intended to bolster trust in the system. The *nodos* were called re-activation nuclei, the credits were printed with greater security measures to prevent forgery, and members could participate only if they carried a plastic card with a bar code and a photograph—in effect, personal identification.

This episode of inflation illustrates one of the big advantages a private currency has compared to currency that represents an official monopoly propped up by law or by force. In the private environment, forgery is punished not only by the judiciary system but also by the attitude of the prosumers themselves, who can decide to stop conducting their transactions through a medium they no longer consider dependable and credible. This, in turn, strongly affects the reputation of the forger and eventually pushes him out of the market.

These competitive currencies constitute a powerful incentive for the adoption of responsible behavior that ensures the preservation of the credits' purchasing power.

Analysis of a Specific Case

We will now analyze in detail a specific case—a club that developed in one of the areas worst hit by the crisis that hit Argentina in late 2001.

Researchers Fabiana Leoni and Mariana Luzzi (2006) describe in minute detail the trajectory of a peripheral *nodo* called El Trueno—the thunderclap. Their research shows that, until summer of 2003, El Trueno met two mornings a week at the headquarters of a social and sports club near the center of the José C. Paz township. This township is one of the communities that form the "fourth belt" of Greater Buenos Aires, an area where the levels of poverty are the highest. Because barter clubs existed in the district before the crisis of 2001, it is possible to get a more detailed view of this club's trajectory.

According to the 2001 National Census of Population and Housing and the Standing Survey of Homes done in October 2002 by INDEC, the rate of unemployment of that fourth belt was 22.3 percent. Families living below the poverty level made ≠up 71.3 percent of the residents, and 35.2 percent lived below the level of abject poverty (INDEC, 2002).

The story of El Trueno is not very different from that of other barter clubs. It was created by a group of women who, between 1998 and 1999, attended a support circle at the First Aid Station in a neighborhood near José C. Paz township. The psychologist who coordinated the support group gave them information about barter clubs and encouraged them to re-create the experience in their neighborhood.

When the club began, in mid-1999, its members gathered at the home of a neighborhood woman. At first, the eight or ten women who formed the group organized a home-style barter system, without contacting the existing networks, practically without advertising their activities, and in a self-managed fashion. The idea behind the enterprise was to strengthen the social bonds between them, rather than create a parallel market.

After six months of operation, because it was difficult to continue within such a restricted circle, one of the participants turned to the Global Barter Network in Bernal. In February 2001, the women set up shop in one of the warehouses of the José C. Paz railroad station. Later, they came to an agreement with the most important sports club in the area to stage a weekly *nodo* that could also attract people from neighboring districts. For a time, that club was the venue for Sunday "megafairs" that attracted 1,800 participants weekly. Then El Trueno moved to a small soccer field, whose manager allowed the women to use it twice a week for no charge, and later it resettled in a social and sports club that became its permanent venue.

In early 2002, as happened in many other *nodos,* the coordinator began to question the GBN's issuance and distribution of credits. The *nodo* subsequently became independent, severing its ties with the GBN and declining to join any of the other networks.

The products offered by the club were similar to those available at barter clubs in the capital and Greater Buenos Aires: clothing and footwear, handcrafted and household items, beverages sold by the glass, prepared foods, household cleaning products, and cosmetics. Among the services were hairdressing and manicures, bicycle repair, health checkups, and the repair of electric appliances.

In mid-2002, El Trueno, like all the other *nodos* and the rest of the national economy, was hit by a serious shortage of supplies, and that reduction in the supply created an exorbitant increase in prices. The number of members dropped noticeably and the club almost ceased to function, until the coordinators decided to "refound" it. A new roster was opened in June 2002 and 60 persons signed up. Thanks to this reorganization, the node's membership rose to 350 within a few months. Success was not lasting, however. Some of the newly implemented measures failed rapidly, and by late 2002 the number of members continued to drop. The *nodo* finally closed in the summer of 2003.

Characteristics of the Club's Members

About two-thirds of El Trueno's participants were women, half of them between 30 and 50 years old and 25 percent of them between 20 and 30. Three-fourths of the members did not graduate from high school, and half of them finished elementary school only. Three-fourths of the members were unemployed. However, only one-fourth of the membership benefited from some sort of social program (basically the Plan for Unemployed Heads of Household), although half of them lived in homes that received some sort of state aid (particularly food programs for newborns).

Compared with other *nodos* in Greater Buenos Aires, El Trueno was remarkable for its organization and the relative cohesion of the coordinating nucleus. Although, as in most clubs, the job of coordinator was held for several years by one person, this person shared the tasks of coordination and control with a group of members that remained stable for a long time and was highly committed to the barter plan.

In contrast to many clubs that use space the way street vendors do, in a more or less random manner and without a clear relationship among the vendors, El Trueno was notable because it followed the model of a supermarket, with fixed stands, grouped products, and labeled sectors.

A strict set of rules that were very clearly advertised (on billboards, on a slate at the entrance, and through loudspeakers) and continuous surveillance by the coordinators completed the image of a formal market, strictly organized.

Although the *nodo* was associated with the GBN, the link to the network was maintained exclusively through the chief coordinator, who visited La Bernalesa weekly to pick up the credit "franchise" and once a month participated in a general meeting of network coordinators. Consequently, most of the participants, even those with seniority in the node, were not involved in the organization of club activities and were not aware of the existence of regional or national barter networks to which they might be linked.

The lack of opportunity for pluralistic decisions and discussions among the participants and the coordinators had diverse consequences. On one hand, because there was no clear division of labor within the club (except with respect to the management of the fairs), as the number of participants grew, the courses and instruction sessions were gradually abandoned. As a result, the number of members who knew and abided by the rules that regulated the club's activities declined notably.

On the other hand, the concentration of tasks and responsibilities—and therefore of power—on the coordinator's shoulders meant that all conflicts were channeled in her direction. As the effects of the crisis were felt in the club, all eyes turned to the coordinator, who was considered by the members to be the person in charge of keeping the club running. Together, these effects explain why some members of the club demanded from the coordinator solutions that could emerge only from shared work, from a collective discussion, and from a reconsideration of the objectives of the barter system.

Finally, early in 2003, the quasi-identification of the *nodo* with its coordinator and her temporary absence from the city led to a halt in the gatherings. None of the "collaborators" or the participants could guarantee that the gatherings would continue.

This situation, which is not unlike the experience of other clubs, shows the degree to which barter clubs operated for a long time on fragile grounds, not only in terms of the exchange of goods and services but also regarding their organizational dynamics.

INFORMAL ECONOMIC ACTIVITY IN THE ARGENTINE ECONOMY

The barter clubs represent only a part of the informal economic activity that plays such an important role in the lives of Argentines and people in other countries of the region. Figures from the National Institute of Statistics and Census (INDEC) show that one of every two jobs in existence is an informal one. As of June 2006, 47.5 percent of the economically active population worked in the informal sector, a percentage equal to 4.7 million people.

Informal economic activity affects different societies in different ways. It has been called an underground or parallel economy in the United States, a black economy in France and England, a second economy or shadow economy in the countries of the former Soviet Union, a submerged economy in Italy, and a replacement economy in Germany, to mention just a few examples (Frediani, 1998).

However, informality is particularly relevant when two factors come together within a social organization. One is the high cost of complying with government regulations. The other is the low observance of those regulations, motivated by the low risk of ignoring the law, because of either a lack of control or the possibility of bribing functionaries at a cost substantially lower than the amount that should have been paid.

The result is a kind of Laffer curve of informality in which, as the cost of complying with the regulations rises, the incentives to act informally also increase. This leads to low compliance with the law.

In Argentina, the cost of operating in the formal market often is twice the cost of doing so in the informal market. Economist Mario Teijeiro (2004) writes that if a private enterprise hires a worker legally, it has to pay nearly twice what it would pay to hire him informally. Much of this difference can be attributed to payroll deductions (employee and management contributions toward retirement and health care, unemployment compensation, and family care). Another important factor is labor legislation, meaning the implicit cost of severance pay and court costs created by on-the-job accidents.

Faced with the high costs and risks of hiring someone, many businesses, such as the textile industry and particularly the construction industry, hire primarily undocumented immigrants, whose only unemployment insurance is their own efficiency and whose lack of legal legitimacy prevents them from suing their employers.

At the same time, given the rules of the game, working informally is an imperative for survival in various sectors, because everybody else in the sector is doing it. Also, to comply with all the regulations would affect any company's ability to be competitive.

In that sense, Teijeiro says, there are other incentives for informality besides high labor taxes and other labor costs. In fact, it is not possible to evade labor taxes without also evading other taxes. This is because the ability to evade controls requires a minimum coherence in what a company declares to the various tax collectors. It is also true that evading other taxes (such as the VAT, or value added tax, and the taxes on gross income, profits, and financial transactions or exports) gives the evader a decisive competitive advantage that allows him to make up for a lack of productivity or to accumulate gains that are tax-exempt.

In brief, the accumulation of tax obligations provides incentives for evasion and informality. The tax burden in Argentina increased from 11 percent of the GDP in 1974 to 25 percent in 2004 because of successive tax packages that raised the rates of taxation, broadened the scope of taxable bases, and created extraordinary taxes.

Although the high taxes imposed by the government affect all the players in a given sector of the economy, in practice there is discriminatory treatment that favors informal businesses, both small and midsized, because they tend to avoid taxes more easily than the larger companies.

The combination of high taxes and discriminatory enforcement affecting big companies creates a dissuasive climate for large investments, especially by foreign capitalists, perpetuating the small-scale size of the economy, even with a small public sector.

As a consequence of this disparity, large companies find the desired profitability through the best legal means possible—by becoming government contractors, whether at the federal, state, or local level, at prices well above those of the market.

Thus, we can observe a close connection between three elements: high taxes, a low level of compliance on the part of small and midsized companies, and a need on the part of large businesses to become profitable by partnering with the government. In this context, barter clubs fit in with the rest of the informal economy that functions outside of the realm of taxpaying businesses. The heavy weight of the government would impede many of the activities that are carried out in the informal economy and deny the survival of the millions of people who depend on informal income.

Thus, the phenomenon of the barter clubs is explained, on one hand, by the failure of the official currency, and on the other by the operation of nontaxable exchanges that are not persecuted by government authorities. Like the barter clubs, other businesses with great visibility and deep roots in society would not be viable if they had to shoulder the tax and regulation burden of the legal economy. As an example, let us look at the market known as La Salada and the activity of the scavengers known as *cartoneros*.

To many, La Salada is considered to be the Eastern City in the urban ring around Buenos Aires. It is a complex of informal fairs in Lomas de Zamora, province of Buenos Aires, and a gathering place for almost six thousand vendors of clothing, CDs, videotapes, toys, and watches, among many other products. Covering an area of 20 hectares (almost 50 acres), it is the nation's largest wholesale market. It is open Monday through Thursday, from midnight to midmorning, and brings in about fifty thousand people a day. More than US$400 million reportedly moves through La Salada each year. Every night, between two hundred and three hundred buses ferry in buyers from all over the country.

La Salada supplies more than a hundred retail fairs with products that are sold at prices that are clearly below those of the formal market. It serves as an outlet for clothing manufactured in clandestine sweatshops near the fair, where people work long hours for "informal" wages. The complex can operate only with the connivance of political and judicial authorities.

The local media say a pact among politicians, police authorities, and judges enables the operation of this million-dollar business that is also supported by neighbors who work in clandestine shops, sell in the fairs, or simply profit from the sales. La Salada has become a small center for illegal development in a very poor and long-ignored sector. It is important to point out that this macrofair has become an efficient organization that functions without any kind of state resource. It is the fair's "managers" who pave the streets using their own resources, operate a lunchroom for children, distribute medicines, guarantee safety on the streets, publish a weekly newsletter with a circulation of four thousand, and support radio station Ribera Sur AM (Krakowiak, 2004).

The other emerging phenomenon is that of the *cartoneros,* or cardboard pickers, who appear on the streets of Buenos Aires once the sun goes down and go through refuse bins, looking for cardboard, paper, plastic, or metals they can sell in recycling markets.

Like the barter clubs, this is a phenomenon that ballooned during the great economic crisis of 2001 and 2002. There were two main causes: the accelerated rise in unemployment, alienation, and poverty, and the increase in price (in pesos) of recyclable materials—such as cardboard, paper, and plastics—that resulted from the devaluation of the peso and the shutdown of imports.

A private study done in the main areas of Greater Buenos Aires where this activity was carried out—Malvinas Argentinas and José C. Paz—estimated that twenty-five thousand pickers crisscrossed the metropolitan area and that this activity therefore supported almost one hundred thousand people directly or indirectly in the city of Buenos Aires and the urban zone (Suárez, 2001).

This socioeconomic phenomenon was accompanied by the appearance of a great number of complementary institutions, such as special trains for *cartoneros,* nurseries for the children of *cartoneros,* dining halls, organizations of *cartoneros,* cooperatives, and others. It attracted the attention and the concern of various social actors, such as waste-management companies, municipal governments, nongovernmental organizations, and even important financial institutions. The magnitude of the phenomenon turned a marginal and economically insignificant activity into a productive socioeconomic activity (Reynals, 2002).

The *cartoneros* rapidly won the respect and support of the people, who saw in them individuals who sought to make a living by performing an unpleasant task without resorting to criminality or requesting state subsidies. In many houses and apartment buildings, the dwellers began to recycle useful materials spontaneously. The counterpart of the *cartoneros* were the *piqueteros,* or pickets, low-income individuals who blocked roads and streets to express their demands. Their source of income was the social aid the national government was able to distribute during the crisis.

In their work "Scavenging and the Refuse Business," Schamber and Suárez (2001) said that the activity of the *cartoneros* begins at dawn or at dusk, because they must stay ahead of the garbage collectors. The *cartoneros* crisscross the city in various ways, depending on their means or resources and the routes of clients they have built. They recycle all inorganic matter, including paper, cardboard, metal, plastic, and glass. Some collectors walk the streets pushing a cart; others ride bicycles or horse-drawn carts. A few of them drive pickup trucks. Often, they are accompanied by members of their family.

The distance covered, the duration of the rounds, and the capacity to collect materials are closely linked to the means of locomotion used by the *cirujas,* as the scavengers also are called. If making the rounds on foot while pushing a cart, a *ciruja* covers from 6 to 9 kilometers and take two to four hours. Using a horse-drawn cart, a *ciruja* can cover 10 to 15 kilometers in four to eight hours, while trucks can cover longer distances. In terms of volume of collection, a hand-pushed cart can carry as much as 200 kilograms; a horse-drawn cart can haul about half a metric ton; and a pickup truck can carry anywhere from 2,000 to 3,000 kilograms, or 2 to 3 metric tons (Schamber and Suárez, 2001).

CONCLUSIONS

The various difficulties that the barter clubs have faced throughout their evolution notwithstanding, it can be said that the clubs are a mechanism that has demonstrated its usefulness and that is ready to continue to provide answers at difficult moments.

Despite a decline that was inversely related to the country's emergence from the economic crisis, barter clubs continue to operate, and the networks are ready if the formal economy should again exclude major groups of citizens.

The principal characteristic of the barter clubs is that they represent a market that can be activated without the need for official money. One must bear in mind the social impact they caused—an impact that was accentuated during the crisis of 2001. In addition to offering an alternative to the formal economy in an attempt to reduce poverty (defined as the lack of money and resources) and to function as a psychological barrier to participants in the face of the grave consequences of the crisis, the barter clubs managed to bring about a change in the way participants viewed money. Barter clubs are living proof that a market can function without utilizing a mandatory currency.

Although the appearance of counterfeit credits (known as *truchos*) was a harsh blow to people's confidence in the system, the system was also strongly affected recently by the institutionalization of political patronage, in the form of state plans for assistance directed at heads of household and unemployed citizens.

Since the end of the convertibility system in Argentina, the country has witnessed a dramatic increase in the issuance of currency, which has caused a return of depreciation as a consequence of the doubling of the monetary base between 2002 and 2005, as shown in Table 5.3.

TABLE 5.3. Argentina's Monetary Base, 2002–2005

Date	Monetary Base ($ millions)
December 2002	27.669
December 2003	45.378
December 2004	50.537
December 2005	55.792

Source: Central Bank of the Argentine Republic

Although the worst of the economic crisis is over, barter clubs today continue to be part of Argentina's reality. They serve as a channel for an interesting portion of the informal activity that is not profitable enough to cover the high costs of the formal system. They also encourage the daily efforts of thousands of citizens who seek a better future and are not willing to live from the abundant charity doled out by the national government through its various subsidy plans.

REFERENCES

Cattana, Rose. 2003. Interview in *Economic Topics* 12, no. 128: 2. Faculty of Economic Sciences of the National University of Río Cuarto.

Central Bank of Argentina at http://www.bcra.gov.ar.

Cervantes Ramírez, Rodrigo. 2004. The Barter Club: A Mechanism to Recycle Goods, Services, and Persons: An Alternative Market Based on Diversity and Plurality. Quoted in *Urban Governance, Diversity, and Social Action in the Cities of the South N-Aerus Annual Conference,* September 16–17, Barcelona, Spain.

de Sanzo, Carlos. 1998. It All Began with a Pumpkin at Midnight: The Official Story. In *Reinventing the Market: The Experience of the Global Barter Network in Argentina,* ed. Heloísa Primavera, Horacio Covas, and Carlos de Sanzo. Buenos Aires: PAR.

Frediani, Ramón. 1998. The Challenge of the Informal Economy. *Techint News Bulletin,* no 252.

González Bombal, Inés, Fabiana Leoni, and Mariana Luzzi. 2002. *New Social Networks: The Barter Clubs.* Paper presented at Answers from the Civil Society to the Social Emergency: Brazil and Argentina Share Experiences, November 4.

Guidebook for Starting a Nodo. 2002. Cited in Beccaria, Luis and others, *Society and Sociability in Argentina in the 90's,* Append 1, Published by Biblos.

Hayek, Friedrich A. 1977. *The Denationalization of Money.* Albuquerque: Transatlantic Arts.

Hintze, Susana, ed. 2003. *Barter and Solidarity-Based Economy.* UNGS.

Hintze, Susana, Alberto M. Federico Sabaté, and José Luis Coraggio. 2003. *Charter of the National Congress on Barter and Solidarity-Based Economy.* Quoted in *Barter and Solidarity-Based Economy,* ed. Susana Hintze. UNGS.

INDEC at http://www.indec.mecon.gov.ar.

Krakowiak, Fernando. 2004. La Salada, *Página 12,* May 8.

Leoni, Fabiana, and Mariana Luzzi. 2006 *Scraping the Canvas: The Experience of a Barter Club in an Urban Area of Buenos Aires.* Center for Latin American Social Policy (CLASPO). Argentina notebooks no. 4, March.

Ministry of Economy and Production of theArgentinean Republic at http://www.mecon. gov.ar <http://www.mecon.gov.ar

National Institute for Statistics and Census (INDEC). 2002. Standing Survey of Homes. Methodological Coordination and Department of Analysis and Thematic Development. Available at www.indec.mecon.gov.ar.

New Majority at http://www.nuevamayoria.com <http://www.nuevamayoria.com.

Primavera, Heloísa. 2001. Social Currency: Gatopardism or Social Coin? *Polis: Academic Magazine of the Bolivarian University* 1, no. 2.

Primavera, Heloísa. 2002. Barter Clubs Must Preserve a Sense of Solidarity. *Clarín,* April 24.

Reynals, Cristina. 2002. *From Cardboard Pickers to Urban Reclaimers.* Paper presented at Answers from the Civil Society to the Social Emergency: Brazil and Argentina Share Experiences, November 4.

Rothbard, Murray N. 1983. *The Mystery of Banking.* New York: Dutton.

Schamber, P., and F. Suárez. 2001. *Scavenging and the Refuse Business: An Exploratory Look at the Informal Circuit of Recycling in the Urban Area of Buenos Aires.* UNGS/UNLA.

Suárez, F. 2001. *Social Actors in the Collection of Solid Waste in the Municipalities of Malvinas Argentinas and José C. Paz.* Thesis for Master in Environmental and Territorial Policies, Faculty of Philosophy and Letters, University of Buenos Aires.

Teijeiro, Mario. 2004. Center for Public Studies. April 30.

Toffler, Alvin. 1980. *The Third Wave.* New York: Bantam.

Freedom, Entrepreneurship, and Economic Growth

JOSHUA C. HALL AND RUSSELL S. SOBEL

INTRODUCTION

Entrepreneurship is the catalyst for economic growth and progress. A primary determinant of entrepreneurship is economic freedom. In this paper we present an overview of the relationship between freedom, entrepreneurship, and economic growth. We then examine the relationship between economic freedom and entrepreneurship across U.S. states and across nations. We find a positive and statistically significant relationship between economic freedom and different measures of entrepreneurship. Policies consistent with economic freedom promote entrepreneurship because they encourage individuals to pursue productive entrepreneurial activities instead of unproductive ones.

It is important to understand the factors influencing entrepreneurship, because it is the competitive behavior of entrepreneurs that drives the market process, thereby leading to economic prosperity and growth (Kirzner, 1973). Minniti (1999) argues that entrepreneurs are the catalysts for economic growth because they create a networking externality that promotes the creation of new ideas and new market formations. Thus, the actions of entrepreneurs lead not only to higher levels of output but to changes in the type of output produced (Holcombe 2003). For example, entrepreneurship not only increases the output of CD players per level of inputs but also leads to the introduction and eventual shift toward MP3 players. Both of these outcomes of entrepreneurial action are examples of why entrepreneurship leads to economic growth and progress.

Empirically, the link between entrepreneurial activity and economic growth is well established at both the international and local levels. For example, Reynolds, Hay, and Camp (1999) show that one-third of the differences in national economic growth rates can be attributed to different rates of entrepreneurship. Zacharakis, Bygrave, and Sheperd (2000) study sixteen developed economies and find that entrepreneurial activity explains approximately one-half of the differences in the countries' gross domestic product growth rates. More recently, Henderson (2002) shows that entrepreneurs significantly affect economic activity at a more local level through fostering localized job creation, increasing wealth and local incomes, and connecting local economies to the larger, global economy. Salgado-Banda (2007) looks at entrepreneurship across Organisation for Economic Co-operation an Development (OECD) countries and finds a positive relationship between a measure of entrepreneurial innovation and economic growth.

Although there are large differences in the rates of entrepreneurial activity across countries, Baumol's (1990, 1993, 2002) theory of productive and unproductive entrepreneurship suggests that these differences are *not* caused by a difference in the underlying entrepreneurial nature of the individuals who populate these countries. Baumol's theory is founded on the idea that entrepreneurial energies are omnipresent but entrepreneurs exploit profit opportunities not only within private markets but also within the political and legal arenas. Entrepreneurial individuals—who are present everywhere—have the choice of devoting their efforts toward either wealth creation in the private sector or toward securing wealth redistribution through the political and legal processes. This decision is influenced by the corresponding rates of return for the two activities. Thus, differences in the measured rates of *private-sector* entrepreneurship are due partially to the different directions in which entrepreneurial energies are channeled by prevailing economic and political institutions, through the rewards and incentive structures they create for entrepreneurial individuals.

In areas where the institutions provide secure property rights, a fair and balanced judicial system, contract enforcement, and effective limits on government's ability to transfer wealth through taxation and regulation, creative individuals are more likely to engage in productive market entrepreneurship—in other words, activities that create wealth (such as product innovation). In areas without strong institutions, these same individuals are more likely to engage in attempts to manipulate the political or legal process to capture transfers of existing wealth through unproductive political and legal entrepreneurship—in other words, activities that destroy wealth (such as lobbying and lawsuits). This reallocation of effort occurs because the institutional structure largely determines the relative personal and financial rewards of investing entrepreneurial energies into productive market activities versus investing those same energies instead into unproductive political and legal activities. For example, a steel entrepreneur might react to competition either by trying to find a better way of producing steel (productive entrepreneurship) or by lobbying for subsidies or tariff protection or filing legal antitrust actions (unproductive entrepreneurship).

As Kreft and Sobel (2005) show, this logic is consistent with the growing body of literature on the relationship between economic freedom and economic growth. This literature has been made possible by the Economic Freedom of the World (EFW) index by economists James Gwartney and Robert Lawson (2007), which was first published in 1996.[1] This index is updated annually and has now been used in hundreds of published studies to examine factors ranging from economic growth to violent conflict.[2] Because state and local policies also affect the degree of economic freedom, authors Amela Karabegovic and Fred McMahon (2006) annually publish their *Economic Freedom of North America* (EFNA) index ranking individual U.S. states and Canadian provinces. These indices measure the degree of economic freedom individuals within a geographic area have, based on data covering a broad range of policies, including the size of government, takings and discriminatory taxation, government regulation, and monetary stability.

Studies using these indices, such as Farr, Lord, and Wolfenbarger (1998); Gwartney, Lawson, and Holcombe (1999); Cole (2003); and Powell (2003) have consistently shown that countries with higher economic freedom scores are more prosperous and have faster rates of economic growth. According to Kreft and Sobel (2005), this clear linkage is present because the index of economic freedom measures precisely those institutional structures that promote productive entrepreneurship over unproductive entrepreneurship in accordance with the ideas of Baumol. Thus, underlying economic freedoms generate economic growth *because* they promote productive entrepreneurial activity, which is the source of economic growth. As economist Dwight Lee writes:

> No matter how fertile the seeds of entrepreneurship, they wither without the proper economic soil. In order for entrepreneurship to germi-

nate, take root, and yield the fruit of economic progress it has to be nourished by the right mixture of freedom and accountability, a mixture that can only be provided by a free market economy. (1991, 20)

The remainder of this essay offers evidence of the positive relationship between economic freedom and entrepreneurship. After providing a framework of how to think about the relationship among economic freedom, entrepreneurship, and economic growth, we turn our attention to presenting empirical evidence of the relationship between economic freedom and entrepreneurship. International evidence, as well as evidence from the United States, is presented showing that economic freedom is positively associated with entrepreneurship.

THE ENTREPRENEURIAL PROCESS AND ECONOMIC FREEDOM

To understand entrepreneurship and the best way for government policy to promote it, we must first delve deeper into the relationship between economic inputs, institutions, and outcomes. An economy is a process by which economic inputs and resources, such as land, labor, venture capital, and natural resources, are converted into entrepreneurial and economic outcomes such as new businesses or patents. This is illustrated in Figure 6.1.[3] As the large arrow in the middle of the figure shows, the entrepreneurial outcomes generated from any specific set of economic inputs depend on the "institutions"—the political and economic rules of the game—under which an economy operates. This model makes it clear that entrepreneurship can be increased either by increasing the inputs into the process or by improving the rules of the game under which entrepreneur operate.

It is important to note, however, that when the rules of the game are unfa-

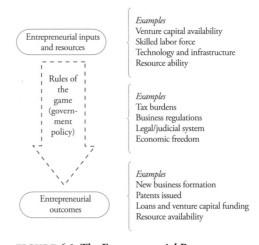

FIGURE 6.1: The Entrepreneurial Process

vorable, increasing the inputs will generally have little impact on the entrepreneurial outcomes. For example, many governments have attempted to promote entrepreneurship and economic growth through massive increases in funding for education and infrastructure. These investments, however, will fail to produce better outcomes when there is an improper and unproductive institutional environment. Consider an analogy of baking a cake by placing the ingredients in an oven. Placing more ingredients in the oven will fail to produce more cake if the oven is not working. Like a cake, a country's economic outcomes are determined by both the inputs to the process (the ingredients) and the policies that set the rules of the game under which the economy operates (the oven).

A growing, vibrant economy depends on entrepreneurs discovering, evaluating, and exploiting opportunities to create new goods and services. The rate at which entrepreneurs undertake such actions is dependent upon the rules of the game, which are consonant with economic freedom. The ability of entrepreneurs to act upon their insights into what customers want without interference from government is at the heart of economic progress. The speed at which ideas are brought to market and labeled as successes or failures is important to economic well-being not only because of the rewards associated with the successes, but also because the quick punishment of business failures frees up productive resources for new ventures. A strong and entrepreneurial economy will not only give entrepreneurs the freedom to try out their ideas in the marketplace, but will give them the freedom to fail as well. New goods and services come into existence because entrepreneurs are always putting new combinations of resources to the market test. A virtually unlimited number of new combinations is possible at any point in time. Successful combinations of resources will be rewarded with economic profits, and unsuccessful combinations will be met with losses. Profits and losses are how a market economy quickly sorts through the new resource combinations discovered by entrepreneurs.

Government intervention into the affairs of entrepreneurs—for example, in an attempt to help save failing businesses—is detrimental to economic growth. A failing business has been told by the profit and loss system that it is wasting resources, since its products cannot be sold at a price above the opportunity cost of those resources. By definition, a failing business is reducing wealth, but its failure is essential to the economic process of trial and error. Attempts by government officials to help struggling companies are antithetical to economic progress because they keep resources tied up in ventures that have failed the market test. A slowing of the rate at which resources are freed up to be used elsewhere in the economy prevents new combinations that may lead to future progress from coming into existence.

This point highlights a main difference between the process view of entrepreneurial outcomes (illustrated in Figure 6.1) and the more activist view of promoting entrepreneurship held by many policymakers. Although policymakers may lament the large number of new ventures that go out of business and use this as a justification for policies to help reduce the number business failures, the process approach suggests that what is important is rather to create an environment that maximizes the number of attempts—new business startups. In a robust, thriving economy, many new things will be attempted, and many of these will not be worthwhile ideas. A thriving economy has both a large number of new startups and a large number of failures.

Governments also attempt to promote entrepreneurship by creating state-run venture funds to help finance new entrepreneurial startups. The incentives faced by these government-run funds, however, are very different than those faced by private venture capital firms. Although different entrepreneurs have different motivations that drive them to bring products to market, their ultimate success or failure in obtaining private financing is determined by whether their product can sell for a price that is above the opportunity cost of the resources employed in its production. Government officials in charge of handing out low-interest loans to struggling entrepreneurs have other interests in mind besides economic progress. For one thing, they are concerned about *where* a new business is located. In the United States, state economic development officials expend considerable resources to keep certain employers afloat in particular geographic areas, or to prevent them from moving to other areas with lower resource costs. Government-run venture funds also tend to be more risk averse than private venture firms, so they tend to "skim the cream" of the new ideas, leaving a weaker investment pool for the private venture capital firms.

Government interventions driven by interest-group politics reduce economic freedom and distort entrepreneurial decision making in a way that is not insignificant. An economic analysis of government suggests that policymakers will push entrepreneurs toward activities that have clearly defined benefits, with little regard for other concerns. A good example is how state economic development offices frequently issue press releases regarding new firms that have been attracted to the state and the number of new jobs created. What is ignored, however, is the effect that a large and active state government intent on picking winners and losers has on small, local entrepreneurs who, with enough luck, might grow into similarly large businesses. For example, in 1999 the state of Michigan offered $27.8 million to the outdoor sporting goods outfitter Cabela's to locate in Dundee, Michigan (LaFaive, 2002). The number of incentives offered to the more than one thousand other sporting goods stores already located in Michigan? Zero.

Even setting aside that government officials often ignore the effect of their "assistance" on other parts of the economy, the evidence suggests that they often make bad choices. On the rare occasions when outside observers check to see if the jobs promised have been created and if growth has occurred, they often find no effect. In an in-depth study of the Ohio Department of Development (ODD), Gabe and Kraybill (2002) studied the impact of ODD tax incentives and found that firms receiving tax incentives to expand had nearly eleven fewer jobs two years after receiving the grant. They found evidence that firms drastically overestimated future job growth in an effort to win tax incentives and that public officials did little independent verification of the accuracy of estimated employment growth because they were more concerned with the benefits accruing from increased "bragging rights."

This discussion should not be taken to mean that entrepreneurs do not make mistakes, because it is obvious that they do. We are all limited in our knowledge about the world around us because of our own mental faculties and the costs of acquiring information. No matter how smart an individual is, he or she can make mistakes. The argument in favor of creating an environment conducive to entrepreneurial action is that we need markets to aggregate dispersed information about the efficacy of a new product into market prices and ultimately into profits and losses. A thriving economy depends on giving entrepreneurs the freedom to try their own ideas, without approval from anyone else, and then letting the profit and loss mechanisms of the marketplace assess the idea once the product is developed. This is one reason why entrepreneurship is stifled in developing countries, where starting a new business requires navigating a years-long process that involves convincing layers of government officials that the idea is worthwhile before an entrepreneur can get the go-ahead to open a new business (de Soto, 2000).

Government regulations are also one of the largest constraints on entrepreneurs in the United States. Although it is fairly easy to start some businesses, regulations frequently prevent entrepreneurs from satisfying consumer wants. Dranias (2006) highlights the absurd and/or protectionist regulations that prevent potential entrepreneurs from reaching their goals. For example, in Minneapolis you need to have a government-issued license to hang a sign. Individuals wanting to become manicurists have to take almost double the hours of training that a paramedic does in order to legally operate. Barbers, plumbers, and taxi drivers are also highly regulated relative to their potential harm to consumers. A similar pattern of regulatory barriers to entrepreneurship could be identified in virtually every country of the world.

There are two big drawbacks to using selective taxes, tax credits, and subsidies to centrally plan entrepreneurial activities. First, by arbitrarily making some industries more (or less) profitable than others, these measures distort economic activity in the private sector. For growth, market-determined returns (profit rates) and market prices should guide these investments, not government taxes and subsidies. Economic freedom is about a fair and level playing field for everyone. This does not mean lower overall levels of taxes and regulations, but it does mean ones that are applied equally to everyone. Second, and perhaps more importantly, these selective taxes and subsidies result in more private entrepreneurial resources being devoted toward capturing them. When it becomes more profitable for entrepreneurs to invest time and resources in lobbying the political process for these favors, we end up with more of these types of destructive activities and less productive activity. Firms begin competing to obtain government tax breaks and subsidies rather than competing with each other in the marketplace. They spend more time lobbying and relatively less time producing.

In the next two sections, we put this model of the entrepreneurial process to the test. We first present empirical evidence of the positive relationship between economic freedom and entrepreneurship, using data from the United States. We use two different definitions of entrepreneurship and analyze two different time periods. We then follow the U.S. evidence with data from the international arena.

EVIDENCE FROM THE UNITED STATES

To get a picture of the general relationship between the institutions of economic freedom and entrepreneurship, we begin by looking at cross-sectional variation within the United States. Our measure of economic freedom is the Economic Freedom of North America (EFNA) index. This index measures the extent of the restrictions that governments place on economic freedom within the U.S. states and Canadian provinces. For example, it measures the extent to which citizens are free to acquire, use, and dispose of property so long as they do not violate the rights of other individuals (Karabegovic and McMahon, 2006). The economic freedom score of each U.S. state from the most recent edition of the EFNA index is provided in Appendix Table 1.

The three core components of the EFNA index are size of government, takings and discriminatory taxation, and labor market freedom. The index is constructed on a scale of 0 to 10, with 0 being the absence of economic freedom and 10 being an extremely high level of economic freedom. Since

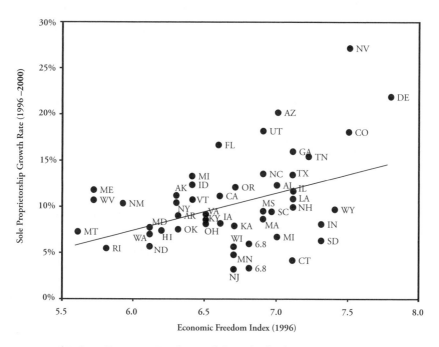

FIGURE 6.2. State Economic Freedom and Growth of Sole Proprietorships (1996–2000)

the EFNA index compares states and provinces to one another, it is a relative ranking in that it does not tell how economically "free" Wyoming is in an absolute sense, but rather how "free" Wyoming is compared to Connecticut. At the same time, however, the index is constructed to be stable over time so that changes in economic freedom can be properly evaluated.

Our first measure of entrepreneurship is the growth in the number of sole proprietors from 1996 to 2000. Figure 6.2 shows the relationship between the level of each state's economic freedom in 1996 and the growth rate of sole proprietors in the state from 1996 to 2000.[4] A simple regression line fitted to the plotted data shows the positive relationship between economic freedom in 1996 and subsequent growth in the number of sole proprietorships.

To further verify this relationship, we gathered additional data on the fifty states related to other factors that have previously been shown to be correlated with entrepreneurial activity. To deal with the problem of causality (i.e., that entrepreneurship might lead to economic freedom as well as freedom leading to entrepreneurship), we used the initial 1996 value to explain a state's subsequent growth in entrepreneurship over the next five years, as well as controlling for other causes of economic growth. The ordinary least squares (OLS) results, presented in Table 6.1, show a positive and statistically significant relationship between a state's economic freedom and its growth in entrepreneurial activity as measured by the sole proprietorship growth rate.

Although the sole proprietorship growth rate is the most common measure of entrepreneurship used in the literature, the Kaufmann Foundation has recently released a new measure of entrepreneurial activity in a new annual report, the *Kauffmann Index of Entrepreneurial Activity*.[5] The Kaufmann index is a new and broader measure of entrepreneurial activity than sole proprietorships because it includes all types of new businesses. Because it is so new, this measure has received very little attention in the literature.

Again, we performed OLS regression analysis using the change in the Kauffman entrepreneurial score as the dependent variable, similar to the approach used with the sole proprietorship data. In addition to including the EFNA measure of institutional quality, we included other standard control variables for which data was available over the sample period. The results are presented in Table 6.2.

TABLE 6.1. Determinants of State Entrepreneurial Growth, 1996–2000

Dependent Variable: State Sole Proprietor Growth Rate 996–2000		
Independent Variable	Coefficient	
Constant	21.011	
	(0.52)	
State Economic Freedom index	3.668	***
	(3.14)	
% of population with a high school diploma	0.033	
	(0.21)	
% of population with a college degree	-0.422	**
	(2.32)	
% of population that is male	-0.508	
	(0.78)	
% of population that is white	0.103	
	(1.52)	
Population median age	-0.949	***
	(2.27)	
Unemployment rate	0.731	
	(1.22)	
% service employment	0.595	***
	(3.22)	
Property crime rate	-0.002	**
	(2.27)	
Observations	50	
R-squared	0.56	

Note: Absolute value of t-statistics in parentheses.

* indicates significance at the 10% level, ** at the 5% level, and *** at the 1% level.

TABLE 6.2. Determinants of U.S. State Entrepreneurial Activity as Measured by the Kauffman Index

Dependent Variable: Change in Kauffman Entrepreneurship index, 2004–05	
Independent Variable	Coefficient
State Economic Freedom index, 2003	4.7346 **
	(2.24)
% of population that is Hispanic, 2005	-0.0230
	(0.21)
% of population with a college degree or higher	0.4314
	1.76
Gross domestic product per capita, 2005 (in thousands)	-0.0549
	(0.27)
Population density, 2005 (in thousands)	0.7820
	(0.13)
% of population that is male, 2005	-0.0594
	(0.03)
Median age of population, 2005	0.8311
	(1.27)
Unemployment rate, 2005	0.1312
	(0.12)
Constant	-80.8634
	(0.63)
Number of observations	50
R-squared	0.28

Note: Absolute value of t-statistics in parentheses.

* indicates significance at the 10% level, ** at the 5% level, and *** at the 1% level.

These results provide additional support for a positive relationship between economic freedom and entrepreneurship. Calculated at the mean, the coefficient on economic freedom from Table 6.2 suggests that if West Virginia were to increase the quality of its institutions to the level of Massachusetts, its change in entrepreneurial activity would be nearly 5 percent higher (about two-thirds of a standard deviation).

Finally, a recent paper by Campbell and Rodgers (2007) confirms the results presented here, using total net new firm creation as the measure of entrepreneurial activity. They find that economic freedom (as measured by the EFNA index) is significantly related positively and statistically to net new firm creation. An increase of one standard deviation in the average state's EFNA score is associated with a 0.34 percent increase in total net new businesses. Campbell and Rogers compare the effect of economic freedom on new firm creation with other policy variables, such as commercial lending, and conclude that increasing economic freedom is the best way to stimulate entrepreneurship.

INTERNATIONAL EVIDENCE

A similar positive relationship between economic freedom and entrepreneurship can be seen internationally. Historically, measuring entrepreneurship internationally was difficult, as there were limited cross-national measures of entrepreneurship or new business formation. In 1999, however, a nonprofit research consortium called the Global Entrepreneurship Monitor (GEM) began to make high-quality data on entrepreneurship available to researchers and policymakers. The consortium annually conducts an extensive survey in a large number of countries. The 2007 GEM survey will include forty-three countries, most of which are developed nations such as the United States, the United Kingdom, France, South Africa, Germany, Finland, and South Korea. Most notably, less developed countries (LDCs) are not included, which is why the other chapters in this book are important.

The availability of the GEM data makes it easier to see if a positive relationship exists between economic freedom and entrepreneurial activity at the international level.[6] In investigating this relationship, we use as our primary measure of entrepreneurial activity what the GEM survey calls total entrepreneurial activity, or TEA. This variable measures the number of individuals out of one hundred who are in the start-up phase of starting a company or are managing a business that is younger than 42 months. The variable is expressed per 100 individuals 18 to 64, and thus in our sample of 21 OECD member countries the sample ranges from 1.81 to 14.52.

We use the Economic Freedom of the World (EFW) index for the year 2002 from Gwartney and Lawson (2007) as our measure of how consistent a country's policies and institutions are with economic freedom. The EFW index is constructed to measure the quality of a country's policies and institutions in five areas: size of government; legal structure and security of property rights; access to sound money; freedom to trade internationally; and regulation of capital, labor, and business. Gwartney and Lawson annually construct the index using data from third-party international sources such as the World Bank and International Monetary Fund. The rankings vary from 0 (no freedom) to 10 (complete economic freedom). In our sample of OECD countries, the EFW score ranges from 5.5 to 8.2. Appendix Table 2 lists the most recent EFW scores for each of the OECD countries included here.

Figure 6.3 is a first look at the question of whether a positive relationship exists between economic freedom and entrepreneurship as measured by the GEM data. In the figure, entrepreneurial activity is on the *y*-axis and economic freedom is on the *x*-axis. There is clearly a strong and positive relationship between these variables in the raw data. In order to test this

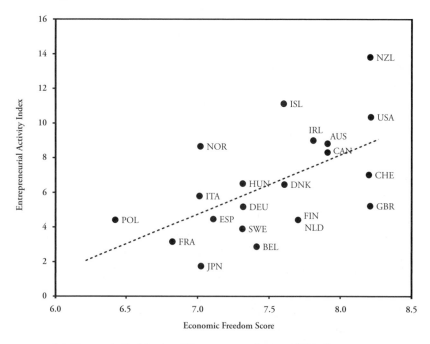

FIGURE 6.3. Economic Freedom and Entrepreneurship in OECD Countries, 2002

relationship more thoroughly, we turned to statistical analysis. We gathered data on other factors that have been found to influence entrepreneurship, such as the percentage of males in a country, the median age, per capita GDP, the unemployment rate, the availability of domestic credit, net foreign direct investment per capita, and a measure of political stability within the country from the World Bank. Table 6.3 presents the OLS results.

TABLE 6.3. Economic Freedom and Entrepreneurship in OECD Countries: OLS Results

Dependent Variable: Total Entrepreneurial Activity

Independent Variable	Coefficient	
Constant	-52.225	
	(1.03)	
Economic Freedom index	2.219	*
	(2.02)	
% of population that is male	1.399	
	(1.43)	
Median age	-0.647	***
	(3.09)	
GDP per capita (in thousands)	0.011	
	(0.10)	
Unemployment rate	-0.121	
	(0.66)	
Domestic credit availability	-0.005	
	(0.30)	
Foreign capital	0.002	**
	(2.40)	
Government political stability	0.496	
	(0.30)	
Observations	21	
R2	0.81	

Absolute t-statistics in parentheses.

* indicates significance at the 10% level; ** at the 5% level and *** at the 1% level.

The results are fairly straightforward. The relationship between economic freedom and total entrepreneurial activity is positive and statistically significant. A 1-point increase in a country's economic freedom score is associated with an increase in the number of entrepreneurs per 100 individuals of 2.219. That represents two-thirds of a standard deviation increase in the TEA of a country.

In a recent paper, Bjørnskov and Foss (forthcoming) also use the GEM data and the EFW index to examine the relationship between economic freedom and entrepreneurship. They disaggregate the EFW index into each of its five component parts and find that the size of government and the quality of monetary policy are the key determinants of entrepreneurship. Bjørnskov and Foss also break entrepreneurship down into "opportunity entrepreneurship" and "necessity entrepreneurship." Opportunity entrepreneurship occurs when individuals become entrepreneurs because of a particular opportunity that they want to act upon, while necessity entrepreneurship occurs when individuals become entrepreneurs because they have few other options. They find that when the level of taxation and transfers and subsides go up, opportunity entrepreneurship goes down. In addition, as government's share of total consumption increases, necessity entrepreneurship falls.

Economic growth is not only about success; it is also about failure. Entrepreneurs need the freedom to try various combinations that they believe customers will want, and policymakers need to allow the profit and loss system to send the appropriate signals as to whether or not a venture is worthwhile. Thus, economic freedom is about having the freedom to fail as well as the freedom to succeed. Any attempts by government to slow or direct

TABLE 6.4. Economic Freedom, Entrepreneurial Activity, and Business Failure

Economic Freedom	Total Entrepreneurial Activity Index	Business Failures per 10,000 Firms
Top half of sample (half with the most economic freedom)	7.51	116.70
Bottom half of sample (half with the least economic freedom)	6.74	67.58

Note: A difference in means tests shows both to be significantly different at a 5% level.

the churn of the marketplace will slow economic progress, not advance it. The quick discarding of bad ideas is as essential to economic growth as the introduction of good ideas, because those with successful ideas have often failed before. Although the statistics may show fewer business closures, because of government intervention, what is not seen is the fact that resources have not been freed to start new ventures that lead to economic growth.

TABLE 6.5. Economic Freedom and Patent and Trademark Activity in Transition Economies, 1995–2000

Dependent Variable: Patent and Trademark Applications per 1,000 Inhabitants

Independent Variable	Coefficient	
Constant	0.76	*
	(1.80)	
GDP per capita (in constant $)	0.31	
	(1.74)	
Infrastructure Reform Index	-0.19	
	(0.04)	
Credit availability (% of loans of GDP)	0.13	
	(0.50)	
Nonperforming loans (% of total)	0.43	
	(0.20)	
Government corruption	0.38	
	(1.07)	
EFW index	0.23	*
	(1.91)	
Net foreign direct investment (% of GDP)	0.14	**
	(2.27)	
Import tariffs (% of GDP)	0.91	
	(0.68)	
Inflation rate	0.25	
	(0.02)	
Observations	52	

Note: Heteroskedasticity corrected t-statistics in parentheses.

To get at the relationship between economic freedom, business failure, and entrepreneurship, we calculated the average number of business failures per 10,000 firms for each country in our sample. We then split the sample into two equal groups: those countries with a level of economic fredom that is above the median for the sample and those with below average economic freedom. Table 6.4 shows our analysis of the relationship between economic freedom, business failures, and total entrepreneurial activity. The table shows that the countries in the sample that have a high level of economic freedom had not only a higher rate of entrepreneurial activity, but also a business failure rate that was nearly twice as high as the countries in the group with less economic freedom! Giving entrepreneurs the freedom to fail is essential to economic progress.

As a final look at the relationship between freedom and entrepreneurial activity, Table 6.5 looks at the effect of economic freedom on patent and trademark activity for a sample of ten transitional economies.[7] Looking at the number of patent and trademark applications from 1995 to 2000 gives some idea of the role that a transition toward economic freedom has on one form of entrepreneurial activity available for that pre-GEM period. The results of the random effects model with group and period effects are consistent with a positive relationship between economic freedom (as measured by the EFW index) and the level of entrepreneurial innovation in a society.

Just as was the case for the U.S. states, the institutions of freedom are associated with entrepreneurship and innovation at the international level—for developed, developing, and transitional economies.

CONCLUSION

The policy implications of the analyses described here are clear. To promote entrepreneurship, the better path, rather than focusing on expanding government programs, such as subsidized loans, workforce education, and programs aimed at increasing "entrepreneurial inputs," is through institutional reform that constrains or minimizes government's role, lowering the return to unproductive entrepreneurship. Government programs too often encourage entrepreneurial individuals to devote effort toward figuring out how to obtain the transfers, rather than toward satisfying consumers and creating wealth.

Government's most important role in promoting a thriving entrepreneurial economy—one that generates prosperity and growth—is to protect property rights, enforce contracts, and provide a stable monetary environment. Well-meaning attempts to centrally plan the entrepreneurial process, through subsidies and tax incentives, are counterproductive, as they encourage more unproductive entrepreneurial activities at the expense of productive entrepreneurial activities. Economies that get their institutions "right" will be able to make the most of the inputs at their disposal, creating economic growth and prosperity for their citizens.

APPENDIX TABLE 1. Economic Freedom in the United States, 2003

Rank	State	Score	Rank	State	Score
1	Delaware	8.6	26	Pennsylvania	6.9
2	Colorado	7.7	27	Wisconsin	6.9
3	North Carolina	7.7	28	Louisiana	6.8
4	Georgia	7.6	29	Michigan	6.8
5	Nevada	7.6	30	South Carolina	6.8
6	Texas	7.6	31	Idaho	6.7
7	New Hampshire	7.5	32	Kentucky	6.7
8	Utah	7.5	33	Ohio	6.7
9	Indiana	7.4	34	Washington	6.7
10	Tennessee	7.4	35	Maryland	6.6
11	Massachusetts	7.3	36	Oregon	6.6
12	Virginia	7.3	37	Alabama	6.5
13	Arizona	7.2	38	Alaska	6.4
14	Illinois	7.2	39	Arkansas	6.4
15	Nebraska	7.2	40	New York	6.4
16	South Dakota	7.2	41	Vermont	6.4
17	Minnesota	7.1	42	Oklahoma	6.3
18	Connecticut	7.0	43	North Dakota	6.2
19	Florida	7.0	44	Rhode Island	6.2
20	Kansas	7.0	45	Hawaii	6.1
21	Missouri	7.0	46	Maine	5.9
22	Wyoming	7.0	47	Mississippi	5.8
23	California	6.9	48	Montana	5.7
24	Iowa	6.9	49	New Mexico	5.7
25	New Jersey	6.9	50	West Virginia	5.3

Source: Karabegovic and McMahon (2006).

APPENDIX TABLE 2. Economic Freedom in Select OECD Countries, 2005

Rank (out of 141 Ranked Countries)	Country	Score
3	New Zealand	8.5
4	Switzerland	8.3
5	Canada	8.1
5	United Kingdom	8.1
5	United States	8.1
9	Australia	7.9
9	Ireland	7.9
11	Finland	7.8
11	Iceland	7.8
15	Denmark	7.7
15	Netherlands	7.7
18	Germany	7.6
22	Hungary	7.5
22	Japan	7.5
22	Norway	7.5
22	Sweden	7.5
38	Belgium	7.2
44	Spain	7.1
52	France	7.0
52	Italy	7.0
56	Poland	6.9

Source: Gwartney and Lawson (2007).

NOTES

1. For a short discussion of the concept of economic freedom, see Gwartney, Lawson, and Clark (2005).
2. For an excellent overview of this research, see Berggren (2003).
3. This section is based on ideas originally developed in Hall and Sobel (2006). See the original work for additional data and references.
4. This section is based on ideas originally developed in Kreft and Sobel (2005). See the original work for additional data and references. The measure of state economic freedom employed includes the impact of federal, state, and local policy.
5. This section is based on ideas originally developed in Hall and Sobel (2007). See the original work for additional data and references.
6. This section is based on ideas originally developed in Sobel, Clark, and Lee (forthcoming). See the original work for additional data and references.
7. This section is based on ideas originally developed in Ovaska and Sobel (2005). See the original work for additional data and references.

REFERENCES

Baumol, William J., 1990. "Entrepreneurship: Productive, Unproductive, and Destructive." *Journal of Political Economy* 98, no. 5: 893–921.

Baumol, William J., 1993. *Entrepreneurship, Management, and the Structure of Payoffs.* Cambridge, MA: MIT Press.

Baumol, William J., 2002. *The Free-Market Innovation Machine: Analyzing the Growth Miracle of Capitalism.* Princeton: Princeton University Press.

Berggren, Niclas. 2003. The Benefits of Economic Freedom: A Survey. *The Independent Review* 8, no. 2 (Fall): 193–211.

Bjørnskov, Christian, and Nicolai J. Foss. Forthcoming. Economic Freedom and Entrepreneurial Activity: Some Cross Country Evidence. *Public Choice.*

Campbell, Noel D., and Tammy M. Rodgers. 2007. Economic Freedom and Net Business Formation. *Cato Journal* 27, no. 1 (Winter): 23–36.

Cole, Julio H. 2003. The Contribution of Economic Freedom to World Economic Growth, 1980–99. *Cato Journal* 23, no. 2 (Fall): 189–198.

De Soto, H. 2000. *The Mystery of Capital: Why Capitalism Triumphs in the West and Fails Everywhere Else.* London: Black Swan.

Dranias, Nick. 2006. *The Land of 10,000 Lakes Drowns Entrepreneurs in Regulations.* Washington: Institute for Justice.

Farr, W. Ken, Richard A. Lord, and J. Larry Wolfenbarger. 1998. Economic Freedom, Political Freedom, and Economic Well-Being: A Causality Analysis. *Cato Journal* 18, no. 2 (Fall): 247–262.

Gabe, Todd M., and David S. Kraybill. 2002. The Effects of State Economic Development Incentives on Employment Growth of Establishments. *Journal of Regional Science* 42, no. 4: 703–730.

Gwartney, James D., and Robert A. Lawson. 2007. *Economic Freedom of the World: 2007 Annual Report.* Vancouver: The Fraser Institute.

Gwartney, James D., Robert A. Lawson, and J. R. Clark. 2005. Economic Freedom of the World, 2002. *The Independent Review* 9, no. 4 (Spring): 573–593.

Gwartney, James D., Robert A. Lawson, and Randall G. Holcombe. 1999. Economic Freedom and the Environment for Economic Growth. *Journal of Institutional and Theoretical Economics* 155, no. 4 (December): 1–21.

Hall, Joshua C., and Russell S. Sobel. 2006. *Public Policy and Entrepreneurship.* Kansas University Center for Applied Economics, Technical Report 06–0717, July.

Hall, Joshua C., and Russell S. Sobel. 2007. *Institutions, Entrepreneurship, and Regional Differences in Economic Growth.* Mimeo.

Henderson, Jason. 2002. Building the Rural Economy with High-Growth Entrepreneurs. *Federal Reserve Bank of Kansas City Economic Review* 87, no. 3: 45–70.

Holcombe, Randall. 2003. Entrepreneurship and Economic Progress. *Quarterly Journal of Austrian Economics* 6, no. 3 (Fall): 3–26.

Karabegovic, Amela, and Fred McMahon. 2006. *Economic Freedom of North America: 2006 Annual Report.* Vancouver, BC: Fraser Institute.

Kirzner, Israel M. 1973. *Competition and Entrepreneurship.* Chicago: University of Chicago Press.

Kreft, Steven F., and Russell S. Sobel. 2005. Public Policy, Entrepreneurship, and Economic Freedom. *Cato Journal* 25, no. 3 (Fall): 595–616.

LaFaive, Michael. 2002. A Tale of Two Sporting Goods Stores. *Michigan Privatization Report* no. 2002–03 (Summer): 8–9.

Lee, Dwight R. 1991. The Seeds of Entrepreneurship. *Journal of Private Enterprise* 7, no. 1 (Fall): 20–35.

Minniti, Maria. 1999. Entrepreneurial Activity and Economic Growth. *Global Business and Economics Review* 1, no. 1: 31–42.

Ovaska, Tomi, and Russell S. Sobel. 2005. Entrepreneurship in Post-Socialist Economies. *Journal of Private Enterprise* 21, no. 1 (Fall): 8–28.

Powell, Benjamin. 2003. Economic Freedom and Growth: The Case of the Celtic Tiger. *Cato Journal* 22, no. 3 (Winter): 431–448.

Reynolds, Paul D., Michael Hay, and S. Michael Camp. 1999. *Global Entrepreneurship Monitor.* Kansas City: Kauffman Center for Entrepreneurial Leadership.

Salgado-Banda, Héctor. 2007. Entrepreneurship and Economic Growth: An Empirical Analysis. *Journal of Developmental Entrepreneurship* 12, no. 1 (April): 3–29.

Sobel, Russell S., J. R. Clark, and Dwight R. Lee. Forthcoming. Freedom, Barriers to Entry, Entrepreneurship, and Economic Progress. *Review of Austrian Economics.*

Zacharakis, Andrew L., William D. Bygrave, and Dean A. Shepherd. 2000. *Global Entrepreneurship Monitor: National Entrepreneurship Assessment: United States of America.* Kansas City: Kauffman Center for Entrepreneurial Leadership.

About the Editor and Contributors

ABOUT THE EDITOR

Alvaro Vargas Llosa is Senior Fellow and Director of the Center on Global Prosperity at the Independent Institute. He is a nationally syndicated columnist with the Washington Post Writers Group and the author of *Liberty for Latin America* (Farrar, Straus and Giroux), which obtained the Sir Anthony Fisher International Memorial Award in 2005.

A native of Peru, Mr. Vargas Llosa received his B.S.C. in international history and an M.A. from the London School of Economics. Previously the host of *Planeta 3*, a weekly television program that aired throughout Latin America, he was the news director at RCN Radio as well as London correspondent for *ABC*, Spain's daily newspaper.

He has been a board member of the Miami Herald Publishing Company and op-ed page editor and columnist at the *Miami Herald*.

In addition to his weekly column, he regularly contributes articles to the *Wall Street Journal*, *New York Times*, *Foreign Policy*, and *New Republic* and is a frequent commentator on international news networks such as the BBC and Univision.

The recipient of several prestigious awards including the Puerto Rican Parliament Award for the Defense of Freedom (1997), the A.I.R. Award for Best Current Affairs Radio Show in Florida (1998), the Peruvian Association of Fishermen Award for the Defense of Freedom (2000), the Association of Ibero-American Journalists Award for Freedom of Expression (2003), and the Juan Bautista Alberdi Award for Defense of Freedom in the Western Hemisphere (2006); Mr. Vargas Llosa was most recently appointed Young Global Leader by the World Economic Forum in Davos (2007).

ABOUT THE CONTRIBUTORS

June Arunga was born in Kenya in 1981. She has a law degree from the University of Buckingham and is now in the film industry as founder and president of Open Quest Media LLC. Ms. Arunga speaks regularly on globalization and development issues.

She wrote and presented the BBC documentary on Africa, *The Devil's Footpath*. She previously studied law at the University of Nairobi in Kenya and directed Youth Programs at the Inter-Region Economic Network-(IREN-Kenya).

In the summer of 2003 Ms. Arunga served as an intern at the United Nations in New York City. She was also featured on a brief *20/20* segment with John Stossel on the WTO. She is also a Member of the Board of Advisors for Global Envision, a pro-market organisation in the United States and Grassroot Free markets, a public policy non-profit in Hawaii.

She holds the following fellowships: H. B. Earhart Fellow; Fellow, Inter-Region Economic Network (IREN-KENYA)—a Kenyan economics think tank; Fellow, International Policy Network (IPN)—a public policy charity based in London; Senior Fellow, Economic Thinking; and E Pluribus Unum Films of Seattle, Washington.

Thompson Ayodele is the Director of Initiative for Public Policy Analysis, a Public Policy think tank promoting the institutions of free society based in Lagos, Nigeria. He attended Obafemi Awolowo University, Ile-Ife, Nigeria, where he got a degree in humanities, and Kwara State Polytechnic, Ilorin, Nigeria, where he also received his Diploma in Law. Prior to his work with IPPA Nigeria, he was a journalist with *The Comet*.

Mr. Ayodele was Deputy Country Director, Students In Free Enterprise (SIFE) Nigeria from 2002 to 2006. He is currently a coordinator of Malaria Free Zones, a Hedge Fund/Free Africa Foundation Project, in Nigeria, Cameroon, and Benin Republic.

Mr. Ayodele is an avid writer and has written several articles. His articles have been published in the *New York Times*, *Financial Times*, *Australia Financial Review*, *This Day Nigeria*, *Daily Independent Nigeria*, and *New Age Newspapers*. He is the author of the upcoming publication: "Why Informal Business Thrives in Nigeria."

Mr. Ayodele has traveled widely and is a Fellow of the International Policy Network, London.

Scott A. Beaulier is assistant professor of economics at Beloit College, Wisconsin, and a Fellow at the Center on Entrepreneurial Innovation at the Independent Institute. He received his Ph.D. from George Mason University. He has conducted field research in Botswana and authored numerous articles on Botswana's economic development.

Most recently he contributed the chapter "Look Botswana: No Hands!" to *Making Poor Nations Rich: Entrepreneurship and the Process of Economic Development* (Stanford University Press in association with the Independent Institute; Benjamin Powell, editor). Another paper (co-authored with Bryan Caplan of George Mason University), "Behavioral Economics and Perverse Effects of the Welfare State" was published in the Fall, 2007 issue of *Kyklos*.

Daniel Córdova earned a Ph.D. in Economics at the Grenoble University, France, in 1994. His Ph.D. thesis was a comparative study of the South Korean and Peruvian paths of development. After his studies Dr. Córdova became an intellectual entrepreneur.

He was the first chairman of the Board of Procapitales, the Peruvian Association to Promote de Capital Market (2001–2002) and the first chief executive officer of Comexperu, the Peruvian Association for External Trade (1997–1999). He spent three years as chief cinancial officer of Milpo, a Peruvian mining company, from 1999 to 2002. Dr. Córdova has been chairman of the Board of El Banco de Comercio (2004), vice chairman of the Board of Copeinca (2004–2006), and member of the Board of Osiptel, the Peruvian Telecom Regulation Agency (2004–2005).

Currently, he serves as Dean of the School of Economics at the Peruvian University of Applied Sciences (UPC), a school he launched in 2003. He recently founded the Invertir Institute a not-for-profit institution that promotes entrepreneurship in Peru. He is member of the Board of three Peruvian Companies (Acetesa, Braedt, and Conductores y Cables).

Dr. Córdova, is author of several academic articles on institutional economics, economic development, and corporate governance. He is co-author of a *Handbook of Corporate Governance for Family Businesses* and author of a book on Public Utilities Privatization and its effect on prices and quality services. Dr. Córdova is also Director of the *Invertir Monthly* magazine and columnist at *El Comercio*, an important Peruvian newspaper.

Gabriel Gasave is Research Analyst with the Center on Global Prosperity at the Independent Institute and Research Fellow with Fundación Atlas 1853 in Buenos Aires. He studied political science at Lock Haven State College in Pennsylvania, received his master's degree in economics and business administration from the Graduate School of Economics and Business Administration (ESEADE) in Buenos Aires, and his law degree from the University of Buenos Aires. He has taught economics and law at the Argentina Chamber of Commerce, University of Buenos Aires, San Jose State University in California, and Instituto Ecuatoriano de Economía Política (Ecuador). In addition, Mr. Gasave has been Academic Secretary for ESEADE, commentator on Cable Channel Política and Economía (Buenos Aires), consultant for Junior Achievement Argentina, and an intern at the Reason Foundation in Los Angeles.

Joshua C. Hall is assistant professor of economics at Beloit College, Wisconsin. He has published numerous scholarly articles in journals such as the *Journal of Labor Research*, *Journal of Economic Education*, *Cato Journal*, and the *Atlantic Economic Journal*. In addition, Hall has authored several book chapters and over a dozen policy reports for state-based think tanks. He received his Ph.D. in economics from West Virginia University in 2007.

Gustavo Lazzari was born in Buenos Aires, Argentina, in 1966. He has studied Politics and Economics at ESEADE and has a Bachelor's Degree in Economics from Universidad Católica Argentina. He is Public Policy Director at Fundación Atlas 1853 and teaches World Economy and Argentinean Economy at the Argentine Chamber of Commerce College. He also has been Associated Professor of Foundations of Economics at the Universidad de Buenos Aires and Principles of Economics at ESEADE.

Martín Simonetta is Executive Director of Fundación Atlas 1853 (Argentina). In 2004 he has elected as "The Outstanding Young Person of Argentina (TOYP)" by the Junior Chamber International and received the "Animarse a Más" (Strive to Excel) award from PepsiCo.

In 1999 he received a British Chevening Scholarship, granted by the British Embassy in Buenos Aires, the British Council and the Fundación Antorchas, for developing a research project at the Institute of Economic Affairs (IEA), London, UK. He also was recognized by scholarships from the Friedrich Naumann Foundation (Gümmersbach, Germany, 2004), Fundación para el Análisis y los Estudios Sociales (FAES, Madrid and Brussels, 2004) and the Foundation for Economic Education (FEE, Irvington-on-Hudson, NY).

Together with Gustavo Lazzari, he edited the books *Public Policy Solutions for a Country in Crisis* (2003), *Successful Market Oriented Policies* (2006) and *Freedom Heroes* (2007). He has a strong presence in the Argentine media.

He holds a bachelor's degree in International Relations (Universidad del Salvador) and an M.A in International Economic Policy (Universidad de Belgrano). Martín is currently professor at the Universidad de Belgrano and the Argentine Chamber of Commerce.

Russell S. Sobel is professor of economics and holder of the James Clark Coffman Distinguished Chair in Entrepreneurial Studies at West Virginia University. He has published over 75 books and articles on economic policy, including a nationally best-selling college-level *Principles of Economics* textbook, and a book on West Virginia policy reform entitled *Unleashing Capitalism*. Dr. Sobel was the founding director of the West Virginia University Entrepreneurship Center, where he established the state's first collegiate business plan competition, helped in the formation of WVU's Business Incubator, and created a minor in entrepreneurship for WVU students.

In addition to his many appearances in West Virginia media, his research has also received national attention, including articles in the *New York Times*, *Wall Street Journal*, *Washington Post*, and *The Economist*, as well as appearances on CNBC, CSPAN, and the CBS Evening News. He has received numerous awards for both his teaching and research. Dr. Sobel gives lectures and teaches economic principles at various seminars across the country each year, including an annual course in economics for U.S. Congressional Staff and another for West Virginia K-12 schoolteachers. He received his Ph.D. in economics from Florida State University, and has been at West Virginia University since 1994.

Index

INDEPENDENT STUDIES IN POLITICAL ECONOMY

THE ACADEMY IN CRISIS: The Political Economy of Higher Education | *Ed. by John W. Sommer*

AGAINST LEVIATHAN: Government Power and a Free Society | *Robert Higgs*

ALIENATION AND THE SOVIET ECONOMY: The Collapse of the Socialist Era | *Paul Craig Roberts*

AMERICAN HEALTH CARE: Government, Market Processes and the Public Interest | *Ed. by Roger Feldman*

ANARCHY AND THE LAW: The Political Economy of Choice | *Ed. by Edward P. Stringham*

ANTITRUST AND MONOPOLY: Anatomy of a Policy Failure | *D. T. Armentano*

ARMS, POLITICS, AND THE ECONOMY: Historical and Contemporary Perspectives | *Ed. by Robert Higgs*

BEYOND POLITICS: Markets, Welfare and the Failure of Bureaucracy | *William Mitchell & Randy Simmons*

THE CAPITALIST REVOLUTION IN LATIN AMERICA | *Paul Craig Roberts & Karen Araujo*

THE CHALLENGE OF LIBERTY: Classical Liberalism Today | *Ed. by Robert Higgs & Carl P. Close*

CHANGING THE GUARD: Private Prisons and the Control of Crime | *Ed. by Alexander Tabarrok*

THE CHE GUEVARA MYTH AND THE FUTURE OF LIBERTY | *Alvaro Vargas Llosa*

CUTTING GREEN TAPE: Toxic Pollutants, Environmental Regulation and the Law | *Ed. by Richard Stroup & Roger E. Meiners*

DEPRESSION, WAR, AND COLD WAR: Studies in Political Economy | *Robert Higgs*

THE DIVERSITY MYTH: Multiculturalism and Political Intolerance on Campus | *David O. Sacks & Peter A. Thiel*

DRUG WAR CRIMES: The Consequences of Prohibition | *Jeffrey A. Miron*

ELECTRIC CHOICES: Deregulation and the Future of Electric Power | *Ed. by Andrew Kleit*

THE EMPIRE HAS NO CLOTHES: U.S. Foreign Policy Exposed | *Ivan Eland*

ENTREPRENEURIAL ECONOMICS: Bright Ideas from the Dismal Science | *Ed. by Alexander Tabarrok*

FAULTY TOWERS: Tenure and the Structure of Higher Education | *Ryan Amacher & Roger Meiners*

THE FOUNDERS' SECOND AMENDMENT | *Stephen P. Halbrook*

FREEDOM, FEMINISM, AND THE STATE | *Ed. by Wendy McElroy*

HAZARDOUS TO OUR HEALTH?: FDA Regulation of Health Care Products | *Ed. by Robert Higgs*

HOT TALK, COLD SCIENCE: Global Warming's Unfinished Debate | *S. Fred Singer*

JUDGE AND JURY: American Tort Law on Trial | *Eric Helland & Alex Tabarrok*

LIBERTY FOR LATIN AMERICA: How to Undo Five Hundred Years of State Oppression | *Alvaro Vargas Llosa*

LIBERTY FOR WOMEN: Freedom and Feminism in the Twenty-first Century | *Ed. by Wendy McElroy*

MAKING POOR NATIONS RICH: Entrepreneurship and the Process of Economic Development | *Ed. by Benjamin Powell*

MARKET FAILURE OR SUCCESS: The New Debate | *Ed. by Tyler Cowen & Eric Crampton*

MONEY AND THE NATION STATE: The Financial Revolution, Government, and the World Monetary System | *Ed. by Kevin Dowd & Richard H. Timberlake, Jr.*

NEITHER LIBERTY NOR SAFETY: Fear, Ideology, and the Growth of Government | *Robert Higgs & Carl P. Close*

OPPOSING THE CRUSADER STATE: Alternatives To Global Interventionism | *Ed. by Robert Higg & Carl P. Close*

OUT OF WORK: Unemployment and Government in Twentieth-Century America | *Richard K. Vedder & Lowell E. Gallaway*

PLOWSHARES AND PORK BARRELS: The Political Economy of Agriculture | *E. C. Pasour, Jr. & Randal R. Rucker*

A POVERTY OF REASON: Sustainable Development and Economic Growth | *Wilfred Beckerman*

PRIVATE RIGHTS & PUBLIC ILLUSIONS | *Tibor R. Machan*

RECLAIMING THE AMERICAN REVOLUTION: The Kentucky & Virginia Resolutions and Their Legacy | *William J. Watkins, Jr.*

REGULATION AND THE REAGAN ERA: Politics, Bureaucracy and the Public Interest | *Ed. by Roger Meiners & Bruce Yandle*

RESTORING FREE SPEECH AND LIBERTY ON CAMPUS | *Donald A. Downs*

RESURGENCE OF THE WARFARE STATE: The Crisis Since 9/11 | *Robert Higgs*

RE-THINKING GREEN: Alternatives to Environmental Bureaucracy | *Ed. by Robert Higgs & Carl P. Close*

SCHOOL CHOICES: True and False | *John Merrifield*

STRANGE BREW: Alcohol and Government Monopoly | *Douglas Glen Whitman*

STREET SMART: Competition, Entrepreneurship, and the Future of Roads | *Ed. by Gabriel Roth*

TAXING CHOICE: The Predatory Politics of Fiscal Discrimination | *Ed. by William F. Shughart, II*

TAXING ENERGY: Oil Severance Taxation and the Economy | *Robert Deacon, Stephen DeCanio, H. E. Frech, III, & M. Bruce Johnson*

THAT EVERY MAN BE ARMED: The Evolution of a Constitutional Right | *Stephen P. Halbrook*

TO SERVE AND PROTECT: Privatization and Community in Criminal Justice | *Bruce L. Benson*

THE VOLUNTARY CITY: Choice, Community and Civil Society | *Ed. by David T. Beito, Peter Gordon & Alexander Tabarrok*

TWILIGHT WAR: The Folly of U.S. Space Dominance | *Mike Moore*

WINNERS, LOSERS & MICROSOFT: Competition and Antitrust in High Technology | *Stan J. Liebowitz & Stephen E. Margolis*

WRITING OFF IDEAS: Taxation, Foundations, & Philanthropy in America | *Randall G. Holcombe*

For further information and a catalog of publications, please contact:
THE INDEPENDENT INSTITUTE
100 Swan Way, Oakland, California 94621-1428, U.S.A.
510-632-1366 • Fax 510-568-6040 • info@independent.org • www.independent.org